INNOCENT WHEN YOU DREAM

TOM WAITS: THE COLLECTED INTERVIEWS

Edited by Mac Montandon
Foreword by Frank Black

An Orion paperback

First published by
Thunder's Mouth Press
An imprint of Avalon Publishing Group
New York in 2005

First published in Great Britain in 2006
by Orion
This paperback edition published in 2007
by Orion Books Ltd,
Orion House, 5 Upper St Martin's Lane,
London WC2H 9EA

3 5 7 9 10 8 6 4

A CIP catalogue record for this book is available
from the British Library.

ISBN-13 978-0-7528-8126-3

Printed and bound in Great Britain at
Mackays of Chatham plc, Chatham, Kent

The Orion Publishing Group's policy is to use papers
that are natural, renewable and recyclable products and
made from wood grown in sustainable forests. The logging
and manufacturing processes are expected to conform to
the environmental regulations of the country of origin.

www.orionbooks.co.uk

This book is dedicated to my brother,
Asher A. Montandon,
whose cassette copy of *Small Change*
I still keep in the car

Bob: "It is a sad and beautiful world."
Zack: "Yeah, it's a sad and beautiful world, buddy."

—*Down by Law,* 1986

CONTENTS

CONTENTS

PART THREE
THESE DAYS:
COME ON UP TO THE HOUSE

CONTENTS

FOREWORD

I first encountered Tom Waits when I was a young teenager in Los Angeles. He was performing for a local news broadcast. I had no idea who he was, but I stopped whatever it was I was doing to look at the television. Thinking back now, I realize the reporter didn't really get it, as she golly gee-ed her way through this segment about the Hawaiian-shirted song man hunched over his little keyboard that was covered in crap. He played it gently and you got the feeling if he hit the keys any harder all his stuff would fall onto the floor. There was a big bottle of booze (almost empty) amongst the debris. He sang to the viewers with a half-smile on his face. I was impressed, and maybe a bit scared.

Apparently the singer lived in this small room where the keyboard was, which was filled with even more crap. It was a motel room in Hollywood. I lived on a street called Western Avenue (the longest street in the world) at the Charles Bukowski–Mike Watt end of things, and I knew that if you kept going north on Western Avenue, through Compton and beyond, you would eventually get to Hollywood. I hadn't been to Hollywood since I lived there as a baby, and I wouldn't start taking that drive until I got my driving permit at fifteen. So for years this was my one image of Hollywood, Tom Waits's motel room.

It wasn't until I was living in Boston some years later that I would really get to hear Tom Waits on a record he had recently released; it was called *Swordfishtrombones*. I've been listening to his records ever since.

When I listen to a Tom Waits record, I want to go and make a record. I get happy. It sounds like so much fun. Not like rollercoaster fun, more like breaking a window kind of fun. More like joining the French Foreign Legion kind of fun. I'm sure some people think Tom is just having a bit of fun when he's clanking on a pipe and singing about a midget from Shanghai, but what they might not realize is that it's all true. I've seen glimpses of that world myself. I used to hang around in Long Beach, near the Port of Los Angeles, at a place called Pike's. It was an amusement park rusted by the fog. The first ride they offered you was a *real* tattoo parlor. They had a freak show, a *real* freak show. And, like Waits, I spent some younger years around San Diego, and I don't recall it as being so beachy. It is crushed by L.A. on the north; Mexico on the south; desert-rat, trailer-park heaven on the east; and the ships coming in to the Pacific Rim port of San Diego on the west pour sailors into the streets. They have *lagoons* there.

Tom Waits may lie about his past, but he does tell you all his secrets. He took his life on the road and wrote the songs that he found/lived. He didn't stay at hotels that had mini-bars; he stayed at hotels that *were* mini-bars. But, of course, it isn't really about the booze. It's really about all the intense layers of beauty and loneliness that Tom Waits saw, breathed, smoked, and chewed. Sure, I know that nowadays he's an upstanding citizen, a country gentleman and all that, but he recorded his last album with his teeth and tongue and voice box as the band—literally—and he recorded it in the Sacramento Delta. Have you ever been to Stockton? The building next to town hall is boarded up and whoever isn't sweating in a suit is lying face down in the park trying to cool off.

This collection of comments on the art of Tom Waits (and his wife, Kathleen Brennan) spans his entire career up to now.

But it's the interviews that will give you a seat at the table with Tom. The interview table is at times an awkward place, rife with tension. Other times, it can be downright cozy. I know, because I've sat there so many times myself. I can't speak for Tom exactly, but I'm sure there are interviews when he feels genuinely good about the opportunity to speak to his patrons via the journalist, only to wind up becoming completely annoyed by the interviewer's line of questioning. Sometimes a journalist can ask you the most basic, boring ten easy questions and the interview takes off like a bird, a delight. At other times the questions are highly original, but you still end up storming off to the men's room because Mr. or Ms. Critic just doesn't get it, doesn't get you. Doesn't get a lot of things. A pure waste of time!

Well, it's not going to be a waste of time for you, the reader. See him at his table, maybe drunk, more than likely high on coffee, trying, trying to get through to you. Trying to make sense of it all himself. It's not so easy to explain something that really is meant to be felt. But take it from me, there are secrets being told here. If you listen closely you can spot them. The horse's mouth. The storyteller's scars. The secret language of musicians.

—Frank Black
March 2005

INTRODUCTION

In 1990, my life was a song. It was a song, that is, if the song was sung by Tom Waits. Here's what was going on. Through May of that year I was a coaster-eyed undergrad at New York University. But by the end of my freshman tour, it was painfully clear that I could no longer justify the high cost of tuition—not when my favorite class was one I'd invented: Malt Liquor and Midnight Village Walks.

With NYU no longer a viable option, my choices were two: return to my hometown of Baltimore and register at U of M, or take a wild leap to Los Angeles and move in with my cousin Aaron, whom I barely knew but liked anyway. So I leapt.

After about two weeks, we found a place on Cherokee, between Hollywood and Franklin. The heart of the Hollywood matter, not far from Vine. We were both new to town so, jobless and friendless, we decorated our junior one-bedroom in what some magazine editors might call "Spartan chic." I called it "two bare mattresses on bad wall-to-wall."

This, it should be noted, was safe squalor—we were middle-class white guys without drug addictions, so our chances of survival were high. Still, for us, that may have been a low point. And because it passed, because we are older now and survived all that, I can't help but get a small surge of nostalgic giddiness for the innocent misery of the scene.

Eventually, we both found day jobs that paid us enough pocket money for the odd drinking night out. Somehow we ended up at the Ski Room one evening, and it became our local bar. I think I read once that Bukowski used to drink there. Waits might have, too. If they never did, they certainly drank somewhere just like it. The place was dark and cheap and dominated by a long battered wooden bar that ran down the spine of the room. The Ski Room was usually half full with mid-life guys bearing broken hearts and hats. They slouched toward the rim of their beer mugs. A few older women without all their teeth laughed too loud. Aaron and I scooted between Cherokee and the Ski Room on the weak little motorcycle I'd bought the day my Dart died, in order to get to work. My tall cousin, perched awkwardly on the yowling Yamaha, seemed always on the verge of tipping us. Maybe the drinks straightened the ride out.

When the bike died, it was time to get practical. I bought a not-too-old VW Rabbit, with a sunroof and cassette player. The cassette player sealed the deal. It was in the Rabbit that I first heard *Small Change,* the brilliant, somewhat overlooked record from 1976 that Waits made in the middle of his Asylum years. The tape was left in the car one day, and I started playing it. Just like that. Pretty quickly I realized what a great L.A. soundtrack the record was: perfect for putt-putting past 1950s strip clubs like Jumbo's Clown Room and the Seventh Veil; for pulling up to the neon gates of the Hollywood bar the Frolic Room; for the beautiful, toxic sunsets. Waits had a song for every L.A. occasion. ("Pasties and a G-String," "The Piano Has Been Drinking (Not Me)," and "I Can't Wait to Get Off Work," fit the bill nicely for the three examples above.) So, strangely, by the time I finally really listened to Tom Waits's music in 1990—and I'm the first to admit I was pretty late to the party—I was already living a Waitsian existence.

Though many will argue excitedly against this idea, I would make a case for *Small Change* as the quintessential Waits recording. From cover to credits, it occupies the Waits universe as strongly and thoroughly as any record I can think of. While it very much supports his early, ballad-leaning, derelict minstrel persona, there are also hints of the future. In songs like "Pasties" and the title track, you can also hear the sturm-und-clang most associated with the middle-period Swordfish trilogy: *Swordfishtrombones, Rain Dogs,* and *Frank's Wild Years.* Meanwhile, "I Can't Wait to Get Off Work" and "I Wish I Was in New Orleans" deliver the open-hearted romance and nostalgia of later, mellower songs, like *Mule Variations*'s "Hold On" and *Blood Money*'s "Coney Island Baby."

I guess all this is just to say that if you have to start someplace with the large load of Waits that exists in the world, you could do a lot worse than *Small Change.* And I did a lot of *Small Change.* Up and down Cherokee, down and down Cahuenga, and back and forth across Santa Monica Boulevard, from our Hollywood apartment dive to my job at a Century City outdoor mall, where I'd watch Beverly Hills matriarchs compare in-store makeovers, their Chihuahuas' moist noses peeking out from inside Fendi handbags. Amazingly, the soundtrack worked there, too.

We should probably talk about the voice now. It's hard not to describe it as gravelly, or raspy, or whiskey-warped. I should know; I have. And so have many of the contributors here. That's not just because we are all a bunch of lazy journalists (insert snide comment here). It's because the voice is big and sometimes loud and uncontainable. Heartsick, lonely, and confiding. It's a feeling, not a word. You can't really know it until you hear it and when you do it sounds, well, gravelly, raspy, and whiskey-warped. But it also sounds tender, melancholy, and in love. Psychotic, desperate, and broken down on the interstate.

As much as Waits's performance persona is just that—a performance—he is also the genuine article. In a conversation with NPR's Terry Gross in the third part of this book, he talks about being a young man, developing the image he wished to project to the world. He bought a cane at a thrift store as a mere affectation. At thirteen, he says he "couldn't wait to be an old man." He'd go to friends' houses to hang out and end up in the den with the dads, listening to Harry Belafonte records. That's who he was, cane or no cane.

Anyone who's never felt exactly right in the world can relate. And, in many ways, I never felt less right in the world than during the two years I lived in Los Angeles, when I first began listening to Waits in earnest. It was the time of the first Gulf War. I watched it flicker on the television from bed. The bed (yes, frame and all) belonged to an older woman I was dating. We'd met at the mall, both working in the Metropolitan Museum shop. She looked a little bit like Faye Dunaway in *Chinatown;* it was a Hollywood affair. I was twenty, twenty-one, she was thirty-two, and I still can't figure out or remember why she felt so alone that she ended up with me. We must have been drinking. She was fragile, depressed, not on speaking terms with her dad, I think. We ordered in, kept the shades drawn, watched the war from her West Hollywood bed. In the morning, I'd drive back to Cherokee in the VW, playing *Small Change* while circling the block looking for parking.

So that's my story about how I came to know and to love Waits's music. It's actually an ongoing tale, the end still not in sight. These days I am slowly introducing my eight-month-old daughter to his strange and wondrous sounds.

In the following pages, you will read thirty-eight stories that cover a lot of ground but, ultimately, are all about knowing and loving Waits's music. And because you are holding this book right now, I think it's a pretty good bet that you have your own story. If for some reason you don't, do me a favor: Put on your headphones and play "All the World Is Green," off of *Blood Money.* If you're not seduced within two minutes, well, I'm not sure I know what to say.

—Mac Montandon
Brooklyn, New York
December 2004

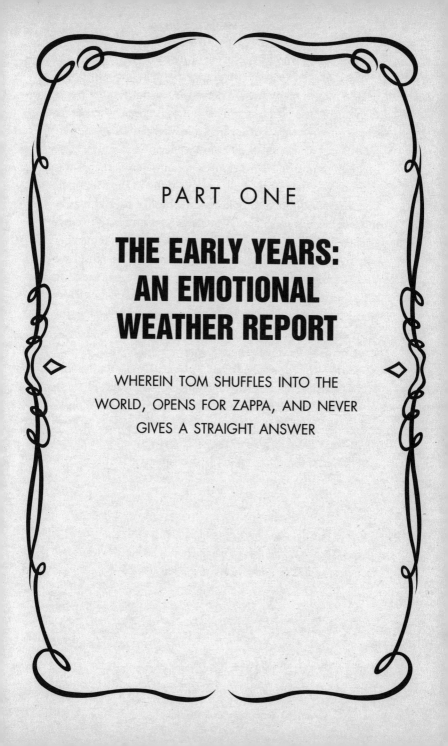

PART ONE

THE EARLY YEARS: AN EMOTIONAL WEATHER REPORT

WHEREIN TOM SHUFFLES INTO THE
WORLD, OPENS FOR ZAPPA, AND NEVER
GIVES A STRAIGHT ANSWER

THE HEART OF SATURDAY NIGHT
PRESS RELEASE

1974

Tom Waits

The blur drizzle down the plate glass and a neon swizzle stick stirs up the night air, as a cueball maverick of a moon rolls across an obsidian sky and the buses groaning and wheezing at the corner of restless blvd. and midnight road, across the tracks from easy street and window shoppers beat the cement stroll and I sit scowling over this week's special Norm's pancakes and eggs $.69 trying to stretch out in the bowels of this metropolitan area. I've tasted Saturday nights in Detroit, St. Louis, Tuscaloosa, New Orleans, Atlanta, N.Y.C., Boston, Memphis. I've done more traveling in the past year than I ever did in my life so far, in terms of my level of popularity, on the night spot circuit, I remain in relative obscurity and now upon the release of a second album, which I believe a comprehensive study of a number of aspects of this search for the center of Saturday night, which Jack Kerouac relentlessly chased from one end of this country to the other, and I've attempted to scoop up a few diamonds of this magic that I see. Musically pulling influence from Mose Allison, Thelonious Monk, Randy Newman, George

Gershwin, Irving Berlin, Ray Charles, Stephen Foster, Frank Sinatra . . .

My favorite writers, Jack Kerouac, Charles Bukowski, Michael C. Ford, Robert Webb, Gregory Corso, Lawrence Ferlinghetti, Larry McMurtry, Harper Lee, Sam Jones, Eugene O'Neill, John Rechy and more. I drive a 1965 Thunderbird that needs a valve job and at least four quarts of Pennzoil a week and gets four miles to the gallon on a long distance, the trunk is busted. And I have three warrants on traffic violations in the Los Angeles metropolitan area alone. I am a pedestrian piano player with poor technique but a good sense of melody. I write in coffee shops, bars, and parking lots. My favorite album is *Kerouac-Allen* on Hanover Records.

Born December 7, 1949, in Pomona, California, I drink heavily on occasion and shoot a decent game of pool and my idea of a good time is a Tuesday evening at the Manhattan Club in Tijuana. I reside now in the Silver Lake area of Los Angeles and am a dedicated Angelino and have absolutely no intention of moving to a cabin in Colorado. I like smog, traffic, kinky people, car trouble, noisy neighbors, crowded bars, and spend most of my time in my car going to the movies.

Now, with two diploma albums, *Closing Time* and *The Heart of Saturday Night,* I trust I will secure enough club dates to keep me moving. I've been an opening act for many artists including Frank Zappa and the Mothers, Buffalo Bob and the Howdy Doody Review, Charlie Rich, John Stewart, Billy Preston, John Hammond, Jerry Jeff Walker, Bob La Beau, Danny O'Keefe, and others and I've met Ed Barbara of Manhattan Furniture.

Your friend and mine,
Tom Waits

THE SLIME WHO CAME IN FROM THE COLD

CREEM, March 1978

Clark Peterson

A pointy, black shoe kicks the motel door open, and in lurches something even the cat would refuse to drag in. It's Tom Waits, looking like a stubble-chinned stumble bum who just traded a pint of blood for a pint of muscatel down at the plasma center. His attire—Frederick's of Goodwill—is appropriately seedy on his meager frame.

"I've got an eagle tattooed on my chest," he growls. "Only on this body it looks more like a robin."

Now that he's made *Time* magazine and has five albums out on Asylum (*Foreign Affairs* is the newest), Tom Waits is the cat's meow (or is it the cat's barf?). When he made his TV debut on *Fernwood 2 Night,* singing "The Piano Has Been Drinking (Not Me)" and then bantered with friend/host Martin Mull, Mull apologized for having only a Diet Pepsi to offer. Waits whipped out a flask from his coat and Mull made a comment about him "sitting here with a bottle in front of him."

"I'd rather have a bottle in front of me than a frontal lobotomy," Waits shot back. Later he offered: "People who can't face drugs turn to reality."

Waits's act is hardly an act at all. He sometimes sleeps in his flea market duds, keeps hours better left to street sweepers, and smokes more than the grill at Joe's Bar-B-Q. He travels in a bus and stays in fleabag joints while his three-piece band chooses classy hotels.

"Blue Oyster Cult and Black Oak Arkansas stayed in the same hotel with me in Phoenix," Waits mumbled, scratching his furry skin and trying to sound sincere. "It was a real *thrill* for me, ya know, being only three doors away from your heroes." (He once said he enjoyed the Cult about as much as listening to trains in a tunnel.) "I like them," he continued. "Of course, I also like boogers and snot and vomit on my clothes."

While he's in hometown L.A., Waits lives at the Tropicana Motor Hotel, once a favorite of Jimi Hendrix and Janis Joplin, and where Andy Warhol's *Trash* was partially filmed. His neighbors are strippers, pimps, Mexicans, "a maniac misfit unemployed actor and a guy named Sparky." Some punks live behind him. Though his music is a mélange of jazz, heart-throbbing ballads, and beat poetry, ironically enough, he has an affinity for punk rock.

"It may be revolting to a lot of people, but at least it's an alternative to the garbage that's been around for ten years," he said. "I've had it up to here with Crosby Steals the Cash. I need another group like that like I need another dick. I'd rather listen to some young kid in a leather jacket singing a song like 'I want to eat out my mother' than to hear some of these insipid guys with their cowboy boots and embroidered shirts doing 'Six Days on the Road.' I like Mink DeVille.

"I was on the Bowery in New York and stood out in front of CBGB's one night. There were all these cats in small lapels and pointed shoes smokin' Pall Malls and bullshitting with the winos. It was good." When he's among outcasts, he's in his own element.

Waits is going to play a piano player in a bar in Sylvester Stallone's next film, *Paradise Alley*, singing three of his own songs. He may have a song in Dustin Hoffman's movie, *Straight Time*, but he won't be on *Starsky and Hutch*.

"I was actually insulted when they asked me," Waits grumbled. "They wanted me to play a satanic figure in a cult group—I said CANCEL. They'd probably put me in a peasant shirt with a bunch of beads and spray paint as devil eyes."

Until he makes the silver screen, watch for tipsy Tom in the sleazy part of town. You won't have any trouble remembering his scruffy, whiskered face.

"I'm usually recognized when I'm talking to some pretty girl in a bar," he sighed, running a few nicotine-stained fingers through his Pennzoil hair. "Some sophomore comes over and drools on my shoulder."

SWEET AND SOUR

Newsweek, June 14, 1976

Betsy Carter with Peter S. Greenberg

An inebriated good evening to you all,
Welcome to Raphael's Silver Cloud Lounge
Slip me a little crimson, Jimson
Gimme the lowdown, Brown
I want some scoop, Betty Boop
I'm on my way into town . . .

Tom Waits is on a darkened stage. A single spotlight illuminates his seemingly wasted body. The cigarette he is smoking has burned down to his fingers while Waits scats his way through his jive repertoire. Wearing a baggy suit, a tattered woolen cap, and yesterday's stubble, he looks more like a guest in a fleabag hotel than a rising new singer with three popular albums.

In a way, Waits isn't a singer at all: he talks a syncopated, stream-of-consciousness tour of the seamy side streets of America, backed by a soulful jazz quartet. All this has already won him a cult following in the music industry, and he has recently been playing to SRO audiences around the country and is currently attracting capacity crowds on his first European tour. "I've got a personality that an audience likes," he suggests, "I'm like the guy they knew—someone raggedy and irresponsible—who never really amounted to much but was always good for a few laughs. A victim, just a victim. But I don't mind the image."

DAY SLEEPER

Waits's sweet-and-sour serenades about eggs-over-easy and the lost American dream place him well beyond his twenty-six years. He is a middle-class southern California kid who dropped out of the hippie generation: "The sixties weren't particularly exciting for me," says Waits, "I wasn't into sand castles and I didn't have any Jimi Hendrix posters on my wall. I didn't even have a black light." After high school in San Diego, he worked as a janitor, dishwasher, and cook. "I would stay out all night," he remembers, "I loved it. I became a day sleeper."

At nineteen, Waits got hip to day sleepers' music—jazz. That's where he discovered Dizzy Gillespie, Mose Allison, the Beat poets, and a broken-down piano that played only the black keys. "I soon taught myself to play everything in F sharp, and little by little I got to be all right." In 1972, Waits took his bluesy, boozy act to amateur night at Los Angeles's Troubadour Club and within a year he had gathered an impressive following, including Elton John, Bette Midler, and Joni Mitchell. When Bonnie Raitt went out on tour last year, she took Waits and his act along—but he went out of his way to spend his nights in seedy flophouses. "Tom's a real original," says Raitt. "He's a window on a scene we never got close to. He's able to make all the double knits both tragic and romantic at the same time."

NAUGAHYDE BOOTHS

Waits's behavior on the stage is just as antisocial. He ignores the audience, shuffles anxiously about, glares at the floor, and lights up one cigarette after another. Once the music starts, his right hand starts snapping while his left foot taps out the beat. Waits's word-clogged monologues about Naugahyde booths, truck stops and platinum blondes stumble from his lips almost unintelligibly. He whips up stories like a short order cook and laces them with a dash of adolescent humor and a sprinkling of word games ("I am a rumor in my own mind, a legend in my own time, a tumor in my own mind"). He flips open a beer, takes a few sips and slips the can into his jacket pocket. The foam dribbles down his leg onto the floor among the countless cigarette butts and crumpled pieces of paper.

This self-conscious, Bowery bum persona only works to hide Waits's talent as an original writer with a unique mixture of blues and jazz in his music. Critics call his style affected and his poetry puerile ("A yellow biscuit of a buttery cueball moon rollin' maverick across an obsidian sky"). But Waits sees himself as the voice of everyman. "There's a common loneliness that just sprawls from coast to coast," he says. "It's like a common disjointed identity crisis. It's the dark, warm, narcotic American night. I just hope I'm able to touch that feeling before I find myself one of these days double-parked on easy street." Right now, Waits is still on the way into town.

Watch Out for Sixteen-Year-Old Girls Wearing Bell Bottoms Who Are Running Away from Home and Have a Lot of Blue Oyster Cult Records Under Their Arm

ZigZag, July 1976

Peter O'Brien

I met up with Tom Waits at nine in the evening outside Ronnie Scott's. He looked just as you would imagine from the sleeve of *Nighthawks*, only tattier. We tried a nearby corner pub. In one door, straight out of the other, into a different street. "Just passin' through," Tom growls at the nonplussed barman. We ended up on the corner of the pub opposite the old *ZigZag* offices on Old Compton Street. Strangely appropriate! Tom sits hunched over a pint of lager, endlessly rocking back and forth while we talk, restlessly turning a silver dollar over and over in his left hand. Much of what follows seemed, in retrospect, a rehearsal for his show that evening. Plenty more was genuine response, particularly his very real concern about the artist, his songs and music. Oh yes, sometimes things come out better if you can read them aloud rather than silently. Try this in your best American, and make it guttural. Then you, too, can share the sore throat my Tom Waits impersonations have left me with.

ZZ: Ok. Now I'll tell you what I was hoping you would do then you can do what you'd like after I've told you! I've never been to America, so I have this great fantasy picture of the country. Take me on a journey across America. Start where you like, take as many little side turns and blind alleys as you like.

TW: You gonna correct the spelling after I'm through? Shit, that's a real hard thing to do because actually I'm working right now on material for a new album called *Pasties and a G-String*. I'm writing all the stuff out here on the road. Where do you want to start? You could start in Seattle or Portland or Cleveland or Phoenix or Albuquerque or Miami or St. Petersburg or Key West or Bangor, Maine or Bloomington, Illinois or Montana or South Dakota. You could start out in Philadelphia or Pittsburgh or New Orleans or east St. Louis or Cincinnati or Dayton or Ashland . . . you could go just about anywhere if you got the bus fare.

ZZ: Where would you go?

TW: If I had a ticket, you mean? I could go anywhere I want. I don't know, I might go to Phoenix. It's close to Los Angeles. I drive with a wild hair up my ass every night, giving the finger to the oncoming traffic and tossing out Miller High Life cans along the way. Drive to Phoenix in a 1954 black Cadillac four-door sedan every now and then. One-eyed jacks across the railroad track. Van Duren road is really the place to be in Phoenix. It's kind of called Hotel Road. There's more hotels than you can shake your dick at. There's a lot of bars. A place called Jenny's Bar. There's the Travellodge Motel. A lot of pavement princesses or women of the evening. You can get just about anything you want. You reach over and scratch your ass and six girls will stop and ask you if you want a date. It's cold in the winter, real cold in Phoenix. In fact I walked all the way from Phoenix to Goodyear one night, which is a fifteen-mile walk. Couldn't get a ride. I don't know what it was. I was well dressed and everything. Laying down in the road pretending I was dead. Nothing happened. I don't know. Depends what you are and what you're looking for. If you're looking for action, or are you looking for girls, do you want to buy a watch, do you want to buy some swamp land in Florida? You got the time and I'll see you at the bottom of a bottle of scotch. I like bars. There's some good bars in Philadelphia, some great bars in New York City. There's a great bar in Denver, Colorado called The Sportsman; it's an after-hours joint. It doesn't open until four in the morning and it's open till about dawn. That swings. This is very difficult for me to give a complete story about the United States. I can't do that. That's what I'm trying to do in my work right now, 'cause I just can't do it sitting here talking in a microphone, 'cos it's really what I'm concerned about right now, and I just can't do it off the top of my head and make it educational as well as entertaining. It was a good idea, but I can't do it.

ZZ: When did you first start traveling around? You must have traveled a helluva lot . . .

TW: Yeah, I have. Worked on the road a long time. Not just traveling to play clubs, I drive a lot. I've had a million cars. The first car I had was when I was fourteen . . . It's kind of an American tradition. Getting a license is kind of like a bar mitzvah. It's nice to have a car, but in winter you gotta have a heater, especially when it's colder than an American Jewish princess on her honeymoon. I've always had cars. Had a '56 Ford Mercury and a '55 Buick Roadmaster, a '55 Special, a '55 Buick Century, a '58 Buick Super, a '54 Black Cadillac four-door sedan, a '65 Thunderbird, '49 Plymouth, let's see, I think I had a '62 Comet. I dunno. Try to stay with Buicks myself.

ZZ: Are these convertibles?

TW: One of them was; it was a pain in the ass. It was busted, and the rain came in all the while, I won't have another convertible.

ZZ: Was it San Diego you came from?

TW: I lived in San Diego, went to high school in San Diego. I was born in L.A. at a very young age. I was born in the back seat of a yellow cab in Murphy Hospital parking lot. I had to pay a buck eighty-five on the meter to move. I didn't have my trousers on yet and I left my money in my other pants. I lived around L.A. and moved around L.A. My dad's a Spanish teacher, so we lived in Whittier, Pomona, La Verne, North Hollywood, Silver Lake, metropolitan areas surrounding Los Angeles. I was working a lot of jobs during school. I didn't find much in school. I was just getting in a lot of trouble so I hung it up.

ZZ: America being so vast, I can quite understand you not being able to do what I hoped. How about California, vast though that is itself? If I was there, what should I visit, what should I look for?

TW: Watch out for falling rocks and eighteen-wheel vehicles. Watch out for the clap. Watch out for sixteen-year-old girls wearing bell bottoms who are running away from home and have a lot of Blue Oyster Cult albums under their arm. Be careful of that . . . If you go to the Tropicana Hotel, watch out for Chuck E. Weiss, 'cause he'll sell you a rat's asshole for a wedding ring. Watch out for Martin Mull. He'll punch-line you to death.

ZZ: Even you?

TW: Actually I'm only afraid of a few things. I'm afraid I'm gonna be walking along some day in Los Angeles and drop into a manhole, and down there's gonna be, like, five hundred unemployed bossa nova musicians and they're gonna "Girl from Ipanema" me to death. Hasn't happened to me yet. I tried to take out some Ipanema insurance, but they won't cover you. Actually the only thing I'm afraid of over here in London is . . . I'm afraid when the moon is high and my hotel room is dark, that I'm gonna start sprouting cameras round my neck, and my trench coat is gonna turn into a flowered shirt, my black slacks are gonna turn into Bermuda shorts. I'm gonna grow some white socks and wing tips that look like old Pontiacs. Then, right next to me is going to sprout a wife, and she's going to be growing larger and larger till she's overweight and she's got bovine perspiration on her upper lip area (and a glazed eye, eh, Tom?), and a see-yourself shine on her forehead, and her feet hurt, she's trying to find a travel brochure and a cigarette, and she wants to sit down, and . . . that hasn't happened yet. Been pretty lucky.

ZZ: And careful.

TW: Yeah, careful. Course, like I told you before, I have been around the block. Slept with tigers and lions and Marilyn Monroe. I got drunk with Louis Armstrong, rolled craps in Las Vegas, been to the Kentucky Derby, seen the Brooklyn Dodgers play at the Ebbets Field, and I taught Mickey Mantle everything he knows.

ZZ: So what are the good things about California? You told me all the terrible things.

TW: Oh, those weren't terrible. That was nothing. Rush hour traffic on the Harbor Freeway on about 110 degrees outside, got no air-conditioning in your car. You got a cigarette, but you ain't got a match. You got hemorrhoids, need a shave and . . . that's fascinating. That can be fascinating.

ZZ: So you don't spend your time at the beach? You're not a surfer, that's for sure.

TW: No, I disavow any knowledge of the world of surfing. I say that without fear of contradiction. I don't know the first thing about surfboards. Which way you ride it, or what side is up, and I don't wanna learn.

ZZ: Do you ever go down to the beach?

TW: Yeah, I've been down there a couple of times. I got lost.

Sure, I go to the beach. Last time I went, I got a tattoo. They told me it would wash off, though, but I've done been scrubbing on that sunbitch, but I'm not using the right soap. It's on my arm. Give me ten bucks and I'll let you see it.

ZZ: I understand you were a doorman at a nightclub in Philadelphia!

TW: Yeah; I was a bouncer and a doorman, which meant I got bounced nightly. In the summer we'd get about twenty-five Hell's Angels coming into town, and I was, like, holding down the fort. They'd give me the arm of a chair to defend myself. It was like a toothpick to a Hell's Angel, so I had my moments. It was a real experiment in terror. Some nightly catastrophes, but I made it through by hook or by crook, come hell or high water. Under the circumstances, I managed to get out alive. But really it was a nightclub kind of fashioned after Gerde's Folk City. They dealt mainly in traditional music. A lot of guitar players—blues and bluegrass mainly . . . I got bluegrassed to death. I must admit that the only thing I . . . I don't mean to sound disdainful, but I guess the only thing I hate is bluegrass played poorly. I guess the only thing I hate more than that is bluegrass played well. That's what really gets me, is when they play it well. I like to see 'em funk it up. I like to see them with the drawers down. It's just got something about it, I don't like it.

ZZ: Is that when you started writing?

TW: I dunno when I started writing really. I was, like, filling out applications and stuff real early. Last name first, first name last, sex . . . "occasionally," stuff like that. Then I was writing letters, filling out forms, writing on bathroom walls. I saw some great graffiti in a bar in Cincinnati. No, it was east St. Louis at a place called The Dark Side of the Moon. It's a club, I don't even know if it's there anymore. Anyway, it said: "Love is blind; God is love; Ray Charles is blind; therefore, Ray Charles must be God." I knew right away I was in a college town! That the lights were on and somebody was home and . . . so . . . but . . . what was I talking about?

ZZ: I don't know. We were just . . . talking!

TW: (Belches loudly) Oh, excuse me . . . actually, I usually vomit. I'm sick all the time, I'm just used to it. I feel bad all the time now so it's . . . bad lungs, bad liver, broken heart, after a while you get used to it. I'm thinking about opening up a nightclub: you can go into the club and, like, the cigarette machine's busted, nobody speaks English, and you can't get change for a dollar. While you're in there, somebody's shipping your wife and stealing your car, and a big sumo wrestler wants to break your neck. All the girls are carrying the disease, and they're really transvestites. The band are six winos that were selected at random and given electronic instruments. It's for people that really don't know how to have a bad time. And there's no cover charge. They don't charge anything to get in, but they charge $100 just to get out.

ZZ: Is recording difficult? Does it come out sounding the way you want?

TW: I'm real awkward in the studio. Don't like it. It's really like pulling teeth. Everything is real fastidious. I dunno, I'm afraid of it. I'm afraid of it, and I'm just a nervous wreck the whole time, because you spend a lot of time working on this material, which is really the crux of it, where the real sweat is. Then you can have major surgery done to something you just busted your chops over. So it's real sensitive, and a lot of heated arguments, a lot of fistfights. I don't look forward to it.

ZZ: I have your three albums here in my bag . . .

TW: They're harmful to swallow. If rash develops, discontinue use and consult physician immediately.

ZZ: Has your writing changed in the way your albums have changed?

TW: Yeah, I really have changed. I've become a little more ambitious about it. For me it's also a craft. It's not something that drops out of the sky. It's not something where you sit at your picture window, and watch the sun glistening off the trees and a deer walks by and whispers in your ear. It's really a craft, and it's hard work. It's just a lot of discipline, and hopefully, you get better with each project. I've just about worked out the stuff for my next album, so what I'm going to do when I get back to Los Angeles is get drunk as a skunk, and stay that way for about three days . . . then I'm going right into the studio.

BLUES

New Yorker, December 27, 1976

James Stevenson

Tom Waits is a twenty-six-year-old composer and performer who looks like an urban scarecrow. He wears a ratty black cap pulled down over his left eye, a coat that is simultaneously too big and too small, paper-thin pointy black shoes, and a couple of days' worth of beard. He appears to have slept in a barrel. His voice is a scabrous rasp, which can become—onstage—an effective instrument, with a wide range of color and feeling. His lyrics reflect a landscape that is bleak, lonely, contemporary: all-night diners; cheap hotels; truck stops; pool halls; strip joints; Continental Trailways buses; double-knits; full-table rail shots; jumper cables; Naugahyde luncheonette booths; Foster Grant wraparounds; hash browns over easy; glasspacks and overhead cams; dawn skies "the color of Pepto-Bismol." His songs—mostly blues—are not everybody's cup of Instant Nestea, but they range from raunchy to beautiful. His fourth album, *Small Change,* recently appeared, and one song in it, called "Tom Traubert's Blues," is extraordinarily moving.

We went out to Roslyn, Long Island, early on a Friday night to see Waits perform at a club called My Father's Place.

It was next to an overpass of Northern Boulevard; with heavy traffic moving eastward above, it was a setting as melancholy as one of Waits's blues. The empty club was low-ceilinged and black-walled; chairs for about four hundred sat upside down on long, narrow tables under dull-yellow lights. A man dollied cases of liquor by; a couple of waitresses at a table stacked with menus were writing in "Pizza $3.50" on each. On a stage in one corner, Waits and his band—bass player, drummer, and sax—were running a sound check, playing fragments of songs. Red and blue spotlights came on, went off. Waits was bent over the keyboard of the piano, a cigarette jiggling from his jaw. "There's no presence," the sax player complained into his mike. Waits, speaking into his mike, said, "Darken the sax." Men started putting the chairs on the floor: slam, crash, jangle. A spotlight cut across the room, hovered on the stage, went out. Waits stepped down from the stage. Because he was wearing black clothes in the dark club, only the small orange glow of his cigarette indicated his whereabouts.

The first show was a full house, and it went very well. Waits included one of his new songs, "Step Right Up," which is a high-speed scat assemblage of unrelated sales pitches ("You, too, can be the proud owner of the quality goes in before the name goes on . . . year-end clearance . . . white sale . . . smoke-damaged furniture you can drive it away today . . . never needs winding"), and did a couple of encores.

Between shows, we went down to a basement room and found Waits seated at a table having a beer. He is a private sort of person, older than his years; skinny, angular, and long-faced; reflective eyes in the shadow of his cap brim. He smiled and growled a pleasant greeting, and told us he was a high-school dropout from Los Angeles and San Diego. His parents were teachers. "When I was in school, I was in trouble a lot. Conflict with teachers. Malicious mischief. I got no sympathy from my folks, being teachers themselves. I was wasted all day, because I worked in a restaurant until four in the morning. I was dishwasher, waiter, cook, janitor, plumber—everything. They called me Speed-O-Flash. Sundays, I'd come in at 6 a.m. and wash, buff, and wax the floors. There was a good jukebox—played 'Cryin' Time' and 'I Can't Stop Loving You.' We had an old piano in our house, but I wouldn't go near it. Scared me. When I was about seventeen, they threw it away, and I put it in the garage. I was an investigator at the keyboard. I was curious about melody. If I wanted to learn a key, I'd write a melody in that key. I went to a predominantly black junior high school in San Diego, where the only music was black hit parade—James Brown, the Supremes, Wilson Pickett—but by then I'd had a lot of incongruous musical influences: jazz, Gershwin, Porter, Kern, Arlen, Carmichael, Mercer, Louis Armstrong, Stravinsky, Reverend Gary Davis, Mississippi John Hurt. During the height of rock and roll, I kept a low profile. I used to read Hubert Selby, Kerouac, Larry McMurtry, John Rechy, Nelson Algren. My reading now is mostly limited to menus and street signs. I liked comedians and storytellers: Wally Cox, Harry the Hipster, Rodney Dangerfield, Redd Foxx, Lord Buckley. I worked in a gas station, didn't do major repairs—Mrs. Ferguson would come in and want her tires rotated; kids want a dollar's worth; fill 'er up; ding, ding—and I worked in a jewelry store, drove delivery trucks, cabs, a Tropic ice-cream truck. Was a firefighter in a town near the Mexican border—brush fires, mostly. Drank coffee, played checkers, looked at *Playboy,* threw darts. Then I got a job as doorman at a night club in L.A., and I listened to all the acts from the door. I heard bluegrass, comics, folk singers, string bands. At the same time, I was picking up people's conversations in all-night coffee shops—ambulance drivers, cabdrivers, street sweepers. I did research there as an evening curator, and I started writing—gingerly. I thought at some point I'd like to forge it all into something meaningful, and give it dignity."

Around that time, Waits began performing. Audiences often made it clear that they couldn't stand him. "There were nights when it was like pulling teeth," he said. Now that is changing. Waits said, "The artist business is merchandise. I see it from the bowel now. One night off in two weeks. The problem with performing is it's repetitive, and unless I can come up with something new each night, I find it gruelling. Like I'm just a monkey on a stick. So I try to stretch out nightly, make something of it. And that's very valuable to me, and a lot of songs come out of that. My creative climate is relatively the same as it used to be. Maybe I keep my eyes open a little longer. I still love living in hotels. Transient hotels. I live in a nine-dollar-a-night hotel in L.A., I know every flop in every town. Cheap hotels remind me of home a lot more than some sanitary-protection place. They're a little more humane. They remember your name, too. If you get hungry at three A.M., you can go downstairs and the desk clerk will give you half his sandwich. They won't do that at a Hilton."

SMELLIN' LIKE A BREWERY,
LOOKIN' LIKE A TRAMP

Rolling Stone, January 1977

David McGee

Smellin' like a brewery, lookin' like a tramp,
the nighthawk digs deep for some small change.

"I'm the type of guy who'd sell you a rat's asshole
for a wedding ring."

Tom Waits—disheveled as usual in his grimy newsboy's cap, wrinkled white shirt, wilted black tie, battered black sports coat, baggy black stovepipe jeans, black roach-killer footwear, with the ever-present Viceroy proud between his long, double-jointed fingers—eyes the packed house at the Other End. Cautiously. Suddenly, the fingers pop in that resonant, clean snap. A deep drag on the Viceroy and he's into "Step Right Up," a word-jazz piece from his newest album, *Small Change.* It's a huckster's ultimate pitch, this "Step Right Up" ("It's effective. It's defective"), and a sophisticated bit of scat phrasing to boot.

How appropriate then that a wry grin should cross Waits's face, for this pitch is being delivered at a press party, and the assembled journalists, record company reps, and assorted hangers-on are, in Waits's eyes, hucksters all, with whom he has a running love–hate relationship. Love—call it grudging respect if you like—for the job they do in bringing him to the public's attention. Hate—and there is no better word—for the countless inane questions he's asked, for the industry's confounding marketing and merchandising techniques which, Waits claims, reduce his albums to "products" destined for a rendezvous with the "Miscellaneous" and "W, X, Y–Z" bins in record stores.

In a dim white spotlight, Waits straps on a battered blond Guild guitar. His band, the Nocturnal Emissions, plays softly, almost inaudibly in the background as he attacks the Guild with a half-strumming, half-fingerpicking style that creates a lonely milieu for a song about old buddies who long for one more shot of youthful insouciance, who cry out hopelessly for an extra step on Father Time, and at last resign themselves to the inevitable.

As the song ends, Waits appears distressed. He mock-staggers, leans away from and back into the microphone, then cries out: "Bartender! The jukebox! Somebody . . . somebody . . . put a quarter in and play me something like . . . something like . . . 'Cupid, draw back your bow / And let your arrow go . . . ' " In his dead-end growl of a voice, Waits forces out an underlying melancholy in the Sam Cooke standard. With the audience on the ropes, Waits delivers a knockout punch, segueing neatly into "(Looking for) The Heart of Saturday Night"— one of the most haunting, exquisite songs ever written about the cruel myth of eternal youth.

Then, quickly, it's all over. Sighs and smiles mingle with thunderous applause. Heads shake and eyes stare forlornly into drinks. Cigarette smoke thickens.

GROWING UP IS HARD TO DO

Tom Waits was born in the back seat of a taxicab outside a hospital in Pomona, California, on December 7, 1949. Growing up was a hit-and-run affair in the various towns where his father taught secondary-school Spanish. While he muddled his way through school ("I really started to shine after school"), Waits discovered his parents' collection of 78s. Como and Crosby, Porter and Gershwin, "I Get a Kick Out of You" and "It's Been a Long, Long Time." In the sixties, California's teenagers rocked to the beat of Brian Wilson's surfing and hot-rod music and, later, blissed out on acid rock from San Francisco and folk-rock from Los Angeles. None of this interested Waits, "I wasn't thrilled by Blue Cheer, so I found an alternative, even if it was Bing Crosby."

"I kept a pretty narrow scope on things," Waits says of those days, as he stretches out on the bed in his disheveled room at the Chelsea Hotel—ill-lit, vomit-green, with copies of *Penthouse*, *Screw*, and *PleaZure* strewn among cigarette butts. "In my formative years, my ambitions didn't go much beyond just working in a restaurant, maybe buying into a place. Music was just such a vicarious thing, I was a patron. No more, no less."

The freedom and intrigue of the nighttime world beckoned to the young Waits, and he found himself taken by a lifestyle that was abundant in fascinating turns and provocative encounters. At one point, he landed a job as the doorman at a small, now-defunct L.A. club called the Heritage.

"I listened to all kinds of music there," Waits recalls. "All kinds of stuff from rock to jazz to folk to anything else that happened to walk in. One night I saw a local guy onstage playing his own material. I don't know why, but at that moment I knew that I wanted to live or die on the strength of my own music. I finally played a gig there. Then I started writing down people's conversations as they sat around the bar. When I put them together I found some music hiding in there."

Later, he discovered and digested the works of Jack Kerouac, Gregory Corso, Allen Ginsberg, and other chroniclers of the Beat Generation with whom he's often identified. And while he doesn't discount their influence, he mentions Irving Berlin, Johnny Mercer, and Stephen Foster as being equally, if not more, important in shaping his world. By the time he auditioned at the Troubadour in 1969, his reading matter was "limited to menus and magazines."

In the audience at the Troubadour that night was Herb Cohen, who managed the Mothers of Invention, Captain Beefheart, and Linda Ronstadt. Cohen was impressed enough to offer the young songwriter—who was living out of his car at the time—a contract. It was an unexpected blow of good fortune, and it forced Waits to reconsider his priorities.

"You bust your chops to get hold of something," he says, "get chumped again and again to where you become bitter and coldblooded, and suddenly someone's saying, 'Okay, here.' And you can't offer any kind of rebuttal. You just have to take it, along with the responsibility. That was frightening."

For over a year, Waits remained "in escrow," subsidized by Cohen, honing his writing and performing skills. He finally signed with Asylum in 1972. Former Lovin' Spoonful member Jerry Yester came along as producer/arranger and Waits cut his first album, *Closing Time*, a relentlessly low-keyed record of gentle pleas for love, solitude and inner peace. One song, "Ol' 55," was later recorded by the Eagles and became a classic ode to freeway flying. Despite notices, *Closing Time* rose and fell quickly on the charts.

By now Waits was on the road with a trio, playing the club

circuit. Today, he looks back disgustedly on this period. "It was the old case of the one-size-fits-all industry-push on a new songwriter—throw you out there and see what you can do," he says, "I didn't know what the hell I was doing."

The final horror came as opening act for the Mothers, whose audiences treated Waits with monumental disdain. Kids crowded around the apron of the stage, spitting and cursing at him, flipping him the bird. "I'd stand there and say 'Well, thank you. Glad you enjoyed that one. I've got a lot of new material I'm going to play for you tonight.' It went right downhill and I never got my fingers underneath to pull it up. It's amusing in retrospect, but there were some nights when, Jesus Christ, does this type of work look interesting to you!?"

Then it was back to L.A. for a second album, *The Heart of Saturday Night*, another critical success, and more of a commercial success than the first one, but still no great shakes on the charts. Waits had begun to play with his language and to inject some swing into his arrangements; images were striking and original; he had matured as a singer. The yearning was still there but it was partially mitigated by the carefree exuberance of "Depot, Depot" and the compelling "Diamonds on My Windshield"—inspired by the Ken Nordine–style word-jazz Waits had begun working into his sets. And Bones Howe, who replaced Yester, had perked up the production.

With two albums behind him, Waits, by 1975, had a solid and growing audience, but was still an opening act. Unable to support himself and a trio on $150 a week, he began working alone. In July of that year he and Howe assembled a quartet, brought an audience into the Record Plant in L.A. and recorded a live performance which became the double album *Nighthawks at the Diner*, his first critical failure—too much talk, too few songs.

But that was a minor problem compared to the nightmares

that lay ahead. First came a disastrous week at the chic Reno Sweeney in Manhattan, followed by an appearance in Passaic, New Jersey, as the opening act for Poco, where he was again confronted by a hostile audience.

"I was sick through that whole period," he mutters, "And I'd get onstage at Reno's and be thrown off by the fancy surroundings. It was starting to wear on me, all the touring. I'd been traveling quite a bit, living in hotels, eating bad food, drinking a lot—too much. There's a lifestyle that's there before you arrive and you're introduced to it. It's unavoidable."

And Waits, on top of all his other problems, was having trouble writing songs. No privacy, he says. Someone always pulling on his coat. No time to sit down at a piano without being disturbed.

The final injustice came last spring in New Orleans when Roger McGuinn, Joan Baez, Kinky Friedman, and some other members of the "Rolling Blunder Revue" as Waits termed Dylan's entourage, took over the stage at Ballinjax Club just before Waits was scheduled to begin his set. "They got up there for an hour just before I was supposed to begin my set," says Waits, "Nobody even asked me; before I knew it, fuckin' Roger McGuinn was up there playing guitar and singing and Joan Baez and Kinky were singing. By the time I got onstage the audience was stoked. They were all lookin' around the room and shit. I don't need this crap—it was my show. I was drinkin' too much on top of everything else."
When he left for Europe in May, Waits had a color photo but no material for his next album. Gigs in Amsterdam, Copenhagen, and Brussels proved inconsequential. But two weeks in London were pivotal. Finally, he found time to be alone. He locked himself away and composed twenty songs, eleven of which are on *Small Change*, the album that details, in

metaphor, his hellish year. Whiskey and cigarettes having taken their toll, his voice is nothing more than a low growl, like Satchmo without the joy, that becomes strangely rich and expressive over the course of several listenings. The songs are structured as finely as those on *Saturday Night*, but the optimism has vanished along with the notion that the night and the open road hold glittering promise.

"I'm learning about stuff, too," Waits says of the album, "Through the songs I'm writing now I'm changing my attitude towards things. I'm becoming a little more shrewd, a little more . . ."

Cynical?

"Yeah. I don't take things at face value like I used to. So I dispelled some things in these songs that I had substantiated before. I'm trying to show something to myself, plus get some things off my chest. 'Step Right Up'—all that jargon we hear in the music business is just like what you hear in the restaurant or casket business. So instead of spouting my views in *Scientific American* on the vulnerability of the American public to our product-oriented society, I wrote 'Step Right Up.'

"I put a lot into 'Bad Liver and a Broken Heart.' I tried to resolve a few things as far as this cocktail-lounge, maudlin, crying-in-your-beer image that I have. There ain't nothin' funny about a drunk. You know, I was really starting to believe that there was something amusing and wonderfully American about a drunk. I ended up telling myself to cut that shit out. On top of everything else, talking about boozing substantiates the rumors that people hear about you, and people hear that I'm a drunk. So I directed that song as much to the people that listen to me and think they know me as much as I directed it to myself."

Asked what's important to him, Waits sits up on the edge of the bed, taps his feet nervously, and takes a draw on his umpteenth Viceroy, "I'm not money oriented except to the point that I have bills to pay and I have to support a trio. I want to be respected by my peers and I want my old man to think that what I'm doing is good. For me, it's more of an internal thing. I'm just trying to do something that I think is viable, that I can be proud of, trying to create something that wasn't there before." A slug of White Horse, "My wants and needs are small and limited," says Waits, who currently lives in Hollywood's sleazy Tropicana Motor Hotel, "I'm not going into real estate or buying oil wells or becoming a slumlord."

A year ago Waits had remarked that he was more concerned about where he would be in ten years than he was about where he would be in one year. Has the satisfaction of *Small Change*, the prospect of his first headlining tour and an emotional turnaround made him more present-minded?

"No, not really. I've got to cinch something before we get out of the seventies. I've got a lot invested in this whole thing—just in confidence—in my development as a writer and all that. I don't want to be a has-been before I've even arrived. That would be hard to live with. Yeah . . . hard to live with. I don't want to think about it, man. Let's go get a pizza."

THE DON LANE SHOW

Channel Nine, April 1979

D: Don Lane (Wearing a wonderful coffee-colored three-piece.)

T: Tom Waits (Tom's wearing a black suit, black shirt with white trim, and porkpie hat. Pointy shoes—possibly boots [can't see them that much, really] with black socks. He's smoking like a chimney, and looks pissed. He also has that under-lip goatee going on.)

The set: normal talk-show set, two chairs with a table between, and a mike between the chairs. Don's sitting down, Tom's not here yet.

D: One of the newest singing phenomenons overseas is a twenty-nine-year-old, gravelly-voiced singer/poet who worked on jobs like a firefighter on the Mexican border and dishwasher just so he could keep working on his music. His name is Tom Waits, and he doesn't work at, or try to be different or unusual—it comes to him naturally.

Film: Tom at a piano, singing "Silent Night." (Presumably a snippet from the "Christmas Card . . ."—looks like a large place.)

D: Heh, ah, that was an unfortunate selection of a piece to show you, right there. I thought I should say that now so I wouldn't have to say it later. He's a mixture of "Satchmo" Armstrong and Humphrey Bogart when he sings—it's an incredible style . . . he sings like no one else does or ever did. He's going to be doing a number for us later tonight, so I think you're really gonna like him, gonna understand the great sensitivity in his work. So would you welcome the very curious and the very talented Tom Waits!

(Tom enters from the right, kinda stumbling. He sits in the chair, proceeding to smoke.)

D: How are you, Tom?

T: Oh, better 'n nothing. Ashtray here?

D: Oh, ashtray, ashtray. We don't have one here . . . I tell ya what . . . use . . . you can use this glass, all right? Just get it in there. How are you? You all right?

T: Yes, yes, I'm fine, thank you.

D: Just wanna check, to make sure you're OK.

T: I'm-a gonna get comfortable here.

D: How long . . . (Tom ashes, missing the cup.) Ah, nice shot. It's OK. We all miss once in a while. How long have you been in Australia?

33

T: I got here last night. I got a plane out from Paris for about twenty-two hours. A fascinating flight.

D: What do you do for twenty-two hours on a flight? Do you have ways of entertaining yourself?

T: Well, they show movies that are not a big success any-where else, they put them on the planes. (Lights another cigarette.)

D: I would do that for you, it's the part of the host that's sup-posed to light the guest's cigarette, but you look like a man who can handle that all by yourself. We got an ashtray yet?

T: S'alright. (Tom looks down between the chairs from now on.)

D: Did you put the butt in there? (Laughs) How long have you been singing?

T: Pardon me?

D: I said how long have you been singing? (They shift in chairs, hunker down closer. Tom appears to not be able to hear too well.) Now I'm right here with you, I'm gonna do this interview. I'm not goin' nowhere. (Stage-hand gives Don an ashtray.) There ya go.

T: Oh, ya got people workin' for ya an' everything.

D: That's right—It never fails, Tom, you can ask for any-thing you want on this show, and we'll have someone go out and get it for you.

T: Christ!

D: I . . . er, we tried to get him, but there wasn't enough money. We didn't know who to call for the booking. I got the wrong agent. (Tom's looking down between the chairs again.) Is there something down here I don't know about?

T: (Tom gestures. It sounds like he says "keep it quiet" or something like that.)

D: Let's move ahead. They tell me you have some kind of a cult following. Do you . . . do you agree with that expression?

T: I have a growing level of popularity throughout the intercontinental United States, Japan, and . . . er . . . I travel extensively in Europe, as well. I don't do half bad.

D: They tell me now you have a new market there in Ireland. Is that true?

T: I've performed in Dublin, I did very well there as well.

D: You look like a leprechaun; you should do well there!

T: Well, I'm also big in Philadelphia. (Grins. Ashes cig, some gets on Don.) Excuse me. I feel like I'm at my grandmother's. (He's talking into a mike between them—he's been progressively slumping closer towards it.)

D: I won't clean anything off. What would you call your singing, your singing style? What kinda music is it that you really like? Is it all your own stuff, or do you do other people's things as well?

T: Occasionally, I'll do a cover version of somebody else's number, but primarily, I like to deal with my own travelogues.

D: And to what kind of an audience do you work? Is there an age bracket to your audience? Or is it a mixture of all?

T: You're starting to sweat, Don. (Don wipes his forehead.)

D: Yeah, yeah . . . If you were in my position, you would be too! I'd like to have a show next week. Question FIVE. (Looks at script—applause—Tom smokes.) I'd . . . (Coughs, waves away Tom's smoke.) If I stay here with you another ten minutes, there's gonna be an Indian raid!

T: You're big here in Australia?

D: (Nods.) Now you know why! At twenty-nine . . .

T: Thank you!

D: Are you twenty-nine?

T: Yes, as a matter of fact.

D: Well, at twenty-nine . . . (As Don leans in, Tom sits back in his chair.) My God! It's the first time I've seen you up straight! Pardon me, I didn't mean to say straight. (Mimes ventriloquy with Tom.) Well, how are you, Tom?

(In funny voice:) Good, thank you, everything's fine! (Back to normal voice:) At twenty-nine, you write about all these things that have happened to you, sorta like these lowlife things that have happened to you . . .

T: You read that right off the page!

D: No I didn't!

T: Ah, you did. It says *lowlife,* right there.

D: Ah, yeah, well I won't mention that. You don't want that question used? You got a pen? Can I borrow a pen? (Stagehand gives Don a pen.) Well, I'll go through the list, Tom, and you can tell me what you'd like to answer and I'll do it. How long have you been singing? You answered that, though, didn't you?

T: I've been on the road for about seven years.

D: Seven years. We got that. (Writes.) Seven years. How does a guy with a voice like that decide to be a singer and succeed?

T: Well, it was a choice between entertainment or a career in air-conditioning and refrigeration.

D: Ah—what about some of your early influences? Early influences on you and your music?

T: I enjoy Rod Steiger.

D: Wait a minute! Wait a minute! Rod Steiger? OK . . .

T: Rod Steiger.

D: I have all of their albums.

T: I . . . er . . . I enjoy Lord Buckley. Lenny Bruce . . .

D: Lord Buckley! You lost the world! Nobody knows who Lord . . .

T: You know who Lord Buckley is!

D: Yes. But we ain't gonna talk about him here. Now we come to the good part. Your acting career.

T: Ah.

D: You remember that? Your acting career? (Waves at Tom.) Yes? We have a clip here with Sylvester Stallone. You know Sylvester Stallone? Big feller. (Makes boxing movements.)

T: I'll try and remember. (Boxes back.)

D: Sylvester Stallone did this movie called *Paradise Alley* in which you had a part.

T: Yes.

D: Did you enjoy doing that movie?

T: Yes. It was like five weeks of work for three lines of dialogue. It was interesting to see the bowels of the film industry.

D: I'm certainly glad you finished the sentence.

T: But it was a totally new challenge for me. (Lights new cigarette.)

D: Let me ask you something. Do you worry about achievement? Does it worry you, or do you just do your own thing and say "here it is, you either accept it or not"?

T: Er, do I worry about achievement?

D: Yep.

T: I worry about a lot of things, but I don't worry about achievement.

D: We'll scratch achievement off there. (Writes.)

T: I worry primarily about whether there are nightclubs in heaven.

D: You wouldn't get a booking there—they'd be over-booked, wouldn't they? Aren't all the greats up there? Where's this heaven you're talking about?

T: Ah, search me.

D: Depends what you've got on ya. OK. We'll take a look at . . . here's Tom in . . . no wait. We do a lot of fooling around here, and believe it or not, somebody at home's gonna say look, gee, they're having a hard time, but we're not! I spoke with him this afternoon and we had a great time, and he's just . . . mad! But he's lovely, he's a great creative man. Look creative! (Tom smiles.) Lovely, Tom. Here's Tom in *Paradise Alley* with Sylvester Stallone, who will be a guest of our show via satellite. Here, have a look at this . . .

Film: (A piano's strings, moving up to show Tom playing. He's singing. The clip cuts, in dialogue, between Tom and Sylvester, finally ending with Sly walking out of the bar.)

T: (Singing) . . . wake at night again, now that Annie's back in town . . .

Sly: Mumbles?

T: Yeah? Whaddayawant?

S: When was the last time you were with a woman?

T: Probably the Depression.

S: What you saving it for?

T: I dunno man, maybe a big finish.

S: Now you better get out a bit more, you're starting to look gray . . . I'm off to visit the best lookin' tomato in the neighborhood. 'Night Mumbles.

T: (Singing) . . . all the corner boys still lollygag, the sailors shoot the breeze . . . well, some things around here never change . . .

(Cuts back to studio. Tom and Don are at a piano, Don seated on the stool, closest. There's a large orange juice on the piano, with a chunky ashtray alongside. Tom starts playing some intro chords.)

D: OK. Have a seat. Where do you get the inspiration for most of your stuff?

T: Well, you know . . . most of my songs are kinda travelogues. It's difficult to say exactly where they come from. You gotta sleep with one eye open. This song here is entitled "On the Nickel." In downtown Los Angeles, there's a place called Fifth Street, it's a place where all the hoboes are, and they call it "on the nickel." There was a motion picture called *On the Nickel* that was written by Ralph Waite and this is a story, kinda a wino's lullaby.

(Ashes his cigarette and proceeds to play "On the Nickel"— it's a great rendition. His voice is very deep and . . . phlegmy. It's a fantastic version, ending with "Waltzing Matilda" that brings the house down.)

(Don walks in, says something to Tom, but it's drowned out by the sound of the crowd's applause.)

D: Tom Waits! Ha! That was great. Listen—we have been warning you and warning you for the past three shows that this was not an ordinary man, and I have never had as good a time interviewing anyone as I have with this man, because he's the ultimate send-up. Lemme tell you where the dates are gonna be. Melbourne, he's at the Palais Theatre on May the 1st and the 7th, and you . . . I can't stress enough that you have to see him. If you can, find a friend who's got a Tom Waits album and have a listen to the kinda stuff this guy creates. The 1st and the 7th—don't blush on me now, by God! (Tom's laughing and blushing.) Sydney, State Theatre, on May 2nd and the 14th Canberra—I want you to come back on the show so everyone sees that this is the way you always are!—Sydney State Theatre May 2nd and the 14th. Canberra Theatre May 4th, Brisbane Main Hall on May the 5th, Adelaide Festival Theatre on the 8th, out at Perth at the Concert Hall—man, you'll love it out there mate, they'll adore you—May the 11th, and if between that, if you can find out a way to come back here and sit down and talk to me, you can come on the show whenever you want. Because I think you're a gas. Thank you for coming out. Tom Waits! And when we come back, Chubby Checker, the big twister that'll knock your brains out . . .

Not So Much a Poet, More a Purveyor of Improvisational Travelogue

New Musical Express, November 29, 1975

Todd Everett

Although he's extremely reluctant to admit it—and will take care to avoid the topic—Tom Waits is a poet.

He'll admit to being a songwriter; he's certainly that, and a fine one.

To his detractors, who can't seem to make a thing of him, Waits is a mumbling soft on stage: a performer who wanders on stage drunk and mutters meaningless multi-syllables at the audience.

To his fans, who safely outnumber his detractors, Waits is that "something different" that we've all been waiting for. Many will tell you that the goateed street rat is a talent far too great to be ignored: the first successful attempt to bring the beat culture of the Greenwich Village fifties into a form meaningful to today's listeners.

Waits, in his early twenties, has absorbed this rich, influential culture with the zeal of a religious convert. He came to it in his mid-teens: a time when some of us discovered Dylan; some of us discovered Swing; and when some of us are discovering Springsteen. The mid-teens are an important, impressionable age.

Waits discovered Jack Kerouac.

"I guess everybody [reads Kerouac at some point in their] life. Even though I was growing up in southern California, he made a tremendous impression on me. It was 1968. I started wearing dark glasses and got myself a subscription to *DownBeat* . . . I was a little late. Kerouac died in 1969 in St. Petersburg, Florida, a bitter old man.

"I became curious about style more than anything else. I discovered Gregory Corso, Lawrence Ferlinghetti . . . Ginsberg still comes up with something every now and again."

The sources became more diverse: comedian Lord Buckley, Ken Nordine, whose "word jazz" was a unique combination of spoken stories and improvised jazz background. Ray Charles, Mose Allison. And James Brown.

"There's a fascinating album that came out in fifty-seven on Hanover Records: *Kerouac-Allen*. It's Jack Kerouac telling stories, with Steve Allen playing piano behind him. That album sort of sums up the whole thing. That's what gave me the idea to do some spoken pieces myself."

"Spoken pieces" are what immediately sets Waits off from most contemporary nightclub performers. It's the same discovery that Bob Dylan made some years ago; that one didn't necessarily have to set all of one's words to music. ("If I can sing it," said Dylan at the time, "it's a song. If I can't, it's a poem.")

"Poetry is a very dangerous word," says Waits, "It's very misused. Most people when they hear the word 'poetry' think of being chained to a school desk, memorizing 'Ode on a Grecian Urn.' When somebody says that they're going to read me a poem, I can think of any number of things that I'd rather be doing. I don't like the stigma that comes with being called a poet—so I call what I'm doing an improvisational adventure or an inebriational travelogue, and all of a sudden it takes on a whole new form and meaning.

"If I'm tied down and have to call myself something, I prefer 'storyteller.' Everybody has their own definition of what poetry is, and of who's a poet. I think that Charles Bukowski is a poet—and I think that most will agree to that."

Waits, raised in various southern California suburbs, was a frequent commuter from San Diego to the Troubadour's Monday night hootenannies when discovered by Herb Cohen. Cohen once managed Lord Buckley and currently handles the affairs of Frank Zappa as well as Waits.

"You arrive at the Troubadour at ten in the morning and wait all day. They let the first several people in line perform that night. When you finally get up there, you are allowed four songs—you can blow it all in fifteen minutes. I was scared shitless." Nevertheless the first night Cohen spotted Waits, a contract was offered to the starving storyteller.

Within relatively short order, Waits was signed to the then new Asylum label with his first album produced by former Lovin' Spoonful member Jerry Yester. *Closing Time*, the album's title, accurately reflected the disc's overall mood—late night in a smoky, all but empty barroom with tinkling piano, discreet rhythm, and Waits's growled lyrics. One of the songs, "Ol' 55," was picked up and recorded by another Asylum act, the Eagles. That and other Waits songs have subsequently been recorded by Tim Buckley, Lee Hazlewood, Ian Matthews, and Eric Andersen, while John Stewart and Bette Midler include Waits's "Shiver Me Timbers" in their stage acts.

A second album, *The Heart of Saturday Night*, produced by Bones Howe, was released, winning even greater critical acclaim than did the well-received first ("I've never gotten any real strong verbal insubordination from any reviewers"). The after-hours mood was preserved, even strengthened.

Waits's third album, a double live set, *Nighthawks at the Diner*, was recorded at the Los Angeles branch of the Record

Plant recording studios, decked up to simulate a nightclub atmosphere, before an invited audience, instrumental accompaniment by a well-rehearsed band of local jazzmen including former Mose Allison drummer Bill Goodwin, pianist Mike Melvoin, bassist Jim Hughart, and tenor saxist Peter Christlieb.

The reedman, who regularly plays with Doc Severinsen's band and leads his own group at North Hollywood's Dante's nightclub, seemed particularly stricken by Waits's gifts. "I'd been going to the club for some time to hear Pete's band. After he played my sessions, he asked me to come down to the club and sit in on 'Vocabulary.' I was very flattered."

Waits describes his relationship with his record company and fellow artists as "All right, I don't invite them over to my house or anything; but I don't really know very many of them. They have a lot of faith in me over there, with the idea that sooner or later I'll do something significant."

His sales are, he admits, "pretty catastrophic" with the income "barely paying production costs." Thanks largely to a constant series of barnstorming personal appearance tours the audience is growing. "In cities like Minneapolis, Philadelphia, Boston, and Denver. I'm a very bizarre cultural phenomenon."

It isn't all that smooth though, even with the exposure. Waits recalls with a sure shudder a series of tours opening the show for Frank Zappa and the Mothers—whose audience, sophisticated though they may be, were not ready for Waits and his "stories."

"I did three tours, until I couldn't stand it any more. It's very difficult for one man [Waits usually plays alone] to come out in front of between five and ten thousand people and get anything but visual and verbal insubordination from the audience. I wouldn't do it again—it makes me look bad, and scares me. People will come and throw produce at you—literally, I could say that I don't mind; that you can throw it at me and I'll pocket the money and run to Venezuela. But after a while it creates a very bitter attitude. It's excruciating."

Waits did learn, though, and his present old suit and loose tie stage costume dates from those tours. "There was no way that I could wear anything and stand out on stage. So I just did a complete 360 degrees. They started calling me 'The Wino.'"

How about the rest of the onstage attitude; the shuffling gait; the ad-lib appearance? "I know what works and what doesn't, strictly by trial and error. People who like what I do have come to expect this narrative; this I-don't-give-a-shit shuffle that I've been doing for a few years. I'm aware that I cut a certain sort of figure on stage. It's the difference between lighting up a cigarette in your living room, and lighting one up on stage—a whole different attitude takes over. Everything is blown up beyond proportion. I want to be able to go up and be a caricature of myself on stage."

Caricature, perhaps. But that's not at all to say that Waits has "sold out." He lives in one of Los Angeles's less expensive districts (Silver Lake), in a home that could be classed by any standards as "modest."

At home Waits drives a huge, black 1954 Cadillac which, he confesses, "costs me more than a new car probably would. I get six miles per gallon long distance; three driving around town. It eats, drips, and burns oil like crazy. It's comfortable for me though, it's roomy and I can put all my garbage in the backseat. I've always had old cars and always enjoyed Body by Fisher and other fine automotive structures."

His friends include his father and drinking buddies at the local bar.

For a while, Tom was getting along fine with his landlord too. But now, there's more than a hint of suspicion in the old man's eyes. "Before I was at home all day and paid the rent on time; he thought that I must be collecting unemployment insurance. But since I've been touring, I'll pay my rent in advance and leave home for a couple of weeks at a time. He can't understand that; thinks that I must be involved in something illegal."

Has success spoiled Tom Waits? Hardly spoiled. But, says Tom, hardly "success" either.

"I'm not concerned about financial success. I just don't think about it. If anything, I've become more comfortable, knowing that I can sleep until two and hang out until ten in the morning; and don't have to worry about losing my job.

"But I'm not a big star. I'm not even a twinkle," Waits's eyes dance.

"I'm just a rumour."

WAITS AND DOUBLE MEASURES

London Trax, March 18, 1981

Johnny Black

Put yourself in my place. Scant hours earlier I'd been regaled with the tale of how, in an interview the previous day, Tom had turned on a somewhat surprised lady journalist and growled, "I don't think I like you," in a voice that would trip the San Andreas Fault. For an hour they glared at each other in almost unbroken silence. So what chance do I have?

There's a favourite scene in gangster movies where the private dick is standing at the bar with the bad guy and the bartender slips him a note with his double brandy. "Look out kid, he's got a gun," it says. I had a similar experience when the phone rang an hour before I left my house and Waits's press officer nonchalantly told me, "You know he just got married?"

"Tom Waits? Married?"

"Yes. Last month, to a script analyst at 20th Century Fox."

Waits's version of how it happened is more appealing.

"Kathleen was living in a convent, studying to be a nun. I met her when they let her out for a party on New Year's Eve. She left the Lord for me."

The encounter is taking place in Dino's, a classless

49

Italian diner, full of South Ken schoolkids, across the road from the hotel. Tom's eyes roam the room until he zeroes in on a waitress.

"Two double brandies and two toasted cheese sandwiches," he orders, then, looking at me knowingly, "You have to have the food to get the drink." It's an apology.

"I've spent ten miserable years looking for her." He means his wife, not the waitress, although his songs might lead you to suspect otherwise. I recall tales of the days when it was not unknown for Waits to arrive at Warner Brothers Records in Los Angeles with a waitress in tow. He'd likely have met her in Reno or San Bernardino, wherever, and now he'd like W.E.A. to find her a job. She could sing like an angel. They all could.

"My wife's part Irish. Brennan. So we spent our honeymoon crawling up and down the shoulders of Ireland for the last three weeks. Best thing that ever happened to me.

"We stayed in an old house, used to be owned by William Blake. Radio was busted, so we called down to the guy on the desk but he'd gone to get parts for the radio. Didn't come back for four days. Just great. They live at my level of incompetence. We fit in real well there."

I notice that he's talking to my tape recorder rather than to me, and I wonder if he distrusts me. Maybe I should ask. I ask. There's a long pause. He coughs. He looks away and, just when I think I'm going to be ignored, he turns to my tape recorder and tells it, "Journalists enjoy creating scenes. You've created a situation here in order to write about it. You mix my words with your feelings and memories. That's what I used to do. I used to feel I had to create a situation where I could live out the life in my songs, but now I know that a distance from it can give you an equally important focus. I used to see Bogart movies and think that someday I'd meet him in the street in an old hat, trench coat, cigarette, smell of whiskey, on his way to a whorehouse, you know?"

It begins to seem possible, that Kathleen, the script-analysing nun, has had her effect on music's most notorious deadbeat. Waits's career has always been bolstered by his authenticity. While others simply wrote about being down-and-out, Waits lived the life. Or appeared to.

Confused, I turn to his three-years-out-of-date self-penned official biography. "It says here that your mother got you your first piano when you were just a kid?"

"Wellllllll," he draws the word out and leans forward to confide in me, "there's a sucker born every minute."

If there's a mental equivalent of a groan, it fluttered through my mind at that moment. How do you talk to a man who'd fake his own biography? I needed a plan and, fortunately, I had one. I'd prepared a long list of references from his songs and I nervously suggest to him that maybe we could, just for laughs, try word association. I'd give him a word and he'd react.

How about it?

"Excuse me." he growled and left the table.

As well as a plan, I needed another drink. Thankfully, he returned moments later and ordered two more doubles. "OK. Let's try it. What you got?"

Relieved, I glance down the list. "Winchell's Donut Shop?"

He coughs. "Part of the urban landscape of Los Angeles. There's one right near the studio. Highway patrolmen live on a steady diet of Benson & Hedges and Winchell's glazed donuts. That's why they're so mean."

"W. C. Fields?"

"I borrowed a line from him. 'Anybody who hates dogs and children can't be all bad.' Right? He was destined to either become a national institution or be locked inside of one."

I begin to relax. Either that second double has just hit him or he's starting to almost enjoy this. I pick another at random.

"Rickie Lee Jones."

"An old friend of mine. Not a good subject."

Panic. Try again. "Tijuana?"

"My father was a Spanish teacher. When I was ten we lived on a chicken ranch in Baja California for about five months. I spent a lot of time in Mexico but I hardly go back now."

That's better. "Francis Ford Coppola."

"I've been working on Francis's new film since last April. It's called *One from the Heart*. A whole catastrophe. I've never taken on anything that big, but I enjoyed it very much. I did songs and underscoring. I really enjoy his creative process."

Kurt Vonnegut Jr. used to do an excellent lecture in which he claimed that there were only three basic plotlines for authors to work with. The first one is: boy gets girl, boy loses girl, boy gets girl back. According to Tom Waits, that's also the plot of *One from the Heart*.

Checking the list again I pick out "Kentucky Avenue." It's a song in which Waits included the lines:

> *Take the spokes from your wheelchair*
> *and a magpie's wings*
> *and tie 'em to your shoulders and your feet.*
> *I'll steal a hacksaw from my dad*
> *and cut the braces off your legs*
> *and we'll bury them tonight in the cornfield.*

"My best friend, when I was a kid, had polio. I didn't understand what polio was. I just knew it took him longer to get to the bus stop than me. I dunno. Sometimes I think kids know more than anybody. I rode a train once to Santa Barbara with this kid and it almost seemed like he lived a life somewhere before he was born and he brought what he knew with him into this world and so . . ." His voice fades off for a moment, then, ". . . It's what you don't know that's usually more interesting. Things you wonder about, things you have yet to make up your mind about. There's more to deal with than just your fundamental street wisdom. Dreams. Nightmares."

"Nightmares?" I perk up. "One of the words on my list is nightmares."

He nods, as if he knew. "I have very violent dreams. A lot of that happens because you're on the road a lot and you wake up in a hotel room and you don't know . . . I used to wake up alone, but now that I'm married there's somebody to turn to before you forget."

Yes, the new Mrs. Waits is having her effect. I try another from the list. "Perrier water."

"The French pulled one over on us. They wash their feet in it and sell it to us for ninety-nine cents a bottle."

And another. "The Jack Kerouac School of Disembodied Poetry?"

"Disembowelled poets?"

"Disembodied Poetry."

"No, I'm not familiar with that. Do they travel in packs, like dogs? At one time, when I was younger, when I was on the, uh, threshold of unravelling my personality," he glances at me to see how I'm taking this and, apparently satisfied with my glazed stare, continues, "I was trying to decide who I was, where I was going, whether I wanted to be a bricklayer or a hairdresser. I was looking for career alternatives and Kerouac just . . . there's a great deal of pressure on you at that age to decide what you're gonna do."

Moving from the sublime to the ridiculous, I try, "Ronald Reagan."

"We [he means America] watched the whole campaign for

the presidency like it was a situation comedy. The Carter administration was a television programme that ran for four years, then the network cancelled it. We look on everything in television terms. When you're a child it's your parents, or at least your babysitter. You don't feel any sense of government control in America. You expect to see anything on television. We wanna hear bad news out of a pretty mouth. Now, they choose announcers like they choose juries, colour coded—Black, Chinese, Jewish, Mexican, Catholic—to suit every taste. Newsreaders are the real personalities."

My list is getting shorter. A misunderstanding of the word "Prez," included as an influence in his biography, caused me to pick Elvis Presley as a topic on my list. (Prez is actually the nickname of saxophonist Lester Young, and my ignorance can only be excused because any interest I might have developed in jazz was systematically pumped out of me by an elder sister who played Kenny Ball's "Midnight in Moscow" ad nauseam. That's Latin for twice.)

After the misunderstanding is cleared up, Waits tells me, "I felt that what they did to him after he died was necrophilia. You don't think of people like that as being mortal. They don't cry or bleed or sleep. I wrote a poem about it after it was over. It felt like something had ended."

"How about the Ivar Theatre?"

"A burlesque house in Hollywood, right next door to the library. It was originally a legitimate theatre. Lord Buckley and Lenny Bruce played there. Now it's just a strip joint, full of transsexuals. Behind the Ivar is another nightclub called the Gaslight. Used to be called the Sewers of Paris."

His visions of the seamy side of Hollywood make Waits unique among Californian musicians. Rather than sun, sand, and surf, or even cowboys, coke, and cactus, Waits sees California as damp, dark, and dangerous.

Next on the list? "Knife fights."

"I stay away from those. There's a lot of Mexican street gangs in Los Angeles. I don't subscribe to gangs of any kind." Guns and knives crop up frequently in his lyrics, so it's no surprise to learn that the first song he remembers hearing was "El Paso" by Marty Robbins.

"Greyhound buses?"

"I've been all over the world, every city in America and I feel like I don't know anyplace. Some name comes up in conversation and I can say, 'Oh, I've been there.' But I don't know anything, never see anything. You're so insulated, usually you get no time to find a neighbourhood where you feel comfortable. You learn to wear your home on your back. It's strange and peculiar mostly. That's why I liked Ireland. My wife and me stayed three weeks."

"Privacy."

"Sure. That's even more important to me now that I'm married. For a writer, it seems that your anonymity is important. *The Devil's Dictionary* defines being famous as being 'conspicuously miserable.' I like to feel I can move around without being noticed."

I see his eye straying continually to the clock. He's been doing interviews all day, sneaking the odd ten minutes between each to slip up to his room and talk to his wife. There's already another hack waiting to invade his privacy in the hotel, and then there's the rehearsal at eight and Europe in the morning. Still, he gives me all the time he can.

"One last question?"

"Sure."

"There's a soft streak in you, isn't there?"

He laughs. It's a deliberately naive question, because there's a soft streak in everybody. I just didn't expect it to be so near the surface in Tom Waits. "Yeah. Right up my back. Charles

Bukowski says, 'As the spirit wanes, the form appears.' The whole creative process is kind of embarrassing sometimes. 'As the spirit wanes, the form appears.' " He repeats it for my benefit, picks up the tab and we leave.

With Waits there's no way to tell what's real and what's imagined. In the flesh, just as on his albums, he's able to evade you, make you wonder what he invented, what he embroidered and where the fact meets the fiction. His whole career, so far, could be straight out of Kerouac, but from here on it might well read more like Flann O'Brien.

"I've spent ten miserable years looking for her." Those words will echo heavily in the hearts of Waits worshippers who will find it as difficult to swallow as Dylan finding God. After all, didn't Waits write "Better Off Without a Wife"?

And so what? He's five years on now, and if it ends in divorce next year I'll applaud as Waits punches the first idiot to say "I told you so." After ten years of nightmares, give him the right to one dream, and who knows, maybe they will live happily ever after.

TOM WAITS

Washington Post, October 29, 1979

Geoffrey Himes

A peculiar kind of poetry is possible very early in the morning. It was forty minutes after midnight when Tom Waits slouched onto the stage of the Warner Theatre early yesterday morning. A crumpled felt hat shaded his eyes; a stained undersized shirt pulled up over his flowery arm tattoo; a jazz quartet swung and bopped behind him. Standing at every angle but straight, Waits muttered, crooned, growled, and wheezed his very peculiar, very powerful poetry.

Waits's songs depict drunks, hookers, petty thieves, small-town refugees, greasy dives, all-night drives, used car lots, hotel shootouts and *The Heart of Saturday Night.* Bruce Springsteen likes to sing about these characters, but Waits sings as one. The clock turned back an hour during Waits's set; time turned back thirty-five years into the films noirs of Humphrey Bogart. Waits played the original connoisseur of cool who supplied Bogart with information and wisdom through his alcoholic haze.

Waits used plenty of props to create a musical theater that put Broadway period pieces like *Chicago* and *Bubbling Brown*

Sugar to shame. Using a cash register as a percussive instrument, Waits launched into an amphetamine litany of advertising slogans in "Step Right Up." Leaning on a battered gas pump, Waits assumed the character of a small-town mechanic telling the story of an all-night cross-country drive taken on impulse. He sang "Putnam County" as fake snow fell around him at an L.A. newsstand. But even sitting alone at the piano Waits managed to wedge the audience into a time and space warp of his own special making.

ONE FOR THE SHOESHINE MAN

Black Sparrow Press, 1977

Charles Bukowski

Note: Waits frequently mentions Bukowski as among his favorite writers. This piece captures the early Waitsian world as well as any Bukowski poem that's been published.

the balance is preserved by the snails climbing the
Santa Monica cliffs;
the luck is in walking down Western Avenue
and having the girls in a massage
parlor holler at you, "Hello, Sweetie!"
the miracle is having 5 women in love
with you at the age of 55,
and the goodness is that you are only able
to love one of them.
the gift is having a daughter more gentle
than you are, whose laughter is finer
than yours.
the peace comes from driving a
blue 67 Volks through the streets like a

teenager, radio tuned to The Host Who Loves You
Most, feeling the sun, feeling the solid hum
of the rebuilt motor
as you needle through traffic.
the grace is being able to like rock music,
symphony music, jazz . . .
anything that contains the original energy of
joy.

and the probability that returns
is the deep blue low
yourself flat upon yourself
within the guillotine walls
angry at the sound of the phone
or anybody's footsteps passing;
but the other probability—
the lilting high that always follows—
makes the girl at the checkstand in the
supermarket look like
Marilyn
like Jackie before they got her Harvard lover
like the girl in the high school that we
all followed home.

there is that which helps you believe
in something else besides death:
somebody in a car approaching
on a street too narrow,
and he or she pulls aside to let you
by, or the old fighter Beau Jack
shining shoes
after blowing the entire bankroll
on parties

on women
on parasites,
humming, breathing on the leather,
working the rag
looking up and saying:
"what the hell, I had it for a
while. that beats the
other."

I am bitter sometimes
but the taste has often been
sweet. it's only that I've
feared to say it. it's like
when your woman says,
"tell me you love me," and
you can't.

if you see me grinning from
my blue Volks
running a yellow light
driving straight into the sun
I will be locked in the
arms of a
crazy life
thinking of trapeze artists
of midgets with big cigars
of a Russian winter in the early 40's
of Chopin with his bag of Polish soil
of an old waitress bringing me an extra
cup of coffee and laughing
as she does so.

the best of you
I like more than you think.
the others don't count
except that they have fingers and heads
and some of them eyes
and most of them legs
and all of them
good and bad dreams
and a way to go.

justice is everywhere and it's working
and the machine guns and the frogs
and the hedges will tell you
so.

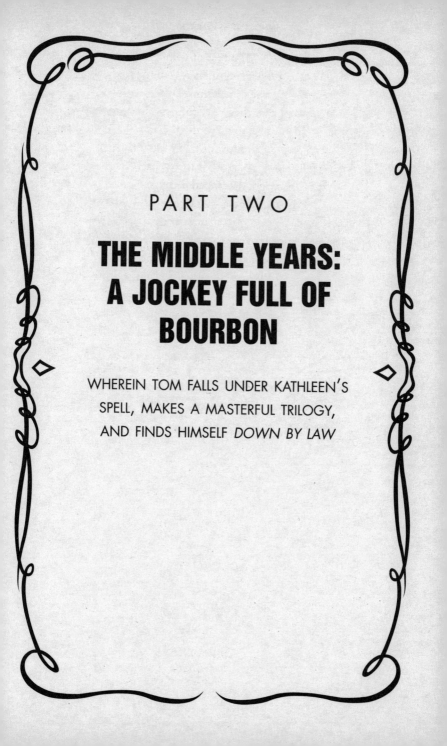

PART TWO

THE MIDDLE YEARS: A JOCKEY FULL OF BOURBON

WHEREIN TOM FALLS UNDER KATHLEEN'S
SPELL, MAKES A MASTERFUL TRILOGY,
AND FINDS HIMSELF *DOWN BY LAW*

TOM WAITS MAKES GOOD: ROCK'S SCAVENGER SONGWRITER HAS BECOME A LEGEND IN HIS OWN SPARE TIME

Los Angeles Times Magazine, February 22, 1987

Robert Sabbag

Parking is not a problem on a Saturday night at 6th and Main in downtown Los Angeles. Jack's "Frolic Room," by the bus station, does not cater to the carriage trade. There is plenty of room on the street and more than enough room at the bar inside, where a quarter will buy you a boiled egg, a Roi-Tan, or a draft.

Tom Waits says, "I think you're going to like this place."

Jack's is refuge to a regular clientele, to the occasional straggler or pilgrim, some dedicated to drinking, some just violating parole. The bartender, a certifiable rickets case, who looks like he would rather be reading the *Racing Form,* has just served a guy wearing a visored, blue polyester cap with crossed anchors on the crown.

"The captain," Waits says. "Just in from Bermuda. All the eccentric millionaires come to Jack's. The idle rich. They all come to Jack with their problems."

Singer, songwriter, actor, composer, something of a legend in his own spare time, Tom Waits, over the years like a wanted man lying in ambush in the musical chaparral, has fortified a shifting position for himself between infamy and obscurity.

A performer frequently associated in the popular imagination with the subject matter of his music—"Christmas Card from a Hooker in Minneapolis," "The Piano Has Been Drinking (Not Me)"—Waits has had a devoted and rather distinctive following from the outset of his career; admirers of his work customarily are greeted with the kindness bestowed only upon the afflicted. Even now, telling many Americans that your favorite singer is Tom Waits is like telling them that your favorite actor is John Wilkes Booth.

Current events threaten to change all that. *Rain Dogs,* issued in 1985 in advance of Waits's first tour in two years, his first U.S. dates in five, was cited by the *New York Times* as "the year's most dazzling and protean pop album." Waits followed it with sold-out concerts in New York, Los Angeles, and London. On the strength of the album, *Rolling Stone* named him songwriter of the year. *Frank's Wild Years,* a play he co-authored with his wife, writer Kathleen Brennan, was produced last summer by Chicago's Steppenwolf Theatre Company. Selected to open the New York Film Festival last fall was *Down by Law,* in which he stars. His next album, *Frank's Wild Years,* will be released next month.

The only witness unimpressed, if not unmoved, by these events appears to be Tom Waits himself. "I like it in here," he says, as the bartender publicly shuts off a guy's credit. "Nobody gives a damn about you. They don't care who you are or where you're from."

Waits is of the scavenger school of songwriting, and at a place like Jack's, salvageable material is found in abundance.

"It's really all around you all the time," he points out. "It's just a matter of framing it, getting thrilled by it. You have to find something to capture it in, make sure your umbrella is upside down."

Waits is always one step ahead of, or one step behind, the

conversation at hand, always alive to the action, his eyes perpetually shifting beneath the brim of his hat. Hanging out with him in public is like keeping company with a man pursued by assassins.

Speaking about the need to impose limitations, about constructing a framework within which to write, he draws an analogy.

"Like the guy in prison who made a tattoo machine out of a Bic pen, a guitar string, and a cassette loader. Some red ink. He wrapped the handle in such a way, with a T-shirt, it felt just like a bird in your hand."

All the while he is speaking, he is scanning the room.

"I'd like to do a movie—forty-eight hours in the life of a guy, he's just been released from a mental institution, New York's an inferno, and he's just got a few pills left."

His attention drifts eventually to the wildlife program on the television over the bar. "They have programs about us, too, you know." He is talking about the animals. He wants to know if you think the world is alive.

"I believe that the earth is a living thing," he announces. "Everything outside is like barnacles on a whale. Someday it's gonna rear up and throw us all off." He shakes his head. "I'm afraid to dig holes in the yard. I won't even cut the grass."

And on that note, the interview takes to the street.

The Travelers Café, on Temple, just off the Hollywood Freeway, featuring "delicious Filipino-Chinese food" in addition to the standard American fare, is serving three neighborhood customers at the counter tonight. The booths in the back are empty. The only traveler in evidence, an elderly gent hunched over a weathered walking stick, is anchored to a cushion on the couch by the door.

If Waits is the Travelers's most celebrated regular, it is only insofar as he is celebrated outside the neighborhood. As far as proprietors Leon and Pauline are concerned, around here he is just Tom. The father of two, Waits is reluctant to open his house to the press, and taking guests to the Travelers, just a few blocks from home, is his variation on bringing out the good china.

He slides into a booth and orders coffee.

"My run-down career?"

"A rundown on your career. On the subject of your career."

"Oh, well, that's another thing entirely," he says.

Does he agree that, in fact, it is taking off like a rocket?

"My career is more like a dog," he concedes. "Sometimes it comes when you call. Sometimes it gets up in your lap. Sometimes it rolls over. Sometimes it just won't do anything."

The theatrical voice, a cross between mellifluous baritone and heavy-equipment breakdown, is only part of what draws one's attention to Waits. An apparently healthy young man, a vigorous performer, Waits works hard to display the visual attributes of a guy on the back end of a drunk-and-disorderly arrest.

His clothing, at best, borders on the nondescript. As a sartorial statement, it crosses that frontier between optimism and delusion. As friend and fellow musical outlaw Kinky Friedman points out, Waits is a guy who "looks like he was put together by committee." Sporting a fedora of the kind associated less with the stalking of vanished missionaries and more with the likes of Hoagy Carmichael, he carries his head low, in the manner of the chronically self-effacing. He speaks at the speed at which forty-weight motor oil circulates in the cold, and with the possible exception of Keith Richards, whom he admires, Waits lays claim to what may be the sorriest posture in rock 'n' roll.

His appearance reinforces that image of him so often painted in the press—the Damon Runyon of downtown Los Angeles, mired in a landscape strewn with the working parts of his music, "hobos, prostitutes, people in trouble, the negative machinery I create to motivate myself." It is an image that his audience has come to embrace. It is not, he admits, an entirely accurate one.

"When you have a certain geography that becomes associated with you," he explains, "people dream you into it. They develop their own ideas about who you are and what you do, and you can only control a certain amount of that."

Meeting every opportunity to look off into the distance, reaching into his pockets, dragging on his jacket's flaps, his hands continually tampering with the structural integrity of his hat, Waits exhibits the body language of a man who is eminently ill at ease when it comes to talking about himself.

"I am not a photojournalist," he continues. "I do not do reportage. You tell someone stories—they come from a lot of places, dreams and memories and lies and things, things you found and heard and saw and read and dreamed and made up."

Waits, who communicates with the world at large most successfully on the strength of his music, and in the absence of that, principally by way of rumor, works hard to remain an outsider.

He plays fast and loose with his biography; his press kit reads like a rap sheet on a guy with nothing but aliases.

"I see the way a lot of people talk to the press. To me it's a bit like talking to a cop." What the media seem to have replaced, he says, is any organic sense of people. "So maybe I pull back. I'm more interested in these types of things"—he does pull back, looks out the window, waves his hand—"these people, I guess, in these neighborhoods. My dad teaches school not far from here, and sometimes I get recognized on my block—that's Frank's boy, over there. I like that; that's more interesting to me."

Tom Waits, the second of three children, as far as anyone can tell, was born in Pomona, eight years to the day after the bombing of Pearl Harbor, the only son of two southern California schoolteachers, neither of whom was a practiced musician.

"All the psychopaths and all the alcoholics are on my father's side of the family," he will tell you. "On my mother's side, we have all the ministers."

School, like any family business, posed its problems for Waits. His formal education was unremarkable at best. What little he picked up that was compelling in school—apart from a desire to leave it—he picked up, he says, at Robert E. Lee Elementary in south Los Angeles. There he picked up a trumpet.

"A Cleveland Greyhound. It was a silver trumpet, and I played taps at the end of the school day and got there early and played reveille as the flag went up."

It was the first and last instrument on which Waits took lessons. From cheap Mexican guitars he moved on to the piano—and from playing Jerome Kern and George Gershwin he moved on to playing around with music of his own. It was not something he was prepared to hook his future on until a succession of jobs after high school left him with little enthusiasm for anything else.

"It's like throwing yourself through a window," he says. "If you don't make any progress, it's kind of embarrassing."

Among the clubs he played was the Troubadour in West Hollywood, where a performance in 1969 landed him a management contract. Three years later he signed with Asylum Records. His first album, *Closing Time,* in 1973, won him an immediate audience and earned him the instant recognition of his contemporaries: "Ol' 55," later recorded by the Eagles, is one of many songs he wrote covered by performers more successful than he.

The Heart of Saturday Night, released in 1974, was followed a year later by a live two-record set, *Nighthawks at the Diner,* the experiment that crystallized various elements of his act: the sophisticated funk, the skid row baritone, the arranged disarray, the rocks upon which he built his musical church.

Waits, at the time, was touring continually, his answer to no-fixed-address the Tropicana Motel on Santa Monica Boulevard, then a nine-dollar-a-night, music-industry hobo palace where rock 'n' roll met Nathanael West—a kind of ranchette manqué, pop-culture landmark haunted by the ghosts of Jimi Hendrix, Janis Joplin, and others and immortalized on celluloid by Andy Warhol in *Trash.*

There Waits's public image began taking on its anatomy. "When I lived at the Tropicana, I wanted to break windows, smoke cigars and stay up late. That was my dream."

It was from the Tropicana that Waits, over a piano in the kitchen, would fulfill his promise as poet laureate of the down-and-out. In 1976, from some fertile lake bed of the imagination where *Naked Lunch* and Stephen Foster uneasily converged, drawing up such sweet odes to misery as "Invitation to the Blues" and "Bad Liver and a Broken Heart," he delivered his fourth album, *Small Change,* the rich, expressive tour de force that established his reputation as an outright original.

Profiles in the *New Yorker* and *Newsweek* were two of many that year. Three albums later, in 1980, Waits was hired to compose the soundtrack for Francis Coppola's offbeat "lounge operetta," *One from the Heart.* "I wrote my first tango. That's always a big moment." The movie did very little business. Waits was nominated for an Academy Award.

It was the success of that endeavor, more than anything else, that enabled Waits to do what he did next. With *Swordfishtrombones* and subsequently *Rain Dogs,* his eighth and ninth albums, it was as though he had finally taken his hat off and let the birds fly out. On top of the guitar, bass, piano, and traditional percussion that had distinguished his music, he imposed marimbas, metal Anglungs, bagpipes, the bowed saw, brake drums under stress, the accordion, and the force applied to a chair.

"You can bang on anything," he is fond of saying.

As Waits's music got further out there, his following curiously grew larger. In its way, this mainstream acceptance contradicts everything he has learned about popular music.

"Most music, in its purest form, has to be gentrified before it reaches the big ear. It's the same thing with fashion. You can't walk into a room wearing nothing but aluminum foil. There has to be something familiar there—you have to be wearing a tie."

On *Rain Dogs,* one of the more flamboyant neckties was Keith Richards's guitar.

"An animal," Waits says. "He's part of the earth. I was expecting a big entourage like a Fellini movie, you know—people that don't speak English, a lot of fur. And they just tumbled out of a limo. He comes in laughing, shoes all tore up. He stands at ten after seven if you can imagine that. Arms at five o'clock, legs at two o'clock, with no apparatus, nothing suspended. He's all below the waist. And if he doesn't feel it, he'll walk away. I was just flattered that he would come. It's kind of like a rite of passage or something."

Waits, whose musical development is probably more typical of jazzmen than of popular musicians—"The geography of the imagination should have a little bit more wilderness to it; I hate when it becomes subdivided"—is no stranger to compromise or the toll it takes.

"Thelonious Monk's brother works in a tollbooth on the Jersey Turnpike. That's who's taking the toll. He gets everything. So you feel better about making those compromises."

"Little Carbon Clean-Out Here on Union Avenue"

Cruising the boulevards of downtown Los Angeles with Tom Waits is like walking the streets of seventeenth-century London with Samuel Pepys. Nothing escapes his very particular interpretation of history.

"I get in the car, I just start to drive, and my mind wanders."

Coleridge blamed it on opium.

"Everything here eventually turns into something else. It's not good if you're insecure. That was a fire station, now it's an Asian market. I bet they still get calls for fires. Which must be uncomfortable. To have to tell a guy whose house is burning down that he's got the wrong number. It must be disturbing."

Even eyesores, such as cigarette billboards, get sucked into the dissertation.

"Now, the Marlboro man, his mom is a night clerk at the Wilmont Hotel in Chicago. I'll swear on a stack of Bibles. I checked in; I told her I was playing a club there. She said, 'You're in show business?' I said yeah. She said, 'The Marlboro man is my son. You probably know him if you're in show biz. Bob Jenkins, works out of Phoenix.' "

This is not information one is likely to find corroborated in travel brochures. It is not the stuff of American legend.

". . . the Silver Lake Motel. That's where Sam Cooke died."

Maybe it was the Hacienda.

"Here it is. Robert Taylor's Car Wash. I do not lie. I shagged cars, pumped gas, I did like a hot wax—that was my specialty. They didn't have a hot wax here until I came in. I said you got to get yourself a genuine Simoniz paste-wax job. They tip their hat to me when I come around here. When I'm playing in town, they put me on the marquee—see the marquee, over there?"

"CAR WASH / 8:30–5:30?"

"TOM WAITS."

"They used to open later. Hi Ho Inn, across the street. You could spend your day here. You wash the car, you get breakfast over at Al's while your car is being washed. You go for cocktails at the Chit Chat. Get a flattop at the barbershop. You go sleep it off at the Hi Ho. The day is complete. Then there's tomorrow. Those were the days."

Tom Waits says it is pretty much goodbye to L.A. According to sources, he has been saying this for years.

"Maybe we'll end up in Missouri. I want a place where I can put a briar patch. Sit on the porch with a shotgun and collect all the kids' baseballs. Go crazy. 'Don't hit one in my yard!' A place where everything I drag home I can leave in the yard, you know."

On Rampart, there is a tree that has grown up around one of the streetlamps. On the way back to the Travelers, Waits points it out.

"You know Poire William?"

"It's a brandy."

"It's a pear brandy," he says. "And it's from France. And every bottle has a pear in it. What they do is, they grow 'em that way. Every pear in the orchard, at a certain point in the maturity of the fruit—they take it and they put a bottle over the bloom. And the bloom matures inside a bottle that's propped up by a crutch. I mean it, you didn't know that?"

"It's bottled on the tree."

"At a certain point, when the pear is full throttle, they snip it. And it's a riddle. It's a riddle, and they allow you to spend the rest of your life solving it."

Tom Waits, a man, it seems, who has finally moved into his season, is content to view such riddles as their own reward. Ask him, was it just a matter of time, did he always know it would happen, and, navigating the traffic of downtown Los Angeles, he will hit the accelerator and tell you, "You can't really look in the mirror that much."

TOM WAITS FOR NO MAN

SPIN, November 1985

Glenn O'Brien

How to act. How to watch *Mr. Rogers.* How to pick a
road manager. How to live in the big city. And more
solid information.

Tom Waits has a voice that could guide ships through dense
fog. He sings songs that are poetic, hilarious, scary,
touching, hallucinatory, and fine. Maybe he's like John Lee
Hooker, Mose Allison, Neville Brand, Francois Villon, Søren
Kierkegaard, Lenny Bruce, and Wallace Beery rolled into one.
Sometimes his band sounds like a Salvation Army combo covering a Stones tune. But nothing really sounds like Waits. Or
writes like. Or looks like. Or talks like.

His new album, *Rain Dogs,* is his tenth. His songs have also
been done by the Eagles, Bette Midler, Jerry Jeff Walker, Lee
Hazlewood, Dion, Richie Havens, Manhattan Transfer, Martin
Mull, and Barbi Benton. His score for Francis Ford Coppola's
One from the Heart was nominated for an Oscar. He has also
acted in Coppola's films: *The Outsiders, Rumble Fish* (pool hall
owner), and *The Cotton Club* (club manager Herman Stark). In
the next year he will star in films directed by Jim Jarmusch and

Robert Frank, and, he hopes, bring the musical play he's been working on for a couple of years now to Broadway.

GO: What's happening with your musical?

TW: It's going to be done in Chicago in the late spring by the Steppenwolf Company, which did *Balm in Gilead* and *Orpheus*. Terry Kinney going to direct it. He's in *Orpheus*. It's called *Frank's Wild Years*.

GO: That was a song on your *Swordfishtrombones* album. Are you using songs from that album?

TW: It's going to be all new, written just for the show.

GO: Are you in it?

TW: Yeah, I'm Frank. I never acted on stage before. I'm studying for it.

GO: What do you have to learn?

TW: I just have to learn honest, truthful behavior, that's all.

GO: How do you learn that?

TW: Just from practice, like anything else. It's kind of early on in the production now. We're going to have a reading of it in a few weeks. We'll find out what sticks to the wall and what doesn't. I'd like it to be as unconventional as possible and still have some focus and structure and credibility. It's going to be stylized. I don't think I've ever seen a musical that I've liked, really.

GO: Did you write the book?

TW: I wrote it with Kathleen Brennan.

GO: How did you collaborate?

TW: With great difficulty.

GO: Did you work together or did you send stuff back and forth?

TW: Well, she's my wife. We sent stuff back and forth. Like dishes, books, frying pans, vases.

GO: Does it start out like the song, with Frank burning his house down?

TW: It actually starts out with Frank at the end of his rope, despondent, penniless, on a park bench in east St. Louis in a snowstorm, having a going-out-of-business sale on the whole last ten years of his life. Like the guys around here on Houston Street with a little towel on the sidewalk, some books, some silverware, a radio that doesn't work, maybe a Julie London album. Then he falls asleep and dreams his way back home. I've been saying that it's a cross between *Eraserhead* and *It's a Wonderful Life*.

GO: Ever work with your wife before?

TW: No, this is a first. And a last.

GO: Do you think it's hard to be critical with somebody that you're close to?

TW: Yeah. Or it's hard not to be critical.

GO: So, what's your day like?

TW: Well, lately it's been a little easier. I get up at about seven o'clock with the baby and I get the Rice Krispies going and the French toast, then I put on *Mr. Rogers*.

GO: How old is the baby?

TW: Two.

GO: Does the baby watch *Mr. Rogers* or do you?

TW: I watch it and I make her watch it with me. I do subtitles. I do a Fourteenth Street version of *Mr. Rogers' Neighborhood*, where everybody's out of work and selling drugs on the corner. When I was a kid the show was *Sheriff John*. He was a policeman. That's who I was forced to get to know.

GO: In New York we had Officer Joe Bolton, an Irish cop; he was the host of the *Three Stooges Show*, which, I guess, was supposed to keep a lid on the knucklehead behavior. What's your baby's name?

TW: Well, we haven't picked a name yet. I told her that when she's eighteen she can pick any name she wants. In the meantime, we'll call her something different every day.

GO: What is she today?

TW: Max today. She's been everything. We just can't seem to make up our minds. When she meets somebody and likes them she takes their name. She speaks seventeen languages. She's now in military school in Connecticut. I only get to see her on weekends. At night when I get home all the kids line up in their uniforms and Joe Bob's got my martini and Max has my slippers and Roosevelt has my pipe. They all say "Hello, Daddy!"

GO: So what happens after *Mr. Rogers?*

TW: Well, I usually go to sleep under the table somewhere. Every day is different. I go over to the seminary on Tenth Avenue a lot. For a couple of hours. Just to relax. It reminds me of Illinois. I've been doing the record for months, so I just got a break. I was getting two or three hours of sleep for a couple of months.

GO: Did you record in the daytime?

TW: Yeah, from about ten in the morning. I was working in midtown. I had to fight all the traffic and all the other commuters. The hardest thing was just getting to the studio. After that I was all right.

GO: This album has really a lot of songs on it.

TW: Nineteen. Everybody says that's too many.

GO: Did you record others that didn't make it on the record?

TW: Yeah, I had about twenty-five all together. There's a religious song that didn't get on the album. It's called "Bethlehem, PA." It's about a guy named Bob Christ. There were a couple of others.

GO: I'm really interested in the songs that don't make it onto albums.

TW: I end up dismantling them. It's just like having a car that doesn't run. You just use it for parts. "The rest of the guys are gonna have to go out there and stick together. Bob, you look out for your younger brother there. And all of you go out there into the world of radio and performance value." I feel like Fagin. It took a long time to record this album, two and a half months. The recording process has a peak, and then it dissipates. You have to be careful that it doesn't go on too long. Then you start to unravel everything. Nowadays, if you want a certain sound you don't have to get it now, you can get it later. When you're mixing, electronically. I wanted to get it now, so I felt I cooked it and I ate it. You can establish percussion sounds later electronically. But I ended up banging on things so I felt that it really responded. If I couldn't get the right sound out of the drum set we'd get a chest of drawers in the bathroom and hit it real hard with a two-by-four. Things like that. That's on "Singapore." Those little things made me feel more involved than sampling on a synthesizer.

GO: How did you wind up getting Keith Richards to play on this album?

TW: I had this thing I used to say. This sound, I didn't know how to identify it, and I used to say, "That Keith Richards–type style thing." So instead of learning how to explain what I meant, I heard he was coming to New York, and it worked out.

GO: Now you're going on tour. Do you pick your tour band just on musicianship or do you try to pick people who are easy to get along with?

TW: In a way, I pick people who are easy to get along with. I just have the road manager make announcements. "Whatever you do, don't go to Tom with all of your problems. If you have problems with girlfriends, if you have problems with your instruments or travel plans, please see the road manager. Do not approach Tom with any personal problems! I repeat: do not approach Tom with any personal problems!" I'm best when I don't get involved. "Do not discuss salary with Tom!" It's going to be good.

GO: Do you ever listen to music?

TW: It's hard for me to sit down and just do that. I like it best when I hear it coming through the wall in a hotel room. I like it best on a bad speaker from a block away.

GO: I find that if I go for a long time without listening to any music, I become vulnerable to what I hear. Like, I'll go around for a whole day whistling "This Bud's for you . . ."

TW: Yeah, you really have to watch your musical diet, especially when you're trying to write something. A couple of years ago on my wife's birthday we heard a song called "Jesus's Blood Never Failed Me Yet," and it stayed in my head for so long.

GO: Have you ever been asked to do a commercial?

TW: A couple. They wanted me for American Airlines. But

we couldn't get the money up. A recreational vehicle company wanted me to do an ad for them. I've had offers for beer commercials.

GO: I could have sworn I saw Robert Gordon in a Budweiser commercial.

TW: Yeah, that was him.

GO: Dr. John does that toilet paper commercial.

TW: Yeah, "Roll all night long." He also does a cookie commercial.

GO: Springsteen turned down $12 million to appear in a Chrysler commercial for three seconds.

TW: Yeah, they came to me first. The same offer, $12 million, but they wanted me to be in it for one second. I said, "Forget it! Go ask Bruce."

GO: Maybe they could get John Cougar. Unless his name identifies him too much with General Motors.

TW: Honda offered me $150,000 to do that commercial. That's twice what Lou got. They said I could write my own copy. Chevrolet! They won't leave me alone. Then a feminine hygiene commercial wanted me.

GO: Summer's Eve Disposable Douche makes you feel fresh as a country lane?

TW: Those were my lines! I just couldn't say them. I tried it so many different ways, I just couldn't make it.

GO: Like Rocky.

TW: It's hard, because we're so product-oriented that our only real spiritual leadership comes from that angle, chasing the dollar. It's like it's OK if you get enough money for it. Selling out is all right as long as you get enough.

GO: I don't hold the toilet paper commercial against Dr. John, though. There's a guy who deserves to make some money.

TW: But I don't know if he got enough!

GO: I've heard that record companies are sick of paying for videos, so they're trying to get companies to pay to have their products displayed in them.

TW: Yeah, you see that all over in films now. Whenever they're in the kitchen you're going to see Nabisco. It's weird, though. You spend all this time on the road and then you realize that in a matter of seconds you can reach more people than you have in the last seventeen years. That's a little hard to swallow.

GO: How do you audition a road manager?

TW: Well, you take a couple of candidates out to the Mojave Desert and you leave the car by the side of the road and you walk for a couple of days, and when you get to a stream, the guys that want to drink from a cup, those are the guys you don't want. It's the guys that throw themselves headlong into the stream and just drink, those are the best soldiers. What I'm really looking for, though, is an all-midget orchestra. They could all stay in the same room and on stage they could all share the same light.

GO: What's your life like on the road?

TW: Well, you get up in the morning, along with millions of other Americans, and you go to the airport. You get to a new town. I go to the chamber of commerce as soon as I get in and talk to whoever is in charge. Sometimes I do. But most of the time you really don't know where you are. It's very possible that you may come out on stage and say, "It's great to be here in St. Louis" and you could very well be in Denver or Seattle. That's happened.

GO: I really hate it when bands come out and say "Hello, New York."

TW: It's an arrogant remark, isn't it? Assuming that everyone of value connected with New York is there. I think it should be against the law for anyone to name a band after a city. Boston, Chicago, any of those.

GO: And those state bands too: Kansas, Alabama . . .

TW: It's criminal.

GO: I was so surprised when I found out that Oregon was a jazz band.

TW: Yeah, that's not right.

GO: When I met you about two years ago you were just sort of visiting New York, and you've been here ever since. Was that a radical change? Being a New Yorker by accident?

TW: We've moved eight times since we've been here. New York is like a ship. It's like a ship full of rats, and the water's on fire. People move to Brooklyn and say, "I feel isolated." That's insane.

GO: This morning I was driving on the Long Island Expressway and I realized that if I was in L.A. that kind of thing would never happen, because there's no rivers to be on the wrong side of.

TW: Yeah, people won't drop you as a friend if you live in Van Nuys or Santa Monica. You can't relate New York and what it requires of you as a citizen to remain civilized and cognizant and liquid . . . it doesn't relate to anyplace in the United States. For what you're paying here to live, if you were in Iowa you could have an estate.

GO: Have you heard any interesting bands lately?

TW: Have you heard of the Pogues? They're like a drunk Clancy Brothers. They, like, drink during the sessions as opposed to after the session. They're like Dead End Kids on a leaky boat. That *Treasure Island* kind of decadence. There's something really nice about them. I heard another record called *Robespierre's Velvet Basement* by Nikki Sudden. That's something to listen to. There's Agnes Bernell. She's a German singer from the forties who just made a record of a lot of her old songs. Elvis Costello was the executive producer. Her lyrics are great. "Father's lying dead on the ironing board, smelling of Lux and Drambuie." That's one of her first lines.

GO: Are you doing any more movies?

TW: I'm doing a picture in New Orleans in November with Jim Jarmusch and John Lurie. It's me and John Lurie and Bill Dana and Bob Wagner and Dean Martin and Sammy Davis, Jr.

GO: A Rat Pack movie.

TW: It's John Lurie and myself and this guy named Benigni who's a really famous comedian in Italy. It's called *Down by Law* and it's about three guys in prison breaking out, through the swamps, through the bloodhounds. They're all innocent victims of blind justice. Then I'm doing a film with Robert Frank, who took the picture on the cover of the record. It's called *There Ain't No Candy Mountain*. It's going to be written by Rudy Wurlitzer and directed by Robert Frank. We're going to do it in the spring. It's about a guy like Les Paul who becomes really famous as a guitar designer and manufacturer. Then he completely abandons everything and disappears. And this young guy goes looking for him.

GO: Are you going to be the young guy?

TW: If it gets done according to schedule. Otherwise, I'll play the old-timer.

GO: How do you write a song?

TW: New York is really stimulating. You can get a taxi and just have him drive and start writing down words you see, information that is in your normal view: dry cleaners, custom tailors, alterations, electrical installations, Dunlop safety center, lease, broker, sale . . . just start making a list of words that you see. And then you just kind of give yourself an assignment. You say, "I'm going to write a song and I'm going to use all these words in that song." That's one way. Or you can get in character, like in acting, and let the character speak. The song "9th and Hennepin" came out like that.

GO: Where's Hennepin?

TW: Minneapolis. But most of the imagery is from New York. It's just that I was on 9th and Hennepin years ago in the middle of a pimp war, and 9th and Hennepin always stuck in my mind. "There's trouble at 9th and Hennepin." To this day I'm sure there continues to be trouble at 9th and Hennepin. At this donut shop. They were playing "Our Day Will Come" by Dinah Washington when these three twelve-year-old pimps came in in chinchilla coats armed with knives and, uh, forks and spoons and ladles and they started throwing them out in the streets. Which was answered by live ammunition over their heads into our booth. And I knew "Our Day Was Here." I remember the names of all the donuts: cherry twist, lime rickey. But mostly I was thinking of the guy going back to Philadelphia from Manhattan on the Metroliner with the *New York Times,* looking out the window in New York as he pulls out of the station, imagining all the terrible things he doesn't have to be a part of.

GO: While other people are looking at New York imagining all the terrible things they can be a part of.

TW: When you see a leg come out of a cab with a $150 stocking and a $700 shoe and step in a pool of blood, piss, and beer left by a guy who died a half hour before and is now lying cold somewhere on a slab, you just take it all in. But it doesn't really apply anywhere else. I don't know how you go from New York to anywhere else. It's like being in a very bizarre branch of the service. "I was in for four years." I read that there's a barge that goes out into the Atlantic with all the limbs from all the hospitals, and it got into a storm and capsized, and all the limbs washed up on Jones Beach. People were swimming and all of a sudden things got a little odd, a little dark. You've got to love it here, though.

GO: Is there anything you want to say to our readers?

TW: Maybe I should say something about the title of the album, *Rain Dogs*. You know dogs in the rain lose their way back home. They even seem to look up at you and ask if you can help them get back home. 'Cause after it rains every place they peed on has been washed out. It's like *Mission Impossible*. They go to sleep thinking the world is one way and they wake up and somebody moved the furniture.

GO: You've got a song called "Bride of Rain Dog." Is that the dog that's following the dog that's supposed to know the way back?

TW: Yeah. That's the one with the hair that goes straight up, with the big blue eyes and the spiked collar and the little short skirt and no underwear.

WAITS NEVER LETS GUARD DOWN

Toronto Star, October 7, 1987

Craig MacInnis

Looking like a hobo who wandered in off the streets, Tom Waits led his musical pals into Massey Hall last night.

Wearing a cheap, slate-gray suit and a wrinkled red shirt, the whisky-soaked songsmith mumbled something about the lousy service at his hotel, a cheesy joint where you have to "grease the palm" of every last bellhop and chambermaid.

He did not explain the reason for the Band-Aid over his right eye or the bandages wrapped around his hand and wrist. (Some things are better left to the imagination.)

So the scene was set, grotty and just mysterious enough to suggest a cheap bordello floor show, redolent of stale perfume, spilled beer and Cuban cigarettes, with a hint of desperation lurking in the far corner.

Appropriate to the mood, some wiseacre in the near-capacity crowd shouted at Waits to sing louder.

"Well, I'm hollerin' my fool head off," rasped the seedy man of the hour. "Ain't screamed so loud since the pigs ate my little brother."

With that, the unruly patron was silenced. Not because Waits had responded to his complaint, but because he had succeeded in turning the issue over on its side.

This was something he did regularly last evening. There was, for instance, his spoof of a lounge singer in "I'll Take New York," a raspy parody of Frank Sinatra, Jack Jones, et al that ended with Waits, in white dinner jacket, coughing uncontrollably through the final notes.

For "Frank's Wild Years" he plunked himself down at a bar table and spun his creepy/comical yarn as if talking to a drunken pal in the back of a Bowery saloon.

Switching between acoustic guitar, upright piano and a police megaphone (which turned his woozy narratives into furious staccato yowls), Waits covered material from his last three albums, *Swordfishtrombones, Rain Dogs,* and *Frank's Wild Years.*

This was performed with the aid of five taciturn sidemen whose quiet skills ran the gamut from inebriated honky-tonk to Mediterranean dancescapes and Brechtian cabaret.

Up, down, sideways, and around—Waits was forever turning the show into something new, revealing another nook in his low-rent pantry.

After opening an empty fridge (which got one of the easiest laughs of the night), he plopped down at the piano for an achingly faithful rendition of "Tom Traubert's Blues."

The weird juxtapositions continued with the wistful "Innocent When You Dream" followed by the jarring instrumental lead-in to "9th & Hennepin." His voice, like the shifting instrumental moods that framed it, was shattered glass one minute, silk soprano the next.

But in the end, it didn't matter. As befits the ragged poet laureate of broken dreams, Tom Waits never let his guard down long enough to be exposed for the artful scam-merchant that he is.

Truth, half-truths and fantastic lies got all balled together, till the only thing that mattered was Waits himself. He returns tonight and tomorrow.

Tom Waits Is Flying Upside Down (On Purpose)

Musician, October 1987

Mark Rowland

> "It's always the mistakes," Tom Waits is saying. "Most things begin as a mistake. Most breakthroughs in music come out of a revolution of the form. Someone revolted, and was probably not well liked. But he ultimately started his own country."

A few years ago, Tom Waits started his own country. Quite literally the born traveler (he debuted in this life from the back seat of a taxi), he proceeded to stockpile the place with the exotic goods of a worldly imagination. A wheezing accordion from a seedy tango palace, blues licks honed on a razor strop. A marimba hijacked to the South Seas during a performance of the *Nutcracker Suite*. A crusty doughnut from an abandoned flophouse, sloshed down with a German drinking song, or something like that. A thousand and one nocturnal images to make your heart race and your head itch, conjured by a rasping voice on the lam from the Surgeon General. Waits planted one flag called *Swordfishtrombones* (demarcating latitude and longitude), then another titled *Rain Dogs*. And while neither has exactly jammed the Voice of

America, they're the kind of signposts you like to have around when someone—maybe yourself—starts to wonder if popular music still has the originality or vitality to really matter.

Waits's latest chapter, *Frank's Wild Years,* first appeared in somewhat altered costume last summer as a one-man opera for the Steppenwolf Theatre Company in Chicago. Waits sees it as the end of a trilogy (the album title and central character are taken from a song on *Swordfishtrombones*), and, like its predecessors, it's an unusually large collection of tunes (seventeen) that invites neither easy assimilation nor casual dismissal. This is music designed to insinuate itself into your consciousness (the context of a play might quicken the process), but, also like *Rain Dogs,* the various puzzle parts eventually align themselves into a theme.

To summarize, *Frank's Wild Years* takes the form of a reminiscence, the story of a guy who decided to let fantasy navigate his life's course (in the original song, he escapes middle-class bondage by torching his house). It's a kind of American dream. Several songs set the tone for fabulous exploits: the murky excitement of a getaway in "Hang On St. Christopher," a tribal rhumba called "Straight to the Top," a siren song about "Temptation." But Frank's fantasy life turns out to be just that; the presence of a more jarring reality occurs during a reprise of "Straight to the Top" as a pathetic lounge number (it's the twisted Vegas parody Waits fans have long fantasized about) and a truly nightmarish "I'll Take New York," which begins as an unwieldy siege and ends with what's left of Frank's hopes careening down an elevator shaft. By journey's end he's become mournful, drowning his sorrows in weepers like "Cold Cold Ground" and the "Train Song," the latter a minor masterpiece that's as timeless as great gospel. The album's coda, "Innocent When You Dream," sounds like a whisper from the hollows of a broken man's memory. It's a strange, funny, and soulful saga, spiced with a cauldron of musical surprises Waits stirs together with shamanistic skill.

He has help. Much of what separates Waits's past three albums from his early career, after all, is the way he's expanded his musical palette, from solo piano man to chief alchemist for a gang of complementary dispositions. Those cohorts include guitarist Marc Ribot, percussionist Michael Blair, bassist and horn arranger Greg Cohen, Ralph Camey on saxophone, and William Schimmel on a variety of equipment, from accordion to Leslie bass pedals. Waits's instruments include pump organ, guitar, mellotron, even something called the optigan, but nothing so astonishing as that voice—here marinating a tender ballad, there howling through a circle of hell, finally settling into a familiarly phlegmatic, lung-crunching groove. He'll never have Whitney Houston's pipes, but he's the better singer.

Of all the pop songwriters who have followed in Bob Dylan's footsteps (that is, everyone), few suggest superficial comparison less than Waits. And yet, more than anyone else, he has done the one deed crucial to Dylan's entire mythology: shattered his chosen form despite deep feeling for its traditions, then found his voice by reconstructing shards from the rubble into a new kind of pop musical language. Dylan's "mistakes" set off an instant revolution; that won't happen with Waits, but it's a good bet he's already planted the seeds for future subversions.

Ironically, part of the tradition Waits deep-sixed includes his first seven albums, from 1973's *Closing Time* through 1980's *Heartattack and Vine*. It's a period of his career he now seems to view as germinal at best, though it produced a wealth of fine songs, some popularized in versions by more conventional singers (Springsteen's "Jersey Girl," the Eagles'

"Ol' 55"), lyrics and melodies spun into webs of deceptively sturdy construction. His former persona—a combination thread of fifties beatnik, forties vaudevillian, thirties melodist, and so on into the nineteenth century—may seem dated, but that was always deliberate. Along with Waits's deprecating humor and the prevailing wisdom that his face-on-the-barroom-floor theatricality accurately reflected a chosen lifestyle, it had earned him a cult following for life, or at least what was likely to remain of it.

But Waits has always shunned clichés, even tragic ones. Subtly at first, he found escape hatches from encroaching stereotypes. His work began to include movie scores (such as the underrated *One from the Heart,* which included duets with Crystal Gayle, of all people) and film appearances—*Rumble Fish, Cotton Club,* and most notably Jim Jarmusch's *Down by Law.* He has a role opposite Jack Nicholson in the forthcoming film adaptation of William Kennedy's Pulitzer-winning novel *Ironweed.* In 1980 he married Kathleen Brennan; they've since become songwriting partners. (She co-wrote the libretto for *Frank's Wild Years* and collaborated on several of the songs.) They have two children.

. Tom Waits recently sat down for talk and a few beers in one of his favorite joints, the Travelers Cafe. A Filipino coffee shop and bar not far from downtown Los Angeles, it's the kind of place that looks closed even after you walk inside. We settled into a weathered booth, as far from the light of afternoon as the middle of a Trader Vic's, though these surroundings emanated considerably more warmth and raffish charm.

The same could be said for Waits. Attired in a black leather jacket, nondescript gray shirt and day-old stubble, he looked and occasionally played the role of house raconteur; as anyone who's followed his career knows, he's a fine storyteller and a funny guy. But he also leavened the humor with insightful observations that, beneath the wisecracking surface, suggested a core of emotional vulnerability and generosity of spirit. He's not the sort you'd presume to "know" after one or two encounters, but it's clear the music of Tom Waits has acquired its special character in large part because he has character. The best mistakes require no less.

MUSICIAN: Your approach to music has changed dramatically over your last three albums, beginning with *Swordfishtrombones*. Can you reconstruct that transitional period?

WAITS: I don't know if I can reconstruct it really—it wasn't religious or anything. You get to an impasse creatively at some point, and you can either ignore it or deal with it. And it's like anything, you go down a road and . . . hopefully, there's a series of tunnels. I'd started feeling like my music was very separate from myself. My life had changed and my music had stayed pretty much its own thing. I thought I had to find a way to bring it closer. Not so much with my life as with my imagination.

MUSICIAN: Was it also a matter of getting more confident?

WAITS: Not so much [with] subject matter. I mean, my voice is still a barking dog at best. You get a little taller, you see a little further; you grow up. Hopefully we all keep growing. That sounds a little corny but . . . you have to decide whether you're going to give this up and start working in the salt mines, or take chances. I never take the chances that I would really like to, if I had more courage. But it's a beginning.

MUSICIAN: Have the results surprised you?

WAITS: No, I knew who I was working with. You surround yourself with people who can know when you're trying to discover something, and they're part of the process. Keith Richards had an expression for it that's very apropos: He called it "the hair in the gate." You know when you go to the movies and you watch an old film, and a piece of hair catches in the gate? It's quivering there and then it flies away. That's what I was trying to do—put the hair in the gate.

MUSICIAN: You've said that when you're writing you'll sometimes put together words by feeling, and later understand why they fit. Do you put together your music that way, or are you following through a fairly concrete plan?

WAITS: It's like when you're in a film and you see where the camera is, and then invariably one will look to the left out of the frame and see something infinitely more interesting. That's what I try to look out for. It's not a science. It's like when you hear music "wrong" or when you hear it coming through a wall and it mixes in—I pay attention to those things. That's the hair in the gate. You can't always do it, and sometimes it's just distraction. Other times it's imperative that you follow the rabbit, and roll.

MUSICIAN: Do you feel by now you've got control of your voice? I don't mean literally your voice, but your ability to communicate.

WAITS: You always work on your voice. Once you feel as though you have one, whatever you tackle will come under the spell of what you're trying to do. You want to be able to make turns and fly upside down—but not by mistake. You want it to be a conscious decision, and to do it well. You don't want somebody to say, "Well, he went for the bank there and lost control and he went right into the mountain and thirty-seven people died." You want 'em to say, "Well, he decided to take his hands off the controls and sacrifice the entire plane and its passengers. And I must say it was a spectacular flight. The explosion set off sparks that could be seen all the way to Oxnard. Remarkable." I think you have to work on yourself more than you work on the music. Then whatever you're aiming at you'll be able to hit between the eyes.

MUSICIAN: You did wait a long time before taking your musical leap. So maybe that was a crucial part of the process.

WAITS: It's strange. It's all a journey. You don't know where it's going to take you, the people that you meet and the changes your life will bring. I can say I wished I'd jumped off earlier, but I don't know if I actually jumped off anything or else, you know, just redecorated. But I know that the last three records are a departure from what I was doing; I'm very aware of that. I don't write the same way. I used to sit in a room with a piano, the Tin Pan Alley approach. I thought that's how songs were written.

MUSICIAN: That's how songs were written.

WAITS: Yeah, you go to work and write songs. I still do that, but now sometimes I break everything I've found. It's like you give a kid a toy and they play with the wrapping. I do that now.

MUSICIAN: Forty years ago the kind of music you played might be more or less dictated by where you grew up.

WAITS: You think you're a victim of your musical environment. To a degree you are.

MUSICIAN: But now it's different. You have access to everything, and what you lose are your roots.

WAITS: Your world is only as large as you make it. What you decide to include and to affect you is very much up to you. What you ultimately do with it is something else. It's like the blind men describing the elephant, you know? "It's a small apartment, it's a trailer, it's a large billfold." As far as influences, it takes a long time for something to find its way into what you do. You have to plant it, water it, let it grow. You know where they say in Genesis that man was made from clay? Now they're saying that clay, genetically, contains all the information of every life form. It's all in the clay. You hit it with a hammer, a light comes from it. They've done experiments with Egyptian pottery made on a wheel thousands of years ago—they play the plates backwards and receive a recording, a very primitive recording of what took place in the room. Your ghosts. So, I'll buy that.

MUSICIAN: So you have to search for your roots, in the right places.

WAITS: The first stroke is always the most important. Kids do that. I watch kids draw and go, Jesus, I wish I could do that. I wish I could get back there. I wish I could go through the keyhole. You become very self-conscious as you get older, and less spontaneous, and you feel very victimized by your creative world, your creative person.

MUSICIAN: What can you do about it?

WAITS: You try and work on it. With music, I mean, some people believe you're cutting off a piece of something that's alive. It's like the guy who had a prize pig with all these bandages over it. And his neighbor asks, "What happened to the pig?" The first guy says, "I use it for bacon. I can't kill such a beautiful pig, I just take a slice off him now and then." So, you don't want to kill the pig.

MUSICIAN: The way you describe it, it seems the process of growing as a musician—or anything—is about finding the doors that let you out of the boxes you put yourself in. And inevitably you're dissatisfied in retrospect no matter what you do.

WAITS: That's just human nature. Somebody has to take it from you, just to allow it to dry. The process of "mixing" makes me insane. I feel like I'm underwater without scuba gear.

MUSICIAN: So who finally puts the cork in the bottle?

WAITS: I do. Or my wife hits me with a frying pan.

MUSICIAN: On *Frank's Wild Years* you two collaborate on several songs. Did that require much adjustment on your part?

WAITS: It's good. She's very unselfconscious, like the way kids will sing things just as they occur to them. It was chemistry. I mean, we've got kids. Once you do that together, the other stuff is simple.

MUSICIAN: Has family life changed your outlook?

WAITS: No, but if you don't get that bug off the back of your seat he's gonna go right down into your pocket [smiles]. That's what I like about this place.

MUSICIAN: It's been a favorite of yours for a while. But you moved to New York while making *Rain Dogs*. Where are you settled now?

WAITS: I don't know where I'm living. Citizen of the world. I live for adventure and to hear the lamentations of the women . . . I've uprooted a lot. It's like being a traveling salesman. People sit at a desk all day—that's a rough place, you know? I've lived in a lot of different towns. There's a certain gypsy quality, and I'm used to it. I find it easy to write under difficult circumstances and I can capture what's going on. I'm moving towards needing a compound, though. An estate. But in the meantime I'm operating out of a storefront here in the Los Angeles area.

MUSICIAN: It seemed you were living on the edge more during the early seventies, in a physical sense. That you've become more settled. Do you worry how that might affect your inspirations?

WAITS: It's never been settled—my life is not what I would call normal or predictable. But yeah, you think about it because what's going on becomes the reservoir for your stuff. You want details? When I was living in New York it was a very insane time. But these songs [*Frank's Wild Years*] were written to be part of a story.

MUSICIAN: Did you sense certain parallels between Frank's life story and your own?

WAITS: No, it's just indicative. A drawing that maybe a couple of people would know where those things match up. Your friends and family know, it's a record of something, but not a photograph.

MUSICIAN: Your father's name is Frank. Is that a coincidence?

WAITS: My dad asked me the same thing. Well, Frank did have his wild years. But this is not verbatim. My dad's from Texas. His name is actually Jesse Frank, he's named after Jesse and Frank James. When you came to California in the forties it was a lot hipper to be named Frankie, after Frank Sinatra, than to go with Jesse—they think you're from the dust bowl. "What did you get here in, a Model A?" But no, Dad, it's not about you.

MUSICIAN: Frank lets fantasies rule his life, but without any direction or sense of reality his life becomes very self-destructive.

WAITS: The laws that govern your private madness when applied to the daily routine of living your life can coagulate into a collision.

MUSICIAN: His "Train Song" is like a mourn of regret, it says, "I ruined my life." And then "Innocent When You Dream" is there to soothe the pain.

WAITS: Well, that's where it starts. When you're young you think everything is possible and that you're in the sun and all that. I always liked that Bob Dylan song, "I was young when I left home and I rambled around and I never wrote a letter to my home, to my home. Never wrote a letter to my home." You don't always know where you're going till you get there. That's the thing about train travel, at least when you say goodbye they get gradually smaller. Airplanes, people go through a door and they're gone. Very strange. They say now that jet lag is really your spirit catching up to your body.

MUSICIAN: So much of the record deals with dreams; they're mentioned in the songs, and the music itself has a dreamlike quality. Is that where some of the album came from?

WAITS: Real life, you know, it's very difficult. These are actually more like daydreams. And sometimes a song may find you and then you find it.

MUSICIAN: "Innocent When You Dream" is a centerpiece of the record and suggests that dreams are a source of rebirth.

WAITS: Sure to be a Christmas favorite. Wait'll you get the promotion guys out on the road with that one.

MUSICIAN: Well, it does have a religious quality. And a love of mystery. The music brings that together: The search for mystery is implicit in the sound of the music, and it takes on the aura of a spiritual quest. Not to solve the mystery, but to find it.

WAITS: Let's face it, all of what we know to be religious holidays fall on what were pagan ritual celebrations. I don't want to get out of my area here, but Christianity clearly is like Budweiser: They came in, saw what the natives were doing, and said, "We're gonna let you guys do the little thing with the drums every year at the same time. You're working for Bud now. Don't change a thing. The words are gonna be a little different, but you'll get used to that. We're gonna have to get you some kind of slacks though, and a sports jacket. Can't wear the loincloths anymore. These are fine, they're more comfortable." I don't want to oversimplify. I do believe very much in Billy Graham and all the real giants—

MUSICIAN: Of the industry—

WAITS: They're like bankers. They understand the demographics, and they feel the country like a giant grid, or a video game. Same way politicians do. But even magic tricks were originally designed to get people to understand the magic of the spirit. Turning wine into water: It's the old shell game.

MUSICIAN: And that aspect is a wonderful thing, I think; it

puts you in touch with the idea of mystery, the unknowable.

WAITS: In this country we're all very afraid of anything that isn't shrink-wrapped with a price on it, that you can take back to the store if you don't like it. So we've pretty much killed the animal in capture.

MUSICIAN: But your music tries to convey that mystery, as voodoo did, or still does, I suppose, in certain places.

WAITS: Yeah. My dad wanted to have a chicken ranch when I was a kid. He's always been very close to chickens. Never happened, you know, but he has twenty-five chickens in the backyard. And my dad was saying there are still places, down around Tweedy Boulevard in South-Central L.A., where you can buy live chickens, and most of the business there is not for dinner. It's for ritual. Hanging them upside down in the doorway for, uh . . . I don't know a lot about it, but at a certain level you get music—the Stones know all about that. You know that tune on *Exile on Main Street,* "I Just Want to See His Face." [laughs] That will put you in a spell.

MUSICIAN: You seem attracted to that side of life, though; the seediness of "9th and Hennepin," or the world of *Nighthawks at the Diner,* or Western Avenue the way Charles Bukowski describes it.

WAITS: I haven't been around 9th and Hennepin in a while, and I only know these things from my own experience. Though I think there must be a place where it all connects. I like where Bukowski says—I'm not quoting exactly—"It's not the big things that drive men mad. It's the little things. The shoelace that breaks when there's no time left." It makes it very difficult for me to drive, you know. 'Cause I'm always looking around. It makes for a very dangerous ride with the family.

MUSICIAN: Do you feel you can impart lessons from your life's experience in a song?

WAITS: You can learn from songs. If you hear it at the right time; like everything else, you have to be ready or it won't mean much. Like going through someone else's photo album.

MUSICIAN: Or if you're in a bad love affair, all the songs on the radio suddenly achieve profundity.

WAITS: Sometimes when I'm really angry at somebody or if I'm in line at the Department of Motor Vehicles, I try to imagine people that I want to strangle; I imagine them at Christmas in a big photograph with their families, and it helps. It's kept me from homicide.

MUSICIAN: You've called this record the end of a trilogy, which suggests you're preparing to move in another direction.

WAITS: I don't know, maybe the next one will be a little more . . . hermaphroditic. But I'm a real procrastinator. I wait till something is impossible to ignore before I act on it.

MUSICIAN: That's surprising, there's enough songs on your

last three albums to make about six normal-sized records.

WAITS: More for your entertainment dollar! That's what we say down at Waits & Associates. Go ahead, shop around, compare our prices. Come back on down.

MUSICIAN: Well, you have written a lot of songs here.

WAITS: And none of them will be used for beer commercials. It's amazing, when I look at these artists. I find it unbelievable that they finally broke into the fascinating and lucrative world of advertising after years on the road, making albums and living in crummy apartments; finally advertising opened up and gave them a chance for what they really wanted to do, which was salute and support a major American product, and have that name blinking over their head as they sing. I think it's wonderful what advertising has done, giving them these opportunities to be spokesmen for Chevrolet, Pepsi, etc.

MUSICIAN: Do you ever get approached by major advertisers?

WAITS: I get it all the time, and they offer people a whole lot of money. Unfortunately I don't want to get on the bandwagon. You know, when a guy is singing to me about toilet paper—you may need the money but, I mean, rob a 7-Eleven! Do something with dignity and save us all the trouble of peeing on your grave. I don't want to rail at length here, but it's like a fistula for me. If you subscribe to your personal mythology, to the point where you do your own work, and then somebody puts decals over it, it no longer carries the same weight. I have been offered money and all that, and then there's the people that imitate me too. I really am against people who allow their music to be nothing more than a jingle for jeans or Bud. But I say, "Good, okay, now I know who you are." 'Cause it's always money. There have been tours endorsed, encouraged and financed by Miller, and I say, "Why don't you just get an office at Miller? Start really workin' for the guy." I just hate it.

MUSICIAN: It's especially offensive if, as you say, you see music as something organic.

WAITS: The advertisers are banking on your credibility, but the problem is it's no longer yours. Videos did a lot of that because they created pictures and that style was immediately adopted, or aborted, by advertising. They didn't even wait for it to grow up. And it's funny, but they're banking on the fact that people won't really notice. So they should be exposed. They should be fined! [bangs his fist on the table] I hate all of the people that do it! All of you guys! You're sissies!

MUSICIAN: I think a lot of people notice, but the resistance isn't organized. Nike claims they only got thirty letters about using the Beatles to sell sneakers.

WAITS: I must admit when I was a kid I made a lot of mistakes in terms of my songs; a lot of people don't own their songs. Not your property. If John Lennon had any idea that someday Michael Jackson would be deciding the future of his material, if he could I think he'd come back from the grave and kick his ass, and kick it real good, in a way that we would enjoy. Now I have songs that belong to two guys named Cohen from the South Bronx. Part of what I like about the last three albums is that they're mine. To that point I didn't own my copyrights. But to consciously sell them to get the down payment on a house, I think that's wrong. They should be embarrassed. And I rest my case.

MUSICIAN: When you began was there concern that your voice lacked the qualities of a classic singer?

WAITS: In terms of what was going on at the time? "Are you gonna fit in? Are you gonna be the only guy at the party with your shirt on inside out?" I was never embarrassed, but I'm liking it more now. Learning how to make it do different things.

MUSICIAN: I like your falsetto on "Temptation."

WAITS: Oh yes, a little Pagliacci.

MUSICIAN: It's true you sang several of the new tunes through a police bullhorn?

WAITS: I've tried to simulate that sound in a variety of ways—singing into trumpet mutes, jars, my hands, pipes, different environments. But the bullhorn put me in the driver's seat. There's so much you can do to manipulate the image, so much technology at your beck and call. But still you gotta make choices. A lot of this stuff is twenty-four-track; I finally allowed that and joined the twentieth century, at least in that regard.

MUSICIAN: Certainly not in the sense of giving the music an aural sheen.

WAITS: I don't want the sheen. I don't know, I'm neurotic about it, and yet Prince is really state-of-the-art and he still kicks my ass. So it depends who's holding the rifle.

MUSICIAN: Prince has complained about not hearing enough "colors" on the radio, that too many talented people deliberately seek to emulate a formula instead of finding their own voice. Do you agree?

WAITS: To an extent. The business machinery has gotten so sophisticated, people want their head on his body. It's a melting pot, and the nutrition gets boiled out. Prince is rare, a rare exotic bird! There's only a few others. To be that popular and that uncompromising, it's like Superman walking through the wall. I don't think we can do it, you know. But this record goes into a lot of different musical worlds. "I'll Take New York" was a nightmare—Jerry Lewis going down on the *Titanic*.

MUSICIAN: I like the North African horn parts on "Hang On St. Christopher," which give it a vaguely menacing quality.

WAITS: [hums a snatch] That just happened in the studio . . . I think in music the intelligence is in the hands. The way your hands rub up along the ends of a table. You begin to go with your instincts. And it's only dangerous to the degree that you only let yourself discover the things that are right there. You'll be uncomfortable and so you'll keep returning to where your hands are comfortable.

That's what happened to me on the piano. I rarely play the piano because I find I only play three or four things. I go right to F-sharp and play "Auld Lang Syne." I can't teach them, so I make them do something else.

MUSICIAN: Are you more free on guitar?

WAITS: Not necessarily. I like picking up instruments I don't understand. And doing things that may sound foolish at first. It's like giving a blowtorch to a monkey. That's what I'm trying to do. Always trying to break something, break something, break through to something.

MUSICIAN: You use a lot of "found" items in the music.

WAITS: That's a trap too. Though there's something in the fact of a studio with instruments you've spent thousands of dollars renting, to walk over to the bathroom and the sound of the lid coming down on the toilet is more appealing than that seven-thousand-dollar bass drum. And you use it. You have to be aware of that. And it makes you crazy. When the intervals and the textures begin to disturb you more than the newspaper, or your rocking chair or the comfort of your mattress, then I guess you're in for the long haul.

MUSICIAN: Well, you still have a few possibilities left.

WAITS: Which is fine if it hasn't been done. You have to feel it hasn't been done until you do it. Tape a bottle of Scotch to the tape recorder. Give a Telecaster to Lawrence Welk. We'd all like to hear what that's like. They're very conscious decisions. You have to believe it's unique to your experience.

MUSICIAN: I think it's encouraging that you're getting more successful as you explore these musical boundaries.

WAITS: What do you mean by success? My record sales have dropped off considerably in the United States. I do sell a lot of records in Europe. It's hard to gauge something you don't have real contact with. We have no real spiritual leadership, so we look to merchandising. The most deprived, underprivileged neighborhoods in the world understand business. Guns, ammo, narcotics . . . But yes, SALES HAVE DROPPED OFF CONSIDERABLY IN THE LAST FEW YEARS . . . and I want to talk to somebody about it. I used to play Iowa. I haven't been to Iowa in some time.

MUSICIAN: Have you considered moving there?

WAITS: Ah, I could never live in Iowa. No offense to people who do. When I tour it's like, people want to see you in one way, and they want to get familiar with you. When I find someone I like, I don't buy every record they ever made. Rarely. But I'm like, "Oh yeah. I know that guy." We all do that. And then it's—"Oh, you're still around, huh?" It's like birdwatching. "The oriole is back at the birdbath, no crows this year." What does that mean? We watch it like weather. We actually think that the media is like cloud formations. And we'll make judgments—"I heard he was up at the Betty Ford Center." And I like folktales, and the way stories and jokes travel. But the media understands it as well. Fashion operates in that world. The top designers for the biggest companies go down into bad neighborhoods to find out how people are rolling their pants. It's all now, NOW. Which gets me railing again.

MUSICIAN: But there's still a funny parallel there with what you do, because even your description of "junk-yard orchestration" implies the gathering of random elements—

WAITS: My personal version of that. The thing is, when you hit a vein, you make a breakthrough, there are a lot of people who want to go through that door. Whether you made it with a screwdriver or an M16, there'll be a lot of traffic. So I don't tap into a national highway. I really think you have to be careful. Everybody looks at the country as this big girl they want to kiss. Like they're courting this big broad, you know? Gonna take the baby out, yeah, show her a good time. Does this sound silly? I'm just talking off the top of my head.

MUSICIAN: Is it upsetting that by taking chances you seem to lessen the likelihood of reaching a wider audience?

WAITS: Music is social, but I'm not making music to be accepted. I think everyone has to go out on their own journey.

MUSICIAN: Is it helpful to have developed a separate voca-tion as an actor?

WAITS: [takes mock offense] What, you don't think I can make a living just playing my music, is that what you're insinuating? But it helps with the groceries?

MUSICIAN: No, I mean does one complement the other? Your acting helps enlighten your music, or vice versa?

WAITS: Like Dean Martin and Jerry Lewis. I don't know; you hope to see things. I think it's part of the same thing. Actors see what they do as conceptually [as musicians], they regard the same bylaws. I can't honestly say I'm accomplished as an actor. I have a lot of respect for those that are.

MUSICIAN: You just worked with Jack Nicholson in *Ironweed*—

WAITS: That was great for me. He's a badass. He lives in the ether, he walks like a spider. Got great taste. He knows about everything from beauty parlors to train guards. Hell kick your ass, he's a giant. He's got himself a place on the board of directors historically, and he does it with his feet. You see him and you know it's not like watching a wild horse. He knows what he's doing. He's like a centaur.

MUSICIAN: You appreciate people that can combine that animal instinct with intellectual control. Keith Richards seems like that.

WAITS: He is, he's the best. He's like a tree frog, an orang-utan. When he plays he looks like he's been dangled from a wire that comes up through the back of his neck, and he can lean at a forty-five-degree angle and not fall over. You think he has special shoes. But maybe it's the music that's keeping him up.

MUSICIAN: Reading *Ironweed*, in the first scene when your character and Nicholson's are on your way to work in the cemetery, reminded me of your song "Cemetery Polka."

WAITS: Did it? Every time I buy a pair of shoes I get nervous. Wondering how long these shoes are going to be with me. Every time I see photographs of dead people, I always look at their shoes. It looks like they only got them a couple of weeks ago, they were the last pair [laughs], "All out of brown, all we have are black Oxford." But that "Cemetery Polka" was, ah, discussing my family in a way that's difficult for me to be honest. The way we talk behind each other's backs: "You know what happened to Uncle Vernon." The kind of wickedness that nobody outside your family could say. That kind of stuff.

MUSICIAN: Do you ever feel your songs should be more personal?

WAITS: I don't like songs that are like some kind of psychiatry. I don't even want to know, in most cases, what the original idea was. Usually I hate pictures of the family and that kind of stuff. Sometimes it catches you in an odd moment you like. But with songs you have to make decisions about what it turns into, and I don't like it too close to what really happened. Occasionally truth is stranger than fiction, but not always.

MUSICIAN: Do you feel part of a fraternity with certain artists?

WAITS: You mean rate my fellow performers? I know the magazine is big on this.

MUSICIAN: Yeah, it's a tic.

WAITS: If you talk too much about people it kind of demystifies them, you know. And it's like watching things that are moving; you may like them today and not tomorrow. People who have careers are moving targets. Who would have known some guy you liked would go and do commercials for Honda? And then you're embarrassed to dig him, 'cause they tampered with their mythology. The guy was doing a beautiful tailspin, he went into a double flip with a camel-hair thing and then—right into the crapper. I like the Replacements, I like their stance. They're question marks. I saw them at the Variety Arts Center downtown; I liked their show. I particularly liked the insect ritual going on at the foot of the stage. There was this guy trying to climb up, and they kept throwing him back, like a carp. No, you can't get in the boat! It was like something out of Mondo Cane. [laughter] And it was really great to watch. And I liked the fact that one of the kids—Tommy?—had dropped out of high school. Being on the road with this band, the idea of all his schoolmates stuck there with the fucking history of Minnesota, and he's on a bus somewhere sipping out of a brandy bottle, going down the road of life.

MUSICIAN: Do you know why you became a musician?

WAITS: I don't know. I knew what I didn't want to do. I thought I'd try some of what was left over.

MUSICIAN: Were you from a musical family?

WAITS: Not like Liza Minnelli, all right? Contrary to popular belief, we don't have the same mother. I took her out a couple of times: Nothing ever happened!

MUSICIAN: Were your folks encouraging?

WAITS: I think when children choose something other than a life of crime, most parents are encouraging. Music was always around when I was a kid, but there wasn't a lot of "encouragement"—which allowed me to carve my own niche. When you're young you're also very insecure, though. You don't know if you can lean on that window, if it'll break. It goes back to what I was saying about flying upside down by choice. There's a time when you don't understand, when you're not focused, not like the sun through a magnifying glass burning a hole in the paper. I used to do that every day when I was a kid. And when the glass broke I'd get another. It was no big deal. I didn't really know what I was doing when I started. I have a better idea now. In a way, I'd like to start now. A lot of great guys, only one third of them is visible, the rest is beneath the ground. Took them ten years just to break the surface. But when I started I thought, "Ah, I'd better get something going here." I still have nightmares about the stage where everything goes wrong. The piano catches fire. The lighting comes crashing to the stage, the curtain tears. The audience throws tomatoes and overripe fruit. They make their way to the front of the stage, and my shoes can't move. And I always play that in my head when I'm planning a tour. The nightmare that you will completely come unraveled.

MUSICIAN: You've suggested taking *Frank's Wild Years* on the road with a "Cuban Dream Orchestra." What does that mean?

WAITS: What will I take on the road? The thing is, in the studio everyone can change instruments, you have cross-pollination. On the road you have to just get up and do it. It makes me nervous. You know those things you play at a carnival, the little steam shovel that always misses the watch? I never get what I really want on the road. It's always vaudeville.

MUSICIAN: So you're more comfortable in a studio?

WAITS: Well, I don't want to do things in there that make it impossible to reproduce onstage. Basically I work with instruments that can be found in any pawn shop, so it's just nuance. I have a band that I trust. They're like having a staff of people that can rob a bank, or they can wear women's clothing if necessary. Be interior designers, or restaurant workers. They're everything. And that's different. I can't do this by myself. But I just hate the way most equipment and instruments look on a stage.

MUSICIAN: The way they look?

WAITS: The wires and all that. These necessary utility items make me feel like I'm in an emergency ward. I want to take the Leslie bass pedals and raise them up to a kitchen table so you can play them with your fists. Which is what we did in the studio on "Hang On St. Christopher." I'm trying to put together the right way of seeing the music. I worry about these things. If I didn't, it would be easier.

MUSICIAN: Do you have any idea what motivates you?

WAITS: I've said for a long time I've been motivated by fear. But I don't really know. And if I ever knew what it was, I don't know if I'd want to tell *Musician* magazine, no offense. If I knew it would probably make me very nervous.

MUSICIAN: Maybe if you knew it wouldn't motivate you anymore.

WAITS: This is really getting metaphysical. Is this for *Omni* magazine? Yeah, I do believe in the mysteries of things, about myself and the things I see. I enjoy being puzzled and arriving at my own incorrect conclusions.

MUSICIAN: Any advice for younger musicians?

WAITS: Break windows, smoke cigars, and stay up late. Tell 'em to do that, they'll find a little pot of gold.

SWORDFISHMEGAPHONES

Tom Waits contends that most of what's played on his records can be found in a local pawn shop; locating some of them in a music store might prove more difficult. The current apple of his musical arsenal, for instance, is a police bullhorn, through which Waits fashioned many of the vocals you hear on *Frank's Wild Years*. Not just any horn, of course, but an MP5 Fanon transistorized megaphone (with public address loudspeaker). "It's made in Taiwan," Waits adds proudly.

Waits also plays a variety of keyboards, including a Brunello di Montalcino pump organ, a Farfisa organ, and the famous Optigan, a keyboard made between 1968 and 1972 and marketed by Penney's stores. The Optigan plays pre-recorded sounds, which can be selected from its library; Tom particularly likes "Polynesian village" and "romantic strings." Not too surprisingly, Waits prefers "mostly tube stuff" to digital equipment.

Microphones of choice include a Ribbon ("Dave Garroway") and RCA high-impedance mikes; Waits usually sings through a Shure Green Bullet (used mostly by harmonica players). Also an Altec 21D vocal mike—"because Sinatra used it."

On guitar, Waits likes his Gretsch New Yorker "with old strings" played through an old Fender tweed basement amp. When recording, he says he uses a lot of heavy compression with room sound; to do that he'll sometimes push the track into the room through Auratone speakers, and then mike that. It's not his only technique, "but I don't want to give away all my secrets."

Option, July 1989

Elvis Costello

THE NATURE OF MUSIC

Over on Temple, near the corner of Union, there's a Chinese restaurant with an unusual name. The Red Eight is a chow mein joint just a short ride west of downtown. Inside, the walls are painted a horrible shade of mental-institution yellow. Nobody goes there. That's what Tom Waits likes about it. Waits, who lives in the neighborhood, is hanging around town while devoting his nights to *Demon Wine,* a play he's appearing in. This afternoon he's got a lunch date with a musician colleague who's in L.A. for the usual round of interviews and gladhandling at his new record company. They've crossed paths on a number of occasions and swapped musicians for their tours and recording dates, cultivating a friendship built on common interests and mutual respect. His friend's name is Declan, but everyone calls him Elvis. Elvis Costello, wearing pointy sideburns, his trademark shades and a black leather car coat, finds his way to the Red Eight first. He's with his wife, Cait O'Riordan. It's an unseasonably warm February day, but the Red Eight is cool inside. Soon, Kathleen Brennan turns up with her husband in tow. Waits is casually eccentric in a too-small suit, his hair colored red for the play. It's grown out and the roots show strands of gray. There's a round of hugs and smiles and greetings, and Kathleen disappears toward home, inviting Cait along. A couple of other hangers-on vanish, and there's nobody in the Red Eight but a waitress, Elvis Costello, and Tom Waits.

ELVIS: I always seem to be watching these nature programs whenever I speak to you . . .

TOM: I love those nature programs. I would love to do some music for a nature program. It's unfortunate that the nature programs themselves ultimately may be perhaps the only record of nature itself. It's like if the camera shifts just a little bit to the left, you'll pick up the condo, right next to the condor on the beach . . .

ELVIS: And the nice little wrapper that's been left there by the previous film crew, probably the Kodak wrapper. I did actually see one about bears, polar bears, where they said, "So the polar bears don't have any natural predators. This far north, there are no hunters up here. In fact, the only thing that interrupts them in their natural idyllic habitat is they're possibly harassed by nature film crews" (laughs). I saw this one thing about the sense that animals have. They showed altered pictures of what insects and birds see, and they showed flowers—the flowers are not the colors we see. Now to my way of thinking, that means we're the ones with the optical illusion, because we don't pollinate flowers, except by accident. Whereas the flowers have evolved and presumably evolved giving off these colors to insects. So really, daisies are not yellow and white, they're really purple and orange or something. Once you start taking that into account in music, then you realize that some people can't physically hear things. A kid that listens to Metallica or something can't hear that, because he's filled himself up with this stuff, he physically can't hear a banjo or a harp or something.

TOM: Well men and women have a different range of sounds that they are sensitive to.

ELVIS: And rhythm. Women hear rhythm differently than men. Do you think there's any kind of biological reason why so many girls play bass?

TOM: I don't know. I always go for the low end. Kathleen's always trying to kick my ass up the scale a little bit because I find that if I'm left to my own devices I will discover various shades of brown. And I'm seeing them of course as red and yellow next to each other. She says, what you've just really created here is sludge, dirty water. So I kind of have to be reminded of that. I'm also colorblind, which is kind of interesting. I juggle with brown and green and blue and red, and green looks brown, brown looks green, purple looks blue, blue looks purple. I don't see the world in black and white, but I'll never make the Air Force.

ELVIS: Do you see it like that? Because I see it definitely in color. The last record I made before this one, it was in red and brown, it was blood and chocolate. That was an actual picture of a room in my head all the way through it, and most of the songs took place in it.

TOM: Do you find that with a record . . . there's a time before it's released when you go through this enormous kind of Lamaze thing with the music, and as soon as you cut it loose you feel like it's grown up and gone to school. Up until the last moment you can change something.

ELVIS: I found with this record I had to really be strong-willed, because in the past I've tended to tinker and add a thing or take a thing away, and nearly always been wrong. That's a neurosis.

TOM: You have to know the difference between neurosis and actual process, 'cause if you're left with it in your hands for too long, you may unravel everything. You may end up with absolutely nothing.

ELVIS: When you're looking further afield than your initial experience for writing, particularly when you consciously narrow your view of the music to create a certain dramatic effect like the last record [*Spike*], I really did do that thing of pulling it all through this funnel and I was hoping that the good stuff didn't kind of get caught on the edge of it. Really the only thing holding a lot of records together is the personality of the singer, and the will to write all of these different things.

TOM: If you can put them all together on the same disc, though, you can perceive them as a collection, that they ultimately will develop a logic, even if you hadn't endowed them with that. Because it's a group of people that just got off the bus, and they seem to be united on some type of a tour. You assume they have relationships. It's like when you make tapes just for your own pleasure, you put Pakistani music and Bobby "Blue" Bland next to each other, you do have some type of logic about it. [But] I can't listen to so much music at the same time. I think you really have to have a diet. You're just processing too much, there's no place to put it. If you go a long time without hearing music, then you hear music that nobody else hears.

ELVIS: I read this thing once in *Finnair* magazine, an article about Jean Sibelius. He couldn't have the window open 'cause if he did he would hear birds in the trees and they'd get into the composition. So his family used to go and have to chase the birds (laughs). But it's quite a comical picture, isn't it? The birdsong would actually enter his composition. Well, there's that other guy, that guy who's still alive, he's eighty, Oliver Messiaen. He's actually an ornithologist, that's the two things he does, he's a composer and ornithologist. And he goes out and records real birdsong, and then transcribes it into compositions.

TOM: Wow. Steve Allen used to take the telephone line, and then when different birds would set at different places on the wire, he would write it out and look at the lines of the telephone wires as a staff, and he would put the notes where the birds would be and he would play it. On a TV show . . .

ANT FARMS & MELLOTRONS

ELVIS: Can you write scores?

TOM: No. I've developed my memory in order to compensate for my inability to . . . you end up with your own languages.

ELVIS: Little hieroglyphics and a set of hand symbols. And humming. I find humming is very useful.

TOM: You always lose a few things, but you also open yourself up to some other things.

ELVIS: If you can divide everything up using a computer, like these machines now that will divide the beat up for you and will even . . . What about these drum machines which can program in mistakes? Program in the human factor? I mean, how human? (laughs) I know plenty of drummers that aren't that human, you know.

TOM: It used to terrify me, the idea of drum machines, and now I've figured it still comes down to who's operating it.

ELVIS: And who programmed it in the first place. That one you showed me? I got one of those to play with and I used it on the next B-side I did, and I just plugged it into an amplifier, which immediately changed it. So there's one thing I've done, I've distorted the natural sound of it . . .

TOM: Crank up the sound, get some dirt on it, and it sounds a lot different.

ELVIS: I like the sound because it sounds like somebody playing bongos with stainless steel gloves on. It sounds completely unnatural. But what kind of ethos does the person who programmed that chip have, that makes him think that those sounds sound like the little drawings on the machine? (laughs) Some of them are really weird. The little cymbals that are supposed to indicate which is an open hi-hat? Some of them are their own sound.

TOM: I love that thing the Mellotron so much. I just used one yesterday. [Its owner] guards it with his life because it's such an exotic bird, it's a complete dinosaur, and every time you play it it diminishes. It gets old and eventually will die, which makes it actually more human, you're working with a musician that is very old, he's only got a couple more sessions left. It increases the excitement of it. And that great trombone sound . . .

ELVIS: I used to go to church with my father, and right next door to the church was this big house that Dickens used to live in apparently. It was one of many houses that he lived in, but this was this guy's claim to fame. He wasn't a musician, he was an executive from the company that made Mellotron originally. And one day he got us outside of the church, and he insisted—he used to lie in wait outside of the church for everybody to come out, and sort of capture them on Sunday morning when they couldn't think of any other excuse—and try and sell 'em a Mellotron. That was how difficult it was to get people to consider them when they first came out. They were such a gimmick. It so happened that a few people who went to that church were musicians, so I guess a few people got this treatment. And one Sunday morning, I must have only been about eleven or twelve, we were dragged into this big sitting room of this big old house, and he had this Mellotron that was like Doctor Fife's organ, it was a huge thing, a big wooden contraption. It had foot pedals, as I recall. Maybe I'm embellishing it now with my cloudish memory. When you go to a childhood house or something, it's always much smaller than the size you remember it.

TOM: Those Mellotrons, the first time I actually played one, it really thrilled me. It's like you touched somebody on the shoulder, every time I touch you on the shoulder I want you to play a note. It was that real.

ELVIS: But this thing did seem big, and I remember my father sat down to play, and he was pushing these buttons on it and engaging different tapes, and saying, "Just listen to that! It's a real trumpet, you know, it's not an imitation like an organ, it's a real trumpet." But the thing about it was, they hadn't really got the mechanism down at that time. It's a prototype we had. The way you hit the key, it engaged like almost a quarter beat late. So you had to play more than slightly ahead of the beat, you had to lurch. You had to have the lurch technique down. But of course it was dismissed. My father, he said, this will never take over because the tone of the instrument never varies, except it gets shriller when it gets higher. And then the fact that it doesn't even engage in time. Within three years of that, they were absolutely the rage and the revolution. People thought that music was coming to an end.

TOM: Yeah, the industrial revolution. This town [Hollywood], which used to have regular, enormous string sessions for films, and now scores are done at home with two fingers. It's essentially done irreparable damage to the whole economics of sessions, of big session players.

ELVIS: I saw a session when we were doing this record where they had a big module outside the studio which must have been like one of those Synclaviers or something like that, like a life support machine. Which in a way I guess it was. I think they just bring the leaders in now, don't they just bring in the leaders now to play the expression over the block? I get suspicious of that sound . . . it sounded like foam rubber and furniture or something. That is silent and deadly, that foam rubber. It's fine while you're sittin' on it, but if your house catches fire, that's the thing that makes it burst into flames. And that sound is the foam rubber filling of music, it doesn't have any meaning at all. You know those cartoons they used to have of people running inside the head? Some of those synthesizers sound like there's a lot of effort. They wheeze almost in a human way, there's an awful lot of effort (laughs). There's a lot of microchips all going at once to create a rather insubstantial sound.

TOM: It's an ant farm. There's some activity inside of it . . .

ELVIS: You know that sampling business where they put those records together, I always think: what a great idea. It's just that somebody hasn't found the right context for it yet. They can only think as far as sampling the best-sounding record that you can think of, or the coolest one, and then juxtapose things that by their very juxtaposition diminish them. Like they'll get James Brown's cool snare sound and they'll juxtapose it with a huge rap bass drum, which makes the snare drum sound silly. Not to mention there's often no logical musical relationship between the samples when they actually sample musical phrases.

TOM: I actually like it. I know that it's controversial in terms of publishing and copyrights and all that, but like you say, they always pick the clichés of things that we're all aware of.

ELVIS: But I want to know what happens to the obsolete sounds. They have obsolescence forced upon them in a way that was never intended for them, because they get eaten up by this voracious pop machinery. It's not the first time it's happened. When rock 'n' roll came in I think it was because enough bad swing bands came that rock sounded vital. People weren't listening to Stan Kenton or Count Basie. Some of them were listening to bands that are well and best forgotten.

TOM: Jazz developed nylon socks, it was out by the pool eventually.

THE CREATIVE PROCESS

ELVIS: Sometimes I write notes that I have difficulty singing. I write them, and when you sing them at home, you're singing them not trying to wake up the neighbors or the kids or something, and you might be, oh, I know I can go to that note, and when it comes to it, and it actually puts you out of breath or something like that well, maybe it's wrong, because I'm gasping for the next line. And you start talking yourself out of the bold melody and start wanting to arrange it in another key or something. Maybe I just never learned my harmony part, because what everybody says sounds odd to them sounds perfectly natural to me. Anyway, it doesn't sound quite so dramatic. I do that all the time, and you sometimes lose the soul a bit of the song by doing that.

TOM: It's like translation. Anything that has to travel all the way down from your cerebellum to your fingertips, there's a lot of things that can happen on the journey. Sometimes I'll listen to records, my own stuff, and I think god, the original idea for this was so much better than the mutation that we arrived at. What I'm trying to do now is get what comes and keep it alive. It's like carrying water in your hands. I want to keep it all, and sometimes by the time you get to the studio you have nothing.

ELVIS: That carrying the water thing is a good description, because when you've got a song and you kind of know how it is, and then you work with certain players—I worked with the same band for ten years, the versatility is different, because of the ability to change it before you've fixed it. I think that's why some bands thrive on the idea of changing instruments. When they're off their real instrument, the ability to go very far from the original idea is reduced. And what if some completely incompetent bands make brilliant records?

TOM: I hate to look at them that way, because there's a certain kind of musical dexterity that you can arrive at that actually punishes a certain point in your development or moves past it. It happens all the time with me. The three-chord syndrome. And then you say, well, if you try to ask a Barney Kessel to cut a simple thing, just a big block brick of chords, just dirty, fat, loud and mean and cryptic—no, he's a handwriter, he's moved and developed to that level. Larry Taylor, this bass player I worked with from Canned Heat, if he can't feel it, he'll put down his bass and walk away and say, that's it, man, I can't get it. And I really respect that. And I said, well, thank you for telling me.

ELVIS: I knew a guy that played drums in a band that if he didn't like the song, he just didn't play it when they came to that number. The rest of the band would play it, and he just wouldn't join in (laughs). I mistrust these people who can be everybody. This is where technology dictates to them, because the boxes, they can be everybody. And the samples and everything, particularly the drummers now—I mistrust that, that in somehow the chips capture the soul of a player, that's patent nonsense. At the other end, you get the idea that a player—I worked that one session with [jazz bassist] Ray Brown, and we had to do bass and voice, first verse of the song, just bass and voice. At first, it was really plain, and I said no, you could really use a little more movement in there. And he played this beautiful series of movements around the melody. It was too much for the record of that song. In the end, he was very patient with me while I sort of outlined what it was I kind of wanted . . . fortunately, before we'd exhausted the possibility and have it become a forced matter.

TOM: It's like seeing a psychiatrist. There you are trying to explain your problem with it, trying to locate a solution and present as many alternatives as you possibly can, and sometimes you end up with gee, I think I'm talking to the wrong guy.

ELVIS: When you're working with the same band you kind of know their style inside out, and even when you've been working for seven years with the same people, suddenly they'll do something you didn't even think they were capable of. It may be a question of what they don't play as well as what they do. It's not always possible to guess exactly. When you work with new people, I think that it throws all of these matters into relief, because you have to explain yourself every time. It's like crossing a new border. They want to see your documents.

TOM: You get a shorthand with people, which is always faster with musicians, because after a while you can tell them with a nod, or you just get in the mood and they know that it was wrong and you don't even have to tell them why.

ELVIS: Did you ever think, though, that in your choice of musicians, several groups of musicians now, they would ever stop you going past that point, when you start to wander away from your own song? Is it ever something they play that puts up the roadblock?

TOM: Sometimes it puts up a roadblock, but sometimes it opens a door. Like the stuff that people are doing in between takes or something, you have to always be aware of what's happening in the room at all times.

Because as soon as the camera's not on and the tape's not rolling . . . the amount of time it takes to discover something, sometimes you discover it on the first moment, sometimes it takes two weeks to find it.

ELVIS: I find that the thing that's been interesting about this record I've just done [*Spike*] was the difference between who I thought the musician was and how they would sound. Just 'cause you write their name on a list of people that play on the track doesn't mean that even if I had to see, I can't write charts—even if I was to write the part out note by note, not only would I deny the possible happy accident or spontaneity, but it would also be kind of like preconceiving exactly how they sound. Particularly in relation to Marc Ribot, say, having seen him play with you, I knew one way he could play, several of the different things he's done. Then I'd seen him play with the Lounge Lizards, and then I'd heard that Haitian record [actually a cassette, *Haitian Suite,* of classical guitar pieces by Frantz Casseus]. That wasn't broadcast all over the world, you know. That opened up something else. I knew he could play delicately, for sure, because I'd heard him play on the records like that. So he really has a lot of scope, but it still didn't prepare me for the reality of him being in the studio playing my songs in the environment that we had already set up for him. We recorded him with a drum machine and maybe there'd be some percussion that Michael Blair had put there. That's back to the thing of the people being slightly different musicians than you'd imagined. Idealizing this kind of combination of players is pretty strange anyway 'cause it's a bit like picking your favorite baseball team. I get a little nervous about that element of it. I've just asked the same musicians I've worked with to conjure up new things in themselves, and sometimes go on a journey even where they don't really trust I've got the map. This time [on *Spike*], I've just gone out and got the people that I really had in mind. As I said, they sometimes turn out to be slightly different than you imagine, and all the better for it.

TOM: It's music by agreement, to a degree. You look forward to the brilliant mistakes. Most changes in music, most exciting things that happen in music, occur through a miscommunication between people—"I thought you said this." Poetry comes out of that too. It's like song lyrics, Kathleen always thought that Creedence Clearwater song "Bad Moon Rising"—she always thought, "There's a bathroom on the right." That's outside, a song about that, because that happens all the time—you go to a club, "There's the bathroom on the right." But I love those mistakes. I salute them and encourage them.

ELVIS: Did you have any bit of a feeling of coincidence that songs might be written in advance of the events? Or songs may be written with people in mind in advance of their hearing them?

TOM: Absolutely. It's like dreams sometimes foretell a particular event.

ELVIS: I've come to believe it in terms of writing songs and having other people who I have no contact with picking them up entirely independently. You know, other singers? Like having [someone] cover songs which I wrote with them in my mind, and I have no way of communicating it to them. Simply because they were out of the picture for that period of time. That's now happened six times to me. You know, I had a very funny experience the other day. This guy from *Rolling Stone* gave me a tape of Chet Baker singing one of my songs. And I didn't know he'd recorded it. "Almost Blue." It was very weird because you always expect to hear about covers, particularly since it's in that movie [*Let's Get Lost,* about Baker] that Bruce Weber made. It almost made me cry, it was such a strange feeling. It was such a feeling of mixed emotions about it. 'Cause I remember giving him the record, not so much to encourage him to record it, but just as an acknowledgment of the debt to him.

TOM: He's got a great singing voice.

ELVIS: He does it great. He sings in a very low register for him. And he doesn't get all the words, he sings the same bridge twice. But the spirit of it's just right. Another guy told me today about it. This guy I know in Paris is doing a book of photographs, I think you're in it as well—of all the people he's taken pictures of over the years, and he's getting all these musicians to write little comments about the other people in it. There's a very tragic picture of Chet Baker in it. I tried to find something that was the opposite of sentimental and sad about it.

THE GLOBAL VILLAGE

ELVIS: You worked with some of the same people all along, but I suppose when you actually have a group, which I have, you don't sort of notice [your own musical] development. Somebody brings along a record they like, and it all becomes a fairly natural growth for a while, particularly when you're working at such a pace that time goes by and you go on little journeys and you go on detours around places. Particularly when you're traveling, you get a tourist kind of . . . You know that shirt that you buy when you're on holiday, you get home and you look in the mirror and go, god, did I ever wear that? You have music like that, I think. I used to buy tapes of music which I was convinced was the greatest thing ever, and it would even have some effect on me. And then I'd get it home and listen to it in a different atmosphere.

TOM: I think it's like when you listen to opera in Texas, it's a very different world. In Rome, you almost ignore it. I've done the same thing, gone out and bought music from Pakistan, Balinese stuff, Nigerian folk songs and all this, and I find that if I bring it with me to unusual places, the place itself is as much a part of the music. Because the music itself was born and nurtured in a particular environment, and came from that environment. It's the same thing with fashion or anything else.

ELVIS: Is there a fallacy in this notion of world music? Is that just a trend, you think? I mean, it would be very sad to be people who developed and refined and nurtured this beautiful thing, and they're invited to display it. You know that Bulgarian group, Balkana? They came and gave a talk. I didn't get to see their concert, the only thing I saw was at the National Sound Archive, which is like something . . . it's the way I imagine when they had Livingstone come back [from Africa], I imagine it was a bit like the talk he gave. It was that alien, slightly stilted, and more than a little embarrassing. Not so much for them, because I think—well, they might have been a little amused by it. But I felt there was a sense of embarrassment, and not a little shame, in some people's minds, at least in my own. What a terrible tragedy if next year these people are invited and nobody comes, not even there to be embarrassed, because [fans] have moved on to something else they've been told to like, and leave these people who are from a real tradition high and dry, without anything. It's like inviting somebody to your house and then moving.

TOM: It almost seems like what is happening in terms of the industrial pop machinery that it, like any business, ultimately feels compelled to go out into the field. It's the Marco Polo effect, it brings home the spices and incorporates them into their own world.

ELVIS: Recently, I've looked to some places which I have some natural connection with, albeit very tenuous. Other places that I can't explain . . .

TOM: Well, your whole molecular structure and what's in your bones and genetically in you also contains musical information. Because the first time I really started listening to Irish music, I had a very strong connection. Strangely enough, there's a great many Japanese melodies and vocal styles that sound very much like Hungarian music. You start seeing all these cross-references and comparative, independent musical cultures . . .

ELVIS: Like when I first heard the Dirty Dozen Brass Band, it was like waking up from a dream where you'd heard the music in your dream, and you woke up to find that it was a reality. It was almost a frightening experience, 'cause it was as if I had known it for a long time. The Dirty Dozen record, the new one, I want to hear that one, 'cause I think this is hopefully a new style for them, with a big label. I think a group like that really needs somebody who can put it in shops everywhere you can find it because inevitably a lot of that stuff is word-of-mouth. Sir Kirk [Joseph], the sousaphone player, is such an obvious star 'cause it's so unusual to have somebody so fluent on an instrument which almost by definition is not fluent, really. He's a one-in-a-million player.

TOM: I love that sousaphone. It's really like dancing with a fat lady, you really have to know what you're doing.

ELVIS: Yeah. I mean you can get stepped on, but it's much more dangerous, because it doesn't ever stop in the same place. It goes out in the air and just stops short, but a little bit more carries on. It's the most wonderful sound, it's everything it should be. It's proper sex music.

ELVIS COSTELLO, TV PERSONALITY

TOM: The pre-play music for this *Demon Wine* is all Tony Bennett music. It's really nice. It serves as kind of a music for the main title of the play. Then out of nowhere I got a call from Tony Bennett, who's doing an album. He wants a song. His son called. I thought, that was great. I've always loved Tony Bennett. That record he did with Bill Evans with just piano and voice, and all those things.

ELVIS: He has the chops, still, that he could do whatever record he wants. I did that show with him, which is basically buried in the vaults of NBC.

TOM: With Count Basie?

ELVIS: Yeah. He was the guy I had to sing with. I'd done three rock 'n' roll shows and had no voice. I was down to that extent and had to go in, and I croaked my way through a ballad, which is fine until the bridge, till it gets into the solo; I was doing fine until I got to that. It was about six months before Count Basie died. He said to me, just at the point when I was about to admit that not only could I not do it even in full voice, I certainly couldn't do it in no voice. And he said, "Listen, son, I'm seventy-five years old and I can't get my arm above here. And you can do it." He just hexed me into doing it. I had to stand about three feet away from him when we went into the finale and watch him take a solo from as close as I am from you, and then guess what happened next? The TV people said, sorry, the cameras weren't rolling, we'll have to take it again. It was actually physically painful for him to play. But that's all in a vault somewhere. I think that is just a question of self-confidence. I don't believe anybody hasn't got a voice, for instance. I just think they haven't found it yet. I believe everybody can write songs in the same way.

TOM: You can discover something out of that, too.

ELVIS: I did. But then I get to say, I sang with Count Basie. And nobody believes me, everybody thinks I'm hallucinating when I say that. Never take on shows just on the basis of being able to tell your great-grandchildren is what I discovered. But we had to do this finale number with Tony Bennett and me, "It Don't Mean a Thing If It Ain't Got That Swing." I mean, his voice is eight feet wide. So you gonna write him a song?

TOM: I'm gonna, when I get some time. I was thinking of maybe trying to do something kind of strange, a subject matter unlike Tony Bennett's.

ELVIS: I'd be very suspicious of anybody that seems to have to move to the next level of expression. I distrust that: now I'm writing a book, now I'm being an actor. It should be a natural thing. I think it's a natural thing for you to act. But I think that people that feel that because they've written one maybe quite beautiful love song that equips them to play Romeo are probably misguided. I don't think that necessarily follows at all, it's an uneven equation.

TOM: You would trust that type of a diversion from somebody with more discipline than you would from somebody who has a complete lack of discipline, has gone into those worlds without a ticket or a passport.

ELVIS: Have you written music in this play?

TOM: No, but there is a great score. It's like an Alex North score. He did a lot of the film noir stuff, he did the music to *East of Eden*. This is really like Pacific jazz stuff, two-track, upright bass, sax, or baritone sax, trumpet, snare drums, real meaty noir stuff that really works. But you're right about the passage, I sometimes think that with music, particularly with pop, you have to put it all in perspective as to what you can sincerely contribute. But you also get a jones about it, and you think well, I'm not doing enough, I'm not challenging myself. I think those are good things.

ELVIS: I went on this television show in Italy. I recommend this one when you're there next time. This is the most extraordinary idea—they have a whole TV studio sort of decked out like a club with layer upon layer of images of musicians. And you've got a picture of Louis Armstrong right next to a picture of somebody from some group in Italy you've never heard of. A picture of Maria Callas next to Mick Jagger, Prince next to Arturo Toscanini. And they've got one of those mechanical balls in the middle of it. I looked at the audience and I thought, this is very strange. This audience is incredibly glamorous. They had these girls with manes of hair and long legs and short skirts, very elegant fellows in suede jackets, striking all kinds of fantastically attractive poses. So when the show starts, there's this young fellow that sings a little bit like Sting, and I go well, this is a happy-go-lucky show, they seem to be enjoying it. What are they gonna make of me? I didn't think I was really fair for this audience. And they go wildly happy the minute I come out. And then Buckwheat Zydeco is the next thing on there. There's Buckwheat and his band completely horrified because the audience is digging them so much, they can't understand why they haven't come to live in Italy before! 'Cause they've never seen girls like this at their shows.

Then I said, what's the scene of this, that all these young people in Italy dig R&B and Zydeco and music like I play, whatever that's called? And they said no, they pay them twenty-five pounds a day each to be on this show. Really genius. He's presenting R&B and jazz. They go [he rants in excited pidgin Italian] and you think they're going to introduce the new George Michael video, and you know what it was? A clip of Ben Webster (giggles).

TOM: That's the beauty of show business. It's the only business you can have a career in when you're dead.

ELVIS: What I think is amazing is this guy's discovered that if you present all this music that he obviously loves, if you present it like it's very hip, not hip as we know it but hip as the kids in Italy know it, then they believe you.

TOM: If you tell them that they're falling down over this three thousand miles from here, you're unhip for not being hip to it. They'll start wearing Ben Webster T-shirts.

ELVIS: The BBC is sort of like, [dryly] "Now we have the only existing clip of the Negro saxophone player, Charles Parker." They make it sound like something really dull. This genius in Italy has really worked out the trick to get people to listen to this music and find what they'd like about it themselves. On this other show in Sweden, that was even wilder in its own way. It didn't have so much to offer, necessarily. I was far and away the most normal thing on the bill. They had the guy that's made millions out of self-assembly furniture, and they had him come on and they said, if you're so damn clever, you assemble your own furniture by the end of the show. Otherwise you'll be denounced.

TOM: And he did it?

ELVIS: Oh yeah, of course he did it. He had a little black designer knife and fork to do it with, or whatever it was, not a knife and fork, a screwdriver. Then they had an interview with the queen of Denmark, who turns out to be this pissed old bat with yellow teeth who chain-smokes. She had this dachshund on her lap who kept looking in her face, and at the end of the interview she said "oh shit" in Swedish, of course a big sensation. And then the star of the show was this enormous guy you know those Swedish beards that don't have mustaches that come with them, just on the chin? This guy had these little beady eyes that darted around, and I noticed he was next to two equally strange-looking people who looked like they were up to no good. One of them had handcuffs on his wrist. I thought, he's an escapologist. This is all going on in Swedish, I don't know what they're saying. He was an actual prisoner! He was being interviewed on Swedish television about this massive credit card fraud which he perpetrated. So they brought him out of prison to have him on television to be inter-viewed 'cause they're all reasonable in Sweden. And better still, he brought his guitar with him and he sang a song about it. Then they handcuffed him again and took him away. He was the star.

TOM WAITS

Thrasher, February 1993

Brian Brannon

No matter what they may claim, few performers let it all go the way Tom Waits does. Screaming, moaning, smashing the ivories, and smacking the strings, he speaks in tongues and plays with abandon, painting bizarre patterns and unraveling tangled memories. His latest works include a skull crackin' CD of primitive clarity that rocks dem bones called *Bone Machine.* Waits also contributed an eerie, earthy soundtrack to *Night on Earth,* a film by Jim Jarmusch.

What do you like to hit the most when you're mad?

I got a bass drum that's about fifty-nine inches across. It's enormous, it's like hitting a dumpster with a sledgehammer. It'll free ya.

Do you ever notice some things feel like they'd be good to throw?

Yeah, I like to do that with family heirlooms, things that have value to others.

I see you have Les Claypool playing bass on this new album.

He came up and played on "The Earth Died Screaming." He was in between fishing trips at the time. He's great, he's got such an elastic approach to the instrument: a fretless, spastic, elastic, rubberized, plasticine approach. He's like a fun house mirror. He can take and elongate his face. He's a real pawnshop weasel, endlessly in pawnshops. I think that's why he tours.

Didn't you do the voice of Tommy the Cat on Primus's "Sailing the Seas of Cheese"?

Yeah, he sent me a tape with him doing it where it sounds like an auctioneer on helium. I said, "Man I can't talk that fast." It was rough.

On that song "The Earth Died Screaming," do you think the earth is dying and we're just living in our own little dreams and ignoring it?

I guess, but I think the world is going to be here a whole lot longer after we're gone. I'm just waiting for the whole world to open up and swallow us all in, scrape us all off its back. I think the world is a living organism. When you stick a shovel in the ground, have you ever heard the earth go "Uhhgm?" And we're living on the decomposed remains of our ancestors, both animal, mineral, and vegetable. So it is a living thing. I don't think it's going to die screaming, I think we're going to die screaming, in the swamp of time.

So I heard that you moved to the country and there's a lot of roadkill out there?

Yeah, roadkill, gun racks, collapsing chicken coops, and organized vultures.

And there's always some killing?

There's always some killing you've got to do around the farm. Barns are painted red because that's where all the slaughtering is done. Originally barns were painted with the blood of dead animals. Before they had paint, there was blood.

A lot of your songs have a certain melancholy, what's that from?

Too much wine. Half of me, I feel like a jackhammer, I love to holler and stomp my feet and throw rocks. But there's another side of me that's like an old man in the corner that's had too much wine. I'm probably too sentimental for my own good sometimes.

What would you say to people who don't know where you're coming from?

I try to nail a lot of different things together. I'm more and more getting interested in rhythm. I like to really kick it hard. I like to play the drums until my knuckles bleed, until I pee my pants. Throw myself against the wall. They think I'm a crazy old man probably, "Check this guy out."

Aren't you using less symphony instruments?

Yeah, I'm getting away from that. Trying to do things with just the essential elements of music. It's like making ashtrays: just put three grooves in it and call it an ashtray. I found a great room to work in, it's just a cement floor and a hot water heater. "Okay, we'll do it here." It's got some good echo.

So going crazy making music goes back forever, right?

I guess so, yeah. Concerts are very tribal and I guess it's the same as an insect ritual, and mating rituals. We all have a drum in our chest from the moment we're born. I think music where the tempo is faster than the heartbeat excites you and music that is slower than the heartbeat calms you down. We all have a constant rhythmic beat going on, whether or not you hear it, it's continuing. You feel it all the time whether you acknowledge it or not.

Did you ever skate?

I used to make skateboards out of plywood and go down to a roller rink called Skate Ranch and buy just the wheels. We used to skate down this hill called Robert Avenue and it was a great curve and you dug up a lot of speed. It went by our neighbor Mr. Stitcha. He lived in the beauty of the curve, where all the momentum culminated in a beautiful slough of cement. It took you right past his house but as close as you could get to his porch. Mr. Stitcha drank to excess. This was common knowledge in the neighborhood. He had the thick glasses and the red face and the red wine stains down the front of his T-shirt. That's like I look now. Anyway it was the only place to get that kind of speed and thrill, so the front of his house became sort of a festival for all the skateboarders in the whole area. On Halloween he had a heart attack and died on his front porch and we were all told he died because we skated by his house and that each and every one of us killed him in our own way. And we were all left with the memory that we all had a hand in his murder. It was like a Shakespeare thing, everybody had their hand on the knife. So I carry this with me, but I just want to say here and now, in *Thrasher* magazine, that I did not kill Mr. Stitcha. It took a lot of therapy and it took a lot of liquor. Mr. Stitcha rest in peace.

20 QUESTIONS

Playboy, March 1988

Steve Oney

Most people know singer-songwriter Tom Waits as the poet of late-night metropolitan areas, the bard of smoky lounges and cueball moons. But lately, Waits has been experimenting, both on his past three albums, which have included songs nailed together from pieces of "found sound"—deafening jackhammers, sirens, strains of an Irish jig—and as an actor (*The Cotton Club, Down by Law, Ironweed*). Writer Steve Oney showed up at a favorite Waits hangout, a seedy café on the fringes of downtown L.A. "Waits, now thirty-seven, arrived looking wild-haired and mystic-eyed and dressed in a parson's black suit and tie," he reports. "He was insistent upon talking into a tape recorder for fear of being misquoted, but he began the conversation with the warning, 'I'm going to pull your string from time to time.' "

1. PLAYBOY: In spite of the fact that your albums have won you a loyal following, your work is rarely heard on the radio. What kind of payola do you think it would take

to get disc jockeys in Des Moines to play a few cuts from *Frank's Wild Years?*

WAITS: Send them some frozen Cornish game hens. That would probably do the trick. Or maybe some Spencer steaks. The people who succeed today essentially write jingles. It's an epidemic. Even worse are artists aligning themselves with various products, everything from Chrysler-Plymouth to Pepsi. I don't support it. I hate it. So there.

2. PLAYBOY: Early in your career, some of your songs—for instance, "Ol' 55," which the Eagles covered—became hits, and almost all of them, no matter how unconventional, relied upon pretty melodies. But lately— especially on your past three albums—you've moved from hummable tunes to what you call "organized noise." Why?

WAITS: I was cutting off a very small piece of what I wanted to do. I wasn't getting down the things I was really hearing and experiencing. Music with a lot of strings gets like Perry Como after a while. It's why I don't really work with the piano much anymore. Like, anybody who plays the piano would thrill at seeing and hearing one thrown off a twelve-story building, watching it hit the sidewalk and being there to hear that thump. It's like school. You want to watch it burn.

3. PLAYBOY: To create a marketable pop song, do you have to sell out?

WAITS: Popular music is like a big party, and it's a thrill

sneaking in rather than being invited. Every once in a while, a guy with his shirt on inside out, wearing lipstick and a pillbox hat, gets a chance to speak. I've always been afraid I was going to tap the world on the shoulder for twenty years and when it finally turned around, I was going to forget what I had to say. I was always afraid I was going to do something in the studio and hate it, put it out, and it was going to become a hit. So I'm neurotic about it.

4. PLAYBOY: Who was Harry Partch, and what did he mean to you?

WAITS: He was an innovator. He built all his own instruments and kind of took the American hobo experience and designed instruments from ideas he gathered traveling around the United States in the thirties and forties. He used a pump organ and industrial water bottles, created enormous marimbas. He died in the early seventies, but the Harry Partch Ensemble still performs at festivals. It's a little arrogant to say I see a relationship between his stuff and mine. I'm very crude, but I use things we hear around us all the time, built and found instruments—things that aren't normally considered instruments: dragging a chair across the floor or hitting the side of a locker real hard with a two-by-four, a freedom bell, a brake drum with a major imperfection, a police bullhorn. He's more interesting. You know, I don't like straight lines. The problem is that most instruments are square and music is always round.

5. PLAYBOY: Considering your predispositions, which modern artists do you like to listen to?

WAITS: Prince. He's out there. He's uncompromising. He's a real fountainhead. Takes dangerous chances. He's androgynous, wicked, voodoo. The Replacements have a great stance. They like distortion. Their concerts are like insect rituals. I like a lot of rap stuff, because it's real, immediate. Generally, I like things as they begin, because the industry tears at you. Most artists come out the other side like a dead carp.

6. PLAYBOY: What do you think of when you hear the name Barry Manilow?

WAITS: Expensive furniture and clothes that you don't feel good in.

7. PLAYBOY: In your musical career, you've tried to retain maximum creative control; yet within the past few years, you've become more and more involved in the most collaborative of all media, theater and film. What's the attraction?

WAITS: It's thrilling to see the insanity of all these people brought together like this life-support system to create something that's really made out of smoke. The same thing draws me to it that draws me to making records—you fashion these things and ideas into your own monster. It's making dreams. I like that.

8. PLAYBOY: In *Ironweed*, you worked with Jack Nicholson and Meryl Streep. What did you learn from them?

WAITS: Nicholson's a consummate storyteller. He's like a great bard. He says he knows about beauty parlors and train yards and everything in between. You can learn a lot from just watching him open a window or tie his shoes. It's great to be privy to those things. I watched everything—watched them build characters from pieces of things in people they have known. It's like they build a doll from Grandmother's mouth and Aunt Betty's walk and Ethel Merman's posture, then they push their own truthful feelings through that exterior. They're great at it.

9. PLAYBOY: Have there been musical benefits from involvement in theater and film?

WAITS: Just that I'm more comfortable stepping into characters in songs. On *Frank's Wild Years,* I did it in "I'll Take New York" and "Straight to the Top." I've learned how to be different musical characters without feeling like I'm eclipsing myself. On the contrary, you discover a whole family living inside you.

10. PLAYBOY: Three years ago, you made much ado about leaving Los Angeles for Manhattan. You praised New York as "a great town for shoes," but now you're back in California. What happened?

WAITS: I was developing Tourette's syndrome. I was blurting out obscenities in the middle of Eighth Avenue. I turned into an eraserhead. But it's been arrested. With research, there is hope.

11. PLAYBOY: If you were to give a tour of L.A., what sights would you include?

WAITS: Let's see. For chicken, I suggest the Red Wing Hatchery near Tweedy Lane in South Central L.A. We're talking both fryers and ritual chickens. Hang one over the door to keep out evil spirits; the other goes on your plate with paprika. For your other shopping needs, try B.C.D. Market on Temple. Best produce in town; also good pig knuckles, always important in your dining plans. Ask for Bruce. Below the Earth, on Hill Street, is the best spot for female impersonators; then you're going to want to be looking into those pickled eggs at the Frolic Room, by the bus station. Guy behind the bar has the same birthday as me, and his name is Tom. Finally, you have to take in Bongo Bean, who plays the sax on the sidewalk in front of the Hotel Figueroa. We're talking *Pennies from Heaven* time. Bongo is tall, good-looking, there most every night. Accept no substitutes.

12. PLAYBOY: While L.A. may be your stomping grounds, your other great love is the wee-hours world of America's big cities. From all your travels, what have been your favorite dives?

WAITS: The Sterling Hotel, in Cleveland. Great lobby. Good place to sit with the old men and watch Rock Hudson movies. Then there's the Wilmont Hotel, in Chicago. The woman behind the desk, her son's the Marlboro man. There's the Alamo Hotel, in Austin, Texas, where I rode in an elevator one night with Sam Houston Johnson. He spit tobacco juice into a cup while we talked. Let's see: The Swiss American Hotel is San Francisco's insane asylum. The Paradise Motel, right here on Sunset in L.A. It's nice in the summer when there's a carnival across the street. And, oh, the Taft. I think they're a chain. You can probably get off a train in just about any town, get into a taxi and say, "Take me to the Taft Hotel" and wind up somewhere unsavory. Yeah, say, "Take me to the Taft, and step on it."

13. PLAYBOY: Despite your reputation and songs that glorify hard living and carousing, you've been married seven years and have two children. How do you balance your domestic and creative lives?

WAITS: My wife's been great. I've learned a lot from her. She's Irish Catholic. She's got the whole dark forest living inside of her. She pushes me into areas I would not go, and I'd say that a lot of the things I'm trying to do now, she's encouraged. And the kids? Creatively, they're astonishing. The way they draw, you know? Right off the page and onto the wall. It's like you wish you could be that open.

14. PLAYBOY: Do you do all-American-dad things, such as go to Disneyland?

WAITS: Disneyland is Vegas for children. When I went with the kids, I just about had a stroke. It's the opposite of what they say it is. It's not a place to nurture the imagination. It's just a big clearance sale for useless items. I'm not going back, and the kids won't be allowed to return until they're eighteen, out of the house. And even then, I would block their decision.

15. PLAYBOY: Your songwriting technique is very unusual. Instead of sitting down at a piano or synthesizer, you

hole up alone somewhere with nothing but a tape recorder. Why do you work that way?

WAITS: I don't want to sound spiritual, but I try to make an antenna out of myself, a lightning rod out of myself, so whatever is out there can come in. It happens in different places, in hotels, in the car—when someone else is driving. I bang on things, slap the wall, break things—whatever is in the room. There are all these things in the practical world that you deal with on a practical level, and you don't notice them as anything but what you need them to be. But when I'm writing, all these things turn into something else, and I see them differently, almost like I've taken a narcotic. Somebody once said I'm not a musician but a tonal engineer. I like that. It's kind of clinical and primitive at the same time.

16. PLAYBOY: While you may strive for musical crudity, lyrically you're quite sophisticated, interior rhymes, classical allusions, and your hallmark, a great ear for the vernacular. In a sense, you're the William Safire of street patois, rescuing such phrases as walking Spanish—inebriated saunter—and even coining some pretty good lingo of your own, such as rain dogs: stray people who, like animals after a shower, can't find their markings and wander aimlessly. What are some of your other favorite bits of slang, phrases you'd like to see get more everyday use?

WAITS: For starters, I'd like to see the term wooden kimono return to the lexicon. Means coffin. Think it originated in New Orleans, but I'm not certain. Another one I like is wolf tickets, which means bad news, as in someone who is bad news or generally insubordinate. In a sentence, you'd say, "Don't fuck with me, I'm passing out wolf tickets." Think it's either Baltimore Negro or turn-of-the-century railroadese. There's one more. Don't know where it came from, but I like it: Saturdaynightitis. Now, it's what happens to your arm when you hang it around a chair all night at the movies or in some bar, trying to make points with a pretty girl. When your arm goes dead from that sort of action, you've got Saturdaynightitis.

17. PLAYBOY: You have said that you'd rather hear music over a crackly AM car radio than over the best sound system. What's the matter with a good CD player?

WAITS: I like to take music out of the environment it was grown in. I guess I'm always aware of the atmosphere that I'm listening to something in as much as I am of what I'm listening to. It can influence the music. It's like listening to Mahalia Jackson as you drive across Texas. That's different from hearing her in church. It's like taking a Victrola into the jungle, you know? The music then has an entirely different quality. You integrate it into your world and it doesn't become the focus of it but a condiment. It becomes the soundtrack for the film that you're living.

18. PLAYBOY: Your score for *One from the Heart* was nominated for an Oscar. Did you enjoy writing it enough to try another?

WAITS: Working on *One from the Heart* was almost a Brill Building approach to songwriting—sitting at a piano in an office, writing songs like jokes. I had always had that fantasy, so I jumped at the chance to do it. I've been offered other films, but I've turned 'em down. The director comes to you and says, "Here, I've got this thing here, this broken toy." And in some cases, he says, "Can you fix it?" Or maybe he just wants interior decorating or a haircut. So you have to be sure you're the right man for the job. Sort of like being a doctor. Rest in bed, get plenty of fluids.

19. PLAYBOY: You've remarked that *Frank's Wild Years* is the end of a musical period for you, the last part of a trilogy of albums that began with *Swordfishtrombones*. Have you turned a corner? Is this album your last experimentation with the scavenger school of songwriting?

WAITS: I don't know if I turned a corner, but I opened a door. I kind of found a new seam. I threw rocks at the window. I'm not as frightened by technology maybe as I used to be. On the past three albums, I was exploring the hydrodynamics of my own peculiarities. I don't know what the next one will be. Harder, maybe louder. Things are now a little more psychedelic for me, and they're more ethnic. I'm looking toward that part of music that comes from my memories, hearing Los Tres Aces at the Continental Club with my dad when I was a kid.

20. PLAYBOY: How far would you go to avoid getting a star on Hollywood Boulevard?

WAITS: I don't think it works that way. It's pretty much that you pay for it. I'm not big on awards. They're just a lot of headlights stapled to your chest, as Bob Dylan said.

I've gotten only one award in my life, from a place called Club Tenco in Italy. They gave me a guitar made out of tiger-eye. Club Tenco was created as an alternative to the big San Remo Festival they have every year. It's to commemorate the death of a big singer whose name was Tenco and who shot himself in the heart because he'd lost at the San Remo Festival. For a while, it was popular in Italy for singers to shoot themselves in the heart. That's my award.

THE FIRE (AND FLOOD)
THIS TIME

St. Louis Post-Dispatch, September 25, 1992

Steve Pick

I listened to the old Captain Beefheart classic *The Spotlight Kid* one day last week in a record store. After the album was over, somebody came up to me and asked, "Say, was that the new Tom Waits album?" No, this is not going to be a rant about how another lost genius has been kept unfairly obscure, though I certainly believe people are genuinely happier for knowing the music of Beefheart. But the point I want to make is how Tom Waits has assimilated so much of what the good Captain did twenty years ago. Though Waits has added much of his own personality, the unusual voicings, oddball rhythms, and strange structural twists of Captain Beefheart are easily found in Waits's work. Or at least his more recent work. The career of Tom Waits can be reasonably neatly divided into everything he did before 1983 (when he was a sort of romantic neo-beatnik poetic singer/songwriter) and all the wilder, more experimental sounds he's played with since then. The genesis of his change came when his voice, always a gin-soaked croak, developed nightmarish qualities, and Waits discovered he could create five or six freakish styles out of the same old set of vocal cords. There followed his trilogy based on the character of Frank, the down-and-out show-biz entertainer who starred in the albums *Swordfishtrombones, Rain Dogs* and *Frank's Wild Years*. After the live album *Big Time*, Waits disappeared from the music biz for five years, until earlier this year, when the soundtrack to *Night on Earth* featured his music, and now, with the release of a new studio album, *Bone Machine*. Forget all the problems poor old Frank used to have. Waits has decided to go after more apocalyptic themes this time. *Bone Machine* is full of end-of-the-world imagery, with fires and floods and constant rain, with angels and devils popping up in people's lives, with the impossibility of beating forces we can't control or even understand. I read an interview a few years back in which Waits said that he's fascinated by music he doesn't quite hear properly. For him, the music somebody is playing down the hall of an apartment building, muffled by the walls, covered by an air conditioner and mingled with traffic sounds, is truly compelling, because so much of what he hears has to be imagined. Waits is not someone who wants all his information handed to him on a single sheet of paper; he wants to work with the bits of information he receives and shape them into something he can imagine. It seems to me that this is at the heart of what he is doing on *Bone Machine*. Many of the songs begin with rough sounds of instruments struggling to find their place before locking in step to play together, and just as many end with the instruments collapsing separately. The percussion, often played by Waits himself, is (to put it mildly) loose, though oddly compelling. The effect is similar to listening to street recordings of parade music, where the sounds build slowly, come together and then pass by. The wonderful working band Waits put together a few years ago is gone. Guitarist Marc Ribot and percussionist Michael Blair, who took these same sorts of ideas and worked them into intricate grooves, are off doing their own various projects (you can frequently find them working with Elvis Costello, who also has been increasingly interested in playing around with the norms of his sound). Most of the time, Waits plays guitar, piano and percussion himself, with very light accompaniment from an upright bass or the occasional saxophone, fiddle, or lead guitar. In this respect, he's doing something Captain Beefheart never did. For Beefheart always employed the most talented musicians he could find and made them play things the way he wanted them played. Waits is clearly more interested in the natural evolution of unusual combinations. On one song, he even trades instruments with Larry Taylor, so that Waits plays bass and Taylor guitar. The primitive results of this switch make the song, "Jesus Gonna Be Here," sound much more like a found piece of gospel ephemera than a calculated imitation of same. Waits has gone so far as to make his song structures abandon rules as well. If he has a couple of extra lines in one verse that aren't there in the next, that's all right with him. If a line has to spill over a couple of extra beats in a bar, that's fine, too. In a strange way, and while always keeping one foot firmly in a modern pop context, Waits is doing what blues artists did in the days before the form became consistently codified. In the past, Waits has worked hard at imitating (and playing around with) the structures of different musical genres. This time, he's just going in there and creating his own. Sometimes he's evoking the gravel cries of Howlin' Wolf, sometimes he's mourning in falsetto and sometimes he's pulling beauty from his straightest, yet still strange, singing voice. *Bone Machine* is a welcome return from a talented musician.

A Mellower Prince of Melancholy

Guardian, September 15, 1992

Adam Sweeting

> He might still dress as though he staggers around
> sniffing under dustbin lids, but now the self-styled
> Oddball Kid refuses to play his old role of roughneck
> rock 'n' roller.

It's the bits Tom Waits leaves out of his conversation that are
the most fascinating. His answers are like shapes drawn in
sand with a stick. You have to guess what's in the middle. I
asked him about a song called "Black Wings," from his new
album, *Bone Machine.*

"Well, it's a bit of a mmmm, er, spoken-word Noriega-type
number there," he slurs, in that raspy bumping-along-the-
bottom voice that haunted a million hangovers. Waits tips his
head back, narrows his eyes, and delivers a searching gaze over
the top of his granny-spectacles, calculating the extent of his
interrogator's gullibility.

"I don't know," he adds (most of his answers begin with "I
don't know"). "The songs are mmmm, ahhh, errr . . . I dunno
. . . the title *Bone Machine,* I guess it's kinda from the fact that

. . . urghhh . . . that there's certain ahhh . . . one of those things that you're not sure what it is, but that's what's good about it. I don't really know what it is, but it kind of reminds me of a superhero."

Grudgingly, Waits ekes out the information that "some of the songs deal with violence and death and suicide and the end of the world, and they're all strung together like old vertebrae."

For our meeting, Waits has picked a place called the Limbo Diner, on a corner in a featureless low-rise district of San Francisco which could be anywhere—Detroit, Miami, Los Angeles. The place seems to have nothing particular to recommend it other than Olympic-sized coffee cups and a corner table from which Waits can keep a beady eye on the door. Waits has made the two-hour drive into the city with his wife and co-writer, Kathleen Brennan, rather than encourage prowlers to come near their home out in the sticks, somewhere in northern California.

"Um . . . I live in a little cow town now," Waits growls. "You probably will too someday. It's over that way." He waves an ungainly arm in a circle above his head. "There's a couple of other people living there, and I'm trying to get rid of them. Put the evil eye on 'em."

If you don't count his recently released soundtrack from the Jim Jarmusch movie, *Night on Earth*, *Bone Machine* is Waits's first album of all-new songs since *Frank's Wild Years* in 1987. But, in the intervening period, he has been busier than ever. In 1988, there was the concert film and live album, *Big Time*. Waits put music to William Burroughs's libretto for the opera *The Black Rider*, produced by Robert Wilson. He has written music for Wilson's production of *Alice in Wonderland*, which will be premiered by Hamburg's Thalia Theatre Company in December. Of the eight movie roles he has notched up in those five years, the most prestigious is Renfield, in Francis Coppola's forthcoming picture, *Bram Stoker's Dracula*. "It's a lurid, torrid film," he reveals.

Although life as a travelling musician must seem like a distant memory, Waits thinks he may eventually be forced to take the *Bone Machine* songs on tour, though he's not sure how. "Sometimes when I think about touring, I would rather be attacked by a school of hagfish. Hagfish eat another fish from the inside out. That's sometimes what touring does to you. You look like you're all right, but you've had all your guts eaten and you have no brain left.

"When I was twenty-one, I was just happy to be on the road, away from home, riding through the American night y'know, out of my mind. Wild-eyed about everything. Now, I think more about it, like what can we do that's cheaper, simpler and better? I think maybe we should just have a stage no bigger than a hatbox. I'll probably go on the road, with devil horns and angel wings and dry ice and a toy guitar. The band will all be cutouts."

His audiences are unlikely to contain the kind of characters who have peopled his songs about the underfed underbelly of American lowlife. He might still dress as though he staggers around sniffing under dustbin lids (porkpie hat, scuffed shoes, torn black jeans, free-range goatee), but Waits is more or less filed under Literature these days, joining the line after Damon Runyon and Raymond Carver.

One could speculate that Waits needed to make his move into film and theatrical work to save himself from becoming a victim of his own seedy mythology. Francis Coppola once described him as "the prince of melancholy" (and hence the perfect choice to write music for Coppola's whimsical fable, *One from the Heart*), but it looked for a while as if Waits was liable to seep away into the margins inhabited by the drunks, bums and con-artists who shuffled through his early albums like *Nighthawks at the Diner* or *Small Change*. On-the-job experience as a dishwasher, bartender, and lavatory attendant had furnished Waits with such priceless kerb-level information as how to get a drink into your mouth when you're rattling with the d.t.s (use your tie as a pulley), or how to render yourself invisible in the presence of policemen. His health was allegedly precarious for a time.

Frank's Wild Years, "un opera romantico in two acts," signalled Waits's acknowledgment that you didn't have to live the life when you could externalize it as theatre. He and Kathleen Brennan wrote the play as a "parable of one accordion player's redemption and baptism" and as a starring vehicle for Waits, and it was staged by Chicago's Steppenwolf Theatre Company. The accompanying album was like a radio dial spinning between Memphis and Tijuana, Detroit and Havana. Waits had reached a pinnacle of the picaresque.

Questions aimed at provoking career analysis or self-assessment get Waits measuring the distance between himself and the exit. "I don't like direct questions, I like to talk," he complains. My suggestion that he's slipped into the arms of the arty, highbrow set is not welcomed. "Hey, highbrow, lowbrow, y'know . . . I'm the Oddball Kid. If you're an artist, you feel there's a shorthand you hope you've developed with whatever the process is. People who try to intimidate you with the vernacular of what they do usually are insecure about what they do."

And what does he love most? "I'm interested in words, I love words. Every word has a particular musical sound to it which you may or may not be able to use. Like for example 'spatula,' that's a good word. Sounds like the name of a band. Probably is the name of a band."

It's logical, then, that Waits should be an enthusiastic fan of rap. "You know what I love about rap? All those guys flunked English. It's so beautiful that it's words that have given them power and strength and courage to articulate the things they're talking about, the anger and the braggadocio and their years of exile and slavery. These are the guys that had real trouble in school, 'cause some of them are real bad kids. Bad bad neighbourhoods, man. Guns there are like fingernails or teeth—you have to have them. I identify with it because I love words."

Waits also heartily approves of sampling records and pilfering noises (*Bone Machine* uses a homemade percussion gadget called the conundrum, and there's hardly a sound on the record that isn't scuzzed and battered and distorted), so it's a pity he felt he had to take action against rappers 3rd Bass for allegedly stealing his song, "Down in the Hole." "They probably think I'm a real prick, but I said listen, you didn't take like boom-ching-boom, you took a whole song."

What about rap's violent, misogynist tendencies? Waits shrugs. "Frank Sinatra is more down on women than the rappers are. People are always gonna step on other people's toes, and they're gonna have to bark and say something about it when it happens. Music is like a big trunkline. It's like a big ocean of blood. It's art versus commerce, ideas versus rhetoric. It's like a freak show sometimes, and other times it's like an emergency room. Other times it's like a church."

And other times it's a good deed, like the benefit concert Waits appeared in after the L.A. riots. It's always as well to expect the unexpected, but an older, more socially responsible Tom Waits is stretching it a bit. I wondered if he felt he was becoming a pillar of society.

"Oh Jesus. A pillar? Goddamn. No." A man of probity, even? "No," he says. "I'm waiting, like a spider."

Tom Waits Meets Jim Jarmusch

Straight No Chaser, October 1992

Jim Jarmusch

I have known Tom Waits now for over eight years. Tom is not only someone whose work has always, for me, been a source of inspiration, but a man for whom I have a very deep, personal respect. I admire him because he remains true to himself in both his work and his life. He follows his own code, which is not always the same one prescribed by laws, rules or the expectations of other people. He is strong and direct. There is no bullshit surrounding the man. Tom is, obviously, also a man whose use of language and ability to express himself are completely unique. I spent half the time while with him laughing uncontrollably, and the other half in amazement at the seemingly endless flow of very unusual ideas and observations pouring out of him. The guy is a wild man. Tom lives with his family in a big, strange house hidden away somewhere in California. I think of it as the Tom Waits version of a gangster hideout; a world in and of itself. For reasons I am very respectful of, its location will remain anonymous. The following conversations were recorded during a one-week period in October of 1992 in and around

Tom's house, in a nearby chicken-ranch-turned-recording-studio, and most often while driving around in either Tom's 1964 Cadillac, or his '65 Chevy El Camino. Our final conversation was abruptly concluded when the El Camino literally caught on fire while we were driving it (with a full load of furniture in the back). Somehow it was an appropriate ending point for an unpredictable adventure with Tom Waits.

—Jim Jarmusch
Los Angeles, October 1992

TOM'S FIRST VISION

Jim Jarmusch: Tell me some stuff about when you were a kid.

Tom Waits: I was in the ocean when I was about seven years old. It was getting dark and I heard my father calling, he has a very unique whistle that he could send anywhere I was and I would hear it and I would know that's my dad whistling and I had to come in.

JJ: My mom had that.

TW: All the kids knew their dad or mom's whistle or call.

JJ: We're trained just like dogs. In fact, in our house our dog used to come back to the same whistle.

TW: [laughs] So I was in the water, up to about my chest, and it was summer, and I was out a little deeper than I should be, and I got that feeling on the beach when it's starting to get dark and you know you've gotta go in. And a fog came over this part of the ocean—this was in Mexico. I was about seven, we had a trailer down there. And a pirate ship, an enormous pirate ship came out of the fog. I was close enough to where I could touch the bow of the ship where there was a cannon, and there was smoke coming off the sails that were burning and there were dead pirates hanging on the mast and falling off the deck. And I was stopped, I was just—because I knew I saw it. It came out of the fog, and I reached to touch it and it turned and it went back into the fog and disappeared. And I told my parents about it, and of course they looked at me like, "Pirate ship, huh? Well, boy. Saw a pirate ship, huh? Honey, Tom saw a pirate ship out there." And I'm like, okay. But I did, I really did, and it was a death ship with a skull and crossbones, the whole thing.

JJ: That's a really ancient thing, seeing the death ship.

TW: Because they used to put people on those ships, you know, the crazy people that were insane, debtors, people that had birth defects.

Alien Life Forms

TW: You know what I'd like to do, I'd like to go into space with a band, have speakers on the outside of our spacecraft, see if we can communicate. Choose a really strange band, develop our own space program where we're gonna actually go up, because right now the only people who are allowed to go up there, y'know, the way they pick them is just like I guess I'm sure the way they picked explorers.

JJ: Sun Ra has been sending signals for some time into space. That's his life.

TW: How does he send them? I mean—

JJ: Well, just through his music.

TW: But I mean get in a spacecraft to go into space, and perform in-space music. Because they're saying that our new program now is to actually find hard evidence of life on other planets. That is the mission and the doctrine of the space program today. And my feeling is that I think that we should communicate through music. We're sending these little things that show the anatomy of man, and our very simple numerical system, and some of our math, and some of our makeup, scientific makeup, but I think we should go out with a group.

JJ: Which means they'd probably send—

TW: They'd send the wrong group, yeah.

JJ: They'd send Michael Jackson, instead of you or Sun Ra.

TW: But speakers on the outside of the spacecraft, can you imagine?

JJ: It's like these kids that have their cars with sound systems so hot that—A mechanic told me that those sub-sonic, sub-woofer bass systems loosen all the bolts and screws in the car, and the whole construction of the car from vibration gradually will just fall apart.

TW: It's beautiful. We recorded in a room that was not sound-proof, you saw the room. When you're on the set and you're recording outside you stop for airplanes or trains or cars or kids coming home from school. You have to stop. But I love that. We didn't stop for anything. I wish we'd had more aircraft flying over on the record because I don't see the point in keeping other sounds out.

JJ: Supposedly on some of the Sun Studio recordings from Memphis in the early fifties you can hear trucks going by outside . . .

TW: It's great.

JJ: Do you think there are aliens or life forms from other planets or other solar systems, other galaxies that have visited earth or at least surveilled it? What do you think about UFOs and aliens and stuff?

TW: No, I believe there is intelligent life, but we are the ones who define what intelligence is, so I'm sure it would fall outside of our intelligence or ability to perceive it, which leads me to believe that they may be here among us and we are unable to see them, or understand that they're here. So y'know, where technology is now as far as tracking other life forms, I don't know. When I was a kid I built radios. My dad was a radio expert in the army, and in addition to bicycle repair, he had me building my own radios and sending away for kits and creating my own little shortwave radios. And I picked up things when I was a child that I swore were extra-terrestrial, and maintain to this day that I made contact, or at least I was on the receiving end of a relationship with an extraterrestrial but was unable to communicate with him because my radio couldn't transmit.

JJ: Were they voices, or sounds or what?

TW: It was a language that did not exist. It was not Russian, I was picking up Russia and Poland and Hungary and China—

JJ: But this was a language?

TW: It was a language, but it was not from around here. And here I was unable to transmit. On earth, we never acknowledge that they exist because it doesn't fit into our beliefs about the creation of the universe. God made the earth in seven days, then he rested. The idea that there would be creatures out there. The government is apparently keeping creatures they found, and in top-secret bunkers in New Mexico, never to be viewed by the public. I believe that.

JJ: Yeah, when we were in Colorado shooting that Bur-roughs documentary, Burroughs was convinced that they were in that area of the Rockies—there were aliens there mining plutonium in the middle of the night. There were all these reports of people seeing guys with silver suits, masks and helmets on, carrying heavy black boxes in the middle of the night in these ghost towns north of Boulder, Colorado.

TW: Wow. I believe it. We're here to go.

JJ: We're all here to go. Burroughs says we have no reason to expect them to be benevolent, you know. Why should we? They're part of the same universe.

TW: Yeah. They come down here and pick us up and suck the blood out of us like plastic juice containers.

Operating on a Flamingo

JJ: Tell me about recording. You just recorded the score for *The Black Rider*?

TW: Yeah. The songs were done, most of them were recorded very crudely in Hamburg in a studio, and then we brought 'em here. So some of 'em are real crude, which I like. I like to hear things real crude, cruder. I think if I pursue it, I don't know where it'll take me, but y'know, it's getting more and more like that. I just like to hear it dirty. It's a natural relation to where we are in technology, because things swing in and swing back. That's normal. And I like to step on it, scratch it up, break it. I wanna go further into that world of texture. That train thing that I played for you came from taking nine pieces and improvising something really quickly, like lining up children and having 'em march and scream out some word. "Real quick, we gotta make it happen right now," it was like real fast sketch, which is real hard to do when people come from (high) music, because that's high music. People who play in all those symphony orchestras, like some guy who plays contra bassoon, it's rare

173

that he's gonna get to do anything. Where it's just free, do something free, y'know, with structure and planning, but very spontaneously from the depths. That's something you don't really get from an orchestra, so I loved doing that. It gave everybody a great feeling. You know that expression "go out to the meadow" . . . orchestra goes out to the meadow?

JJ: I don't know that expression.

TW: You know, when you leave the room, you leave the music, everyone is just like a ship, a strange ship, and everyone feels essential to it . . . I love that. And those are the things I keep looking for in the studio, and how to do it. There are certain variables that are possible to control, but that's what frustrates me when I'm in there all the time, because I'm thinking about something in here that was alive an hour ago, and now it's just . . . blood is all over the walls, and the fucking thing will never breathe again, and then who's responsible? You! And you point to one of the musicians, and you accuse him of murder. And then we have little mock trials where the guy is found guilty of, whatever, murdering a particular song, and sometimes there's a punishment, and it's a little too high for some of these guys to pay. I've taken fingers off. I'm not proud of it, but it's just part of—one accordionist I worked with just eats the music. He eats the music, and you find him, it's all over his shirt, down his chin, it's just been murdered . . . Accordionists will sometimes take a part and they'll just play the hell out of it until it's dead. But y'know you're always fighting those things, the same thing on a film set. You've got to turn it around. You're responsible for navigating through strange places. I've had these terrible dramas about the expedition, and they remind me of music, of operations where sometimes you lose a patient, and I'm despondent over it, I'm so fucking mad about it. I leave the room like a doctor must feel after he's lost a patient. Of course it's not that bad, but—

JJ: During the recording stage or the performing stage?

TW: Both. And it frustrates me. I don't mean to say that it's like somebody dying, I'm just using that. But that's how it feels sometimes, that it's an expedition and we fail. Other times we really soar. You know how that feels. It's a great feeling. It can't happen every time, and if it did you'd probably (stop doing it) . . . The democratic approach to sound expedition is always a mystery where you're going to wind up. But the best thing is to work with people who respond to suggestions, just like you would tell actors, you have to know something about them, and you have to share some common desire for mystery and danger, and then you can say things to them that they will take you someplace. We'll all go someplace together.

JJ: Do you sometimes sketch out your songs with other musicians?

TW: Yeah. We had a session a week ago where we took just viola, double bass, and cello, and we created a pointillist kind of ant colony. It just happened very spontaneous and thrilling. Conceptually, working with suggestions is usually the best way for me. We made up a train, a monster—sometimes it's good to combine high music with low music, orchestral guys with guys that play in the train station. Then, through the conflict of background you go to a new place. And there's a lot of orchestral guys who rarely get an opportunity to just, to abandon their history on the instrument, just play free, go to a totally free zone, and you fall into these Bermuda triangles of rhythm, melody. And lately those are the places that I like to go to. But most of the songs I write are very simple. They're three-legged chairs, and you make 'em very fast. You provide just enough for them to be able to stand up . . . You paint 'em, let 'em dry, and move on to the next one. I mean the songs on *Bone Machine* are all really simple songs, "Murder in the Red Barn," "That Feel," "In the Coliseum," "Earth Died Screaming," mostly written with just a drum in a room, and my voice, just hollering it out, until—like the other day when we were in there making photos.

JJ: There was a song right on that tape. When I was cleaning up the room I rewound it and listened to it.

TW: Enough ectoplasm to construct an organism.

JJ: You collect a lot of wild sounds, and sound effects, right?

TW: Yeah. There are so many sounds I want to record. Carnival stuff. All the sounds on the (midway), you know . . . I still haven't got a really good metal sound—when you see like swords in a real sword fight, or a real anvil with a real hammer. I'm still looking for the ultimate sound of a real stress metal clang. I wanna hear, really hear, really the clang of all clangs. Real clang.

JJ: I used to work in a sheet metal factory, and there were some great sounds, tossing the stuff around, moving it, the metal scraps and stuff. Explain the Chamberlin. The first keyboard sampling instrument. The Chamberlin 2000.

TW: It's a seventy-voice tape loop, it's a tape recorder, an elaborate tape recorder with a keyboard.

JJ: What year was it made?

TW: I think maybe '60, '61, or '62. Musicians were afraid it was gonna put 'em out of business, because it was too real. It was like, oh my god . . . And if somebody had one of these, why ever hire a band? It's too perfect . . .

JJ: I like the Chamberlin because it sounds like it breathes somehow. Maybe it's the action of the keys that you once showed me that cause a delay, so that it changed the way you played.

TW: It changes the physicality of your approach to the instrument, because the keyboard is not easy (to play). It goes down too far, your fingers get stuck down there and can't get back up.

JJ: They were made in L.A.?

TW: Yeah. By Richard Chamberlin. Not the actor (laughs). There's a bicycle chain in it, and if the tape gets on the other side of the chain it can damage the tape. There are no gamblers in "Chamberlin Pass." You get decorated for valor. It's like operating on a flamingo. You don't even know where the heart is, nothing. If you touch

177

there, you know, the world will end. If you touch this tape here, I dunno, you may lose your hand. It has that kind of danger about it.

JJ: How do you program tapes on it?

TW: They just move to a different place on the tape. They give you about a twelve-second sample that's the length of time it takes for the tape to move through the head, and give you about three feet of quarter-inch tape.

JJ: You've got two of them, right?

TW: I've got one Mellotron and one Chamberlin, and the Chamberlin I have is a prototype. So it's made with found electronic objects.

JJ: Did you use it on *Bone Machine*?

TW: Only on two songs, on "The Earth Died Screaming" and "The Ocean Doesn't Want Me."

JJ: What other stuff did you use it on previously?

TW: I used it a lot on *Frank's Wild Years*.

A Proscenium of Beat Boxes

JJ: Have you played live recently?

TW: We played on a bill with Fishbone in L.A., and I was worried, that oh god, I'm gonna have to play for their

178

audience and they're gonna have to play for mine, and I think they're two totally different audiences, because they have a mosh pit and the whole thing, they're hanging off the rafters. I was afraid to play on the bill with them, and I got there, I met 'em, and they were great. The show they did just changed me, it really changed me. It was so loud, it was so electric, it was just loaded. Really, it combed my hair and gave me a sunburn. They fly, yeah. That's when you realize that music, it does something physically to you. It can actually lift you and throw you around.

JJ: Some songs of yours are well-suited to a simple, say slightly country-tinged backdrop, songs that don't need to have radio signals from Mars coming into them. You seem to find what's appropriate for the worlds you create. A lot of your songs are like little films for me.

TW: Oh, how about this, Jim. You know sound systems in theatres? I hate 'em. Get beat boxes, just start collecting 'em, a wide variety of 'em, and use their speaker systems, and make a proscenium of beat boxes, you know, your own sound system, it's all wired into a main box, and you just, you create this whole world of sound, but it's all found stuff, because people throw those things out. And it's just dirt plastic, the lowest material, the cheapest material, cheaper and cheaper to them. They're getting worse and worse, but they're getting on another level, better and better. But they vanish after they've been around awhile.

JJ: They're disposable.

TW: People throw 'em away like cigarette lighters.

JJ: But the speakers usually still work.

TW: Yeah. So mount all these speakers in this strange thing and travel with that. Travel with your own sound system. You don't use any of these Marshall stacks or any of this bullshit.

JJ: Not only that, but you could build a proscenium of the boxes, like an arch.

TW: Yeah. And that's what becomes your stage set. And you walk out, and the curtain comes down off of that. It's just like making the theater go away. You make everything smaller and go into that world.

JJ: That's a great idea. The (*Frank's Wild Years*) tour (in smaller) theaters was really strong.

TW: We had the light boxes?

JJ: Yeah.

TW: Yeah. The nightclub.

JJ: You had the refrigerator, too.

TW: I liked that. And the bubble machine . . . I rebel against all these conventions. I'm going on the road this spring and I'm having to think about it. You know, I think I'm gonna ask Robert Wilson maybe also his opinions because he has a wonderful sense—he has no limitations when it comes to his understanding of the limits of theater.

JJ: Did you write "That Feel" with Keith Richards or did he just play on it?

TW: No, we wrote it together.

JJ: You've written stuff with him before.

TW: Yeah, he's all intuition. I mostly play drums, he plays guitar. He stands out in the middle of the room and does those Chuck Berry splits, y'know, and leans over and turns it up on ten and just grungg! I mostly just play drums. He plays drums, too, he plays everything. It was good. I'm just recently starting to collaborate in writing and find it to be really thrilling. And Keith is great 'cause he's like a vulture, he circles it and then he goes in and takes the eyes out. It was great. I guess we maybe wrote enough for a record, but everything didn't get finished, so—there was one called "Good Dogwood," about the carpenter that made the cross that Jesus hung on. (Sings:) "Made the other two out of pretty good pine, they all seemed to be doing just fine, but I hung my lord on good dogwood, huh! (forty ton) . . . And I made my house myself, and I know he likes the workmanship 'cause he's a carpenter himself, and I made the other two out of pretty good pine, they all seemed to be doing just fine, but I hung my lord on good dogwood." Dogwood is what the cross was made out of. And they say after Jesus went up to heaven that the blossoms on the dogwood developed a red cross in the bloom, and you can see it in the dogwood blossom. And that wasn't until after he had risen. So, uh, that was a good one.

JJ: There's a lot of strange religious imagery in your house. But on a kind of grotesque level.

TW: Yeah, "The Earth Died Screaming" was an attempt at some of that. "Rudy's on the midway, Jacob's in the hole," that's all from the Book of Rudy, which is one of the lost books of the Bible, the Book of Rudy.

JJ: I'm not familiar with the Book of Rudy.

TW: No, it's the uh, it's still being held in a library in Russia. Give 'em back, give 'em back! So it's great to go into a room with somebody you really love and have known for a long time.

JJ: What songs on *Bone Machine* did you collaborate with Kathleen on?

TW: About half of 'em. I don't know which ones, they all seem mixed up to me. "I Don't Wanna Grow Up," "The Earth Died Screaming." "All Stripped Down" is kind of a religious song, 'cause you can't get into heaven until you're all stripped down.

JJ: Tell me about the drummer you used on the *Night on Earth* score.

TW: Mule Patterson?

JJ: Yeah. How'd you meet Mule?

TW: Well, for a man who has not bathed ever in his life,

studio work with him has started to become a problem and people just won't play with him.

JJ: He's the first drummer I've seen who shows up (with no instruments) and says, "Whaddya got?"

TW: Whaddya got. Mule "Whaddya got" Patterson.

JJ: And the gun thing kind of made me nervous.

TW: Yeah, y'know, I've talked to him, and we can't seem to reach him on that. That it's just no, y'know, you're gonna lose work.

JJ: Yeah, the loaded gun . . .

TW: The waving of guns around in the . . . studio, and you have people there . . .

JJ: The gun in the gym bag just kind of made me nervous.

TW: Yeah. The gun in the gym bag.

JJ: There's a couple of beers in there and a loaded .38.

TW: Yeah.

JJ: And some of those dry roasted peanuts, but in the small bags that you can't really buy, the ones that you get on the train or a plane or a bus.

TW: And that was his dinner.

JJ: That's what he had in the bag. No drumsticks.

TW: And the gun was also held together with string. There was a place where the whole handle mechanism was coming off the handle, and the hammer was loose.

JJ: I know that the grip was just electrical tape.

TW: Just tape, there was no more wood.

JJ: And also that the studio was way out in the middle of nowhere, but he didn't drive.

TW: He has no car.

JJ: Then he left.

TW: Some men fear him. Others admire him. Because he steals his promise, he'll steal his promise from being there. He'll show up, and if he doesn't like what's going on in the session, he'll walk out. He won't work it.

JJ: Right in the middle of a take?

TW: Oh yeah. Oh yeah. You hope, you wanna keep him happy. That becomes the whole point of the session. Larry Taylor (from Canned Heat) is the same way. He'll just walk away, "Hey man, I just don't get it. I'm sorry," and he'll just walk away. That's it, he'll just give up . . . He had a gig the night after we finished the album, and his bass broke. It was just, it was like John Henry, the whole neck snapped and the strings came out, it was in the middle of the first song, he ended up finishing it on electric, but—

JJ: What about working with guitarist Marc Ribot?

TW: Well, he's big on the devices. Appliances, guitar appliances. And a lot of 'em look like they're made out of tinfoil and, y'know, it's like he would take a blender, part of a blender, take the whole thing out and put it on the side of his guitar and it looks like a medical show . . . that look. And the sound seemed to come from, the way it looked and the way it sounded seemed to be the same. (He works with) alternative sound sources, he turns his guitar into an adventure.

JJ: Yeah, nobody plays like Ribot. Maybe that's a good thing.

TW: Yeah, he also gets himself whipped up into a voodoo frenzy. He gets the look in his eye that makes you want to back off. Y'know? It's like, "goddamn!" We were in some after-hours place in, I dunno, Holland, in the corner, there was no stage, it was a club with normally no live music. We just got into the corner and plugged in and started to play. And everybody just pushed the tables and chairs back and it was real wild. And Ribot banged into a speaker box, and there was a bottle of Vat 69 on it, and it tipped over, and it was full, and it just kept spilling out onto the floor, and he was getting under the stream of liquor, which was splashing onto the floor, and liquor was going everywhere, and you looked at his face and it was like an animal, he'd been, like worked up—

JJ: Whipped up.

TW: Whipped up, whipped up into a place where he was gonna do something. He was gonna bite somebody, he was gonna do surgery without knives. Like those guys who can reach into your chest and pull your heart out, he went (big grunt) and then put it back in. There's guys that say they can do that.

JJ: They do that in martial arts films, kung fu movies . . .

TW: Yeah (laughs) . . .

JJ: . . . pull your heart right out.

TW: And you just see it.

JJ: But there's a certain protocol thing that goes with it. (String of Chinese-style grunts.)

TW: It was pretty scary . . .

JJ: What about the sax player Ralph Carney? Like me, he's from Akron, so we're like brothers.

TW: Yeah, well, you'll always be bound together by Akron. Ralph's parents still live there, so when we played there . . .

JJ: You played in (Akron)?

TW: Yeah. It was a good night, it was a real good night. Next day Ralph wouldn't come to sound check and when he finally did show up, it was about fifteen minutes before the show. And I said, "What happened, where you been?" And he said, "Well, I went home. I haven't been home in a couple of years." He said, "My dad had me rakin' leaves . . ." (laughs) He had to rake leaves all fucking day.

JJ: How would you describe your artistic relationship with Francis Thumm?

TW: Oh. Frannie's um—

JJ: He was around for the recording of *Bone Machine*, right?

TW: Yeah. Security guard. He did a lot of security on the album because there were a lot of kids in the area that were coming out, curious, and we normally, we bring somebody from out of town. Frannie got security guard. No, seriously. He wasn't sure how he was going to be involved, so he stayed on the edge and waited to find out how he might be used. He has a very regimented background. He comes from discipline. I come from the opposite, which gets me in trouble sometimes. Frannie comes from the discipline which gets him in trouble sometimes, so it's like if two people had come from the same background, one of them is unnecessary. Like I bring something to the music that I couldn't bring if I had the same kind of background that he has. I curse it sometimes, y'know . . .

JJ: We talked about Ribot, we talked about Ralph Carney, we talked about Francis Thumm. How about Greg Cohen? You've worked a lot with Greg Cohen, too, the bass player.

TW: Greg's also an arranger and a stamp collector. He has a strong, very peculiar personal mythology he brings to all of his musical exploits. It's really great to watch Greg play both bass and drums at the same time. That's really something. His left hand on the fingering board, his right hand has two drumsticks in it, and he has the little kit he puts together, and he hits the one on the drums and the two on the bass, goes back and forth, and creates an independent sound board with four legs.

I remember once I asked you about this: if there's Cuban-Chinese (food), then there must be Cuban-Chinese music. But Cuban must be like the dominant trait. If two people marry and have a child, the dominant genes still prevail in appearance and personality sometimes. It must be the same with music, right? So if Cuban-Chinese music is more Cuban music, the Chinese did not win in the war of music between those two cultures. Somewhere there are Chinese guys playing in Cuban bands.

JJ: Then what's the musical equivalent of nouvelle cuisine? New age music?

TW: New age-elle, I guess. It's a little tasty, and looks nice on a plate.

JJ: It's decorative.

TW: Decorative, it's like food elevated to a place where it never should have been allowed.

JJ: It's like wallpaper.

TW: It's part of an interior design. (pause) Hey, that pygmy stuff that you sent me really flipped me! It really got me listening, because we struggled for a couple days with getting the sound of a stick orchestra inside the studio for "Earth Died Screaming." We tried every configuration and position of the microphone, and finally I said, "Well, why don't we go outside, isn't that where all these recordings are made?" And five minutes later we had a mike up, we were hitting it, it was there. It was that simple.

JJ: Like out in the parking lot of the studio?

TW: Right outside the door, yeah.

JJ: What kind of sticks were you using?

TW: Just two-by-fours, anything we could find, logs from the firewood. About nine people. Just different people walking by. We'd say, "Come on, play some sticks!" But that pygmy music really sent me. There were a couple of rhythms on there that I listened to . . . that just really, boy, I went into a Bermuda Triangle of rhythm, where you vanish in some—You feel the power of it, and you realize why there are no drums in church, you know? There are no drums in church music . . . Gospel people . . . They don't like drums . . . There's certainly no tribal drums. If there are, there's a country-western high hat, cornball—kit drums, like a redheaded stepchild. I went through Mississippi when I was twenty-three playing a tour, and they (the radio station) wouldn't play anything with saxophone on Sunday. You know, those Bible Belt things. Forget about it. You had to deal with it, you know.

JJ: In a lot of counties in southern states there's no dancing on Sunday. Blue laws. It's still illegal.

The record company is promoting *Bone Machine* as your "first studio album in five years," so I just wanted to list all the things you've done since *Frank's Wild Years.* You did the soundtrack to *Night on Earth,* which is an entire album's worth of material, even more, really, 'cause we didn't even use it all. You did a cover of a Fats Waller song for another film.

TW: *American Heart.*

JJ: Directed by the guy who did *Streetwise,* Martin Bell. What's the Fats Waller song?

TW: "Crazy About My Baby." Then we wrote a closing song for the film, also, called "I'll Never Let Go of Your Hand." And I did a play at the LATC, downtown L.A., called *Demon Wine,* that was written by Thomas Babe, it's kind of a gangster play.

JJ: Was Carol Kane in that one?

TW: Yeah, she was. Bill Pullman. And also Philip Baker Hall was in it, who played my father.

JJ: And you acted in *At Play in the Fields of the Lord* with Aidan Quinn and Tom Berenger, directed by Hector Babenco, who you'd previously worked with in *Ironweed.* You just acted in the new Robert Altman film which is still in production.

TW: Yeah, I play a limo driver who's married to Lily Tomlin, and I live in a trailer. It was a great experience.

JJ: You acted in *Queen's Logic*.

TW: Yeah, with Joe Mantegna. Then *Dracula*.

JJ: You play Renfield in Francis Ford Coppola's *Dracula* and you did the voice of the DJ for *Mystery Train*.

TW: Oh right, let's not forget that.

JJ: You did *The Fisher King,* the Terry Gilliam film. You also composed the music for, and collaborated with Robert Wilson and William Burroughs on *The Black Rider,* for which you just recently recorded the score.

TW: The songs from *Black Rider* are now finished. They will be out in the spring.

JJ: You're also preparing now to do another collaboration with Robert Wilson for his *Alice in Wonderland,* composing the music for that, which you are already starting on. And there's even more.

TW: Oh yeah, a song for John Hammond called, uh, what the hell's the name of that? Oh. "No One Can Forgive Me but My Baby." Then I did two songs on Teddy Edwards's album. One was called "Little Man," and the other one was called "I'm Not Your Fool Anymore."

JJ: Then you wrote that stuff with Keith Richards, too. You recorded a song with Primus.

TW: Oh yeah. "Tommy the Cat" with Les Claypool. He's really jungalian, primitivo.

JJ: I saw on MTV or somewhere a little documentary and interview with him. It was great. I'm sure there's more stuff we're forgetting, even more things. But it just shocked me to see "first studio album in five years," and me knowing you I knew I didn't even know all the things you did, but even knowing half of them, it made me laugh, like people thinking, "What's he been up to?" Your productivity in the last few years, plus with your family, is quite amazing to me.

TW: Make hay while the sun shines. Well, I had a good rain, and so it always—you know, when it's really coming down there's not enough to catch it in, and then you go through dry spells, too, y'know.

JJ: Yeah, while we were driving to San Francisco yesterday you were making up songs and I wish I'd had a recorder. There were songs you were making up—

TW: In the car?

JJ: Yeah, that song about tobacco, about smoking. That was a great song you were writing. They just seem to pour out of you these days.

TW: Well, it's been a good period. So I'm anxious to start work on another original album of new songs. I've got backed up with material for new songs.

JJ: I think you should put some EPs out, some short things with collections of those. You did a version of "Sea of Love" for the film. It's one of my favorite songs of all time, that version. I carry it with me, I have it here on that cassette.

TW: Oh, thanks.

JJ: And I'm sure we're forgetting other things. Ken Nordine. Did you do some stuff with Ken Nordine?

TW: Yeah. He's most known for his records, *Word Jazz, Sound of Word Jazz, Colors.* He worked with a small jazz group and made records in the fifties, and they're really stories, those strange little stories, little *Twilight Zone*s from the dark recesses of his brain. Little worlds you go into. He has little conversations with himself, as if he's got the little guy with the pitchfork on his shoulder that's telling him, "Yeah, kiss her." "Well, I don't know." "Go ahead, kiss her."

JJ: . . . and the voices overlap.

TW: Yeah, Ken Nordine.

JJ: Yeah, Ken Nordine. Where does he live, in L.A.?

TW: Chicago.

JJ: He's a strange little addition to American culture.

TW: Yeah, he's really remarkable.

JJ: An overlooked one for most people.

TW: Yeah, he is. So they put out that album, and we did a little kind of word duet. I don't know how else to describe it. I did a little story and he talked in the pauses, and I talked in his pauses, and it was kind of a little woven duet.

JJ: And how can one find that stuff, is it out?

TW: Yeah, let's see, I've forgotten the title of it.

JJ: It is released, though?

TW: Oh yeah.

JJ: Even his name, Ken Nordine, makes you hear his voice right away.

TW: "Hi, it's Ken." On the phone, "Nordine here, how are you? In town for a couple of days, hope we can get together. Later."

JJ: I'm sure we're forgetting other things you've done. In any case the point is that you've been so amazingly prolific recently, and people aren't aware of it because you don't necessarily choose things according to how high profile, or mainstream they might be. You are, for a lot of people, very important just because your sensibility doesn't fall in the mainstream. It's who you are, the kind of things that strike you about life on this planet, the kind of characters that you write songs about, and the way you live yourself. You inspired me long before I met you. Then there are things you've done that have become mainstream in a way because of the soul of them, like the song "Jersey Girl," the Springsteen cover of that, or "Downtown Train" covered by Rod Stewart.

TW: I'm in shoe repair, really, Jim. I'm like a cobbler, they come in, they've worn 'em out. I work on the instep.

JJ: What things draw you to roles you play as an actor?

TW: Well, I'm not really in a position where I make all of those choices myself. I mean actors get to a point where their involvement immediately insures the film will be both financed and distributed and seen. So, I'm not at that position in acting, so it's usually smaller parts that I'm thought of for. Sometimes it's smaller parts that I'm interested in. Y'know, they say there's no small parts just small actors. But believe me, there are small parts. (laughs)

JJ: I think that sometimes smaller parts are much more difficult because you don't have time to develop the character. To create a character in three minutes on screen is not an easy thing.

TW: It's true. You don't have fifteen scenes with a character where it's like, if I drop it here I can pick it up later, or if I didn't get a chance to develop that aspect, I have a much fuller realized scene later on that I get to do those things in. Sometimes it's like sending your design to a big toy company, and it may end up you're just the ears and the feet, and you don't get the full anatomically correct character. But you still have to pursue it, you have to do a lot in a few scenes. I like limitations. If I don't have limitations I'll impose them on myself naturally, just to narrow it down. Immediately time is always an element. If we were going to write a song right here now, and we had only a half an hour to do it it would take on certain characteristics. I find myself usually having more in common with the directors than maybe sometimes the actors. A lot of directors look at actors as insecurities with arms and legs, they're just children, and they need to be constantly reassured and directed and given rewards and discipline.

JJ: That's part of them, though. I think that actors that don't have a childish quality are dangerous.

TW: Yeah. That's where a lot of those things live. You can't approach them intellectually with the tools that you use for other things in your life. You can't see the tools that you need to use in order to massage the ideas out of it. It's sometimes in the most obvious place, and you're looking right at it and you can't see it. You have to use truthful behavior, and you have to use what's in your life. You have to use what you're going through right now, and out of that comes, you say, "Oh my god I can't do this, I'm having all these problems in my life and I can't handle this right now," and you say, "Well, use all those things, 'cause those are the things you'll use to make this. Don't think they're encroaching on your work. They are your work, or whatever." You find ways of integrating your other struggles into it. Then it gets like a tributary, and you realize it gets like an irrigation system, and if you water here it'll also water this, also water that, so it's always good, it always feeds you, and it always shows up in other areas. If you make a breakthrough as an actor it'll help you make a breakthrough in music. Because I think all things really do aspire to this condition of music. Everyone keeps saying, well, it has a musical quality to it, or want to find the music in this. You do it yourself in film, you're very sensitive to music, to finding the music in the pictures. So I'm always ready to incorporate all those things into making it have balance and life.

LANGUAGE

JJ: Have you ever written stuff that would end up being like a text, that would exist as a book or as writing rather than as music or as acting?

TW: No, I haven't. I've got some lyric books of my lyrics out in Spain and Italy and a few other places. I don't know; you see I'm always going for the sound of things, even like recently when I was trying to write down different little memories for an article. I was going to do an interview, and I told the interviewer to go home. I couldn't talk to him, I couldn't even look at him. I said just leave the questions and I'll deal with them, and I'm doing that at night. But I have a hard time just writing things out, I have to hear them first. Sometimes I put it on a tape recorder, but then I transcribe it and it's lost its music.

JJ: When I was a kid and first read Jack Kerouac, when I was fifteen or something, I read *On the Road,* and it didn't speak to me. I didn't get it. I mean I liked the adventure of it, but the language of it seemed slapped together and shoddy to me. And four or five years later I hear Kerouac on tape reading stuff, and suddenly I got it, immediately I got it, and I went back and I read that and *The Subterraneans,* and I understood. But without that first understanding his voice and his way of hearing language, it was hard for me to get it off the page. Now it's permanently in me, I can read it, I can pick up Kerouac and I hear his voice. Breathing and phrasing and bebop and sound influenced his way of thinking about language.

TW: Yeah, I agree. It's like for Robert Wilson, words are like tacks or like broken glass. He doesn't know what to do with them. He lays down on them and it's always uncomfortable. He wants to melt them down or just line 'em up and use 'em as design, or whatever, because he doesn't like to deal with them. I love reference books that help me with words, dictionaries of slang or the *Dictionary of Superstition,* or the *Phrase and Fable, Book of Knowledge,* things that help me find words that have a musicality to them. Sometimes that's all you're looking for. Or to make sounds that aren't words, necessarily. They're just sounds and they have a nice shape to them. They're big at the end and then they come down to a little point that curls. Words, y'know, for me are really, I love 'em, I'm always lookin' for 'em, I'm always writin' 'em down, always writin' down stuff. Language is always evolving. I love slang, prison slang and street idioms and—

JJ: You like rap music because of that, right?

TW: Oh yeah, I love it. It's so, it's a real underground railroad.

JJ: It keeps American English living. Rap, hip-hop culture, and street slang is to me what keeps it alive, and keeps it from being a dead thing.

TW: Yeah, it happens real fast, too. It's . . . and it moves on, in like three weeks maybe something that was very current is now very passé. As soon as they adopt it, they have to move on.

JJ: It's an outsider's code, in a way.

TW: Well, it's all that dope talk that came because you had to have conversations, that whole underground railroad thing where you had to be able to talk to somebody in the presence of law enforcement, and have law enforcement totally unable to understand anything of what you were saying. I don't know if people really acknowledge as much as they should how the whole Afro-American experience, how it has given music and lyricism, poetry to daily life. It's so ingrained that most people don't even give it credit. A lot of those Alan Lomax records that he did, song collecting in the thirties, captures that. He also captured just sounds, sounds that we will no longer be hearing, eventually, like he captured just the sound of a cash register that you really don't hear anymore.

JJ: Yeah, manual typewriters will be obsolete. Certain things that we're so accustomed to now, most phones don't ring anymore, they have that electronic beep beep beep. That ringing sound will be archaic. It almost is already.

TW: Yeah, that's true. But, yeah, I love language. Like you yourself do, and put it into the dialogue of the characters in your films as well.

JJ: What writers do you like?

TW: 'Course Bukowski, the new collection is great, the *Last Night of the Earth Poems*. The one called "You Know and I Know and Thee Know" . . . there's some beautiful things in there, very mature, and (with an) end-of-the-world sadness. And Cormac McCarthy I like. He has a new novel called *All the Pretty Horses*.

JJ: You worked with William Burroughs on *The Black Rider*. What do you think about Burroughs? Burroughs has always incorporated the language of criminals and junkies and street stuff into that like process that he runs the words through.

TW: Yeah, I love Burroughs. He's like a metal desk. He's like a still, and everything that comes out of him is already whiskey.

A FEW OF TOM'S MEMORIES

TW: I had a midget prostitute climb up on a bar stool and sit in my lap when I was about eighteen in Tijuana. I drank with her for about an hour. It was something. Changed me. Tender, very tender. It was like I didn't go off to the room with her. She just sat in my lap.

JJ: Have you ever been arrested in Mexico?

TW: Oh many times, yeah. Bought my way out. As a kid, as a teenager down there raising hell. It was such a place of total abandon and lawlessness, it was like a Western town, going back two hundred years—mud streets, the church bells, the goats, the mud, the lurid, torrid signs. It was a wonderland, really, for me, and it changed me. I used to go down there for haircuts with my dad, and he would go into the bars and drink, and I would sit on those stools with him and have a special Coke.

JJ: What do you mean special Coke?

TW: You know, just a Coca-Cola with some lemon juice in it, a cherry. But I had a lot of fun, saw a lot of things down there that stayed with me. Mexican carnivals are the best. You find the rides are driven by car engines that are mounted on just these wood blocks. And an old guy, mentally ill, covered with tattoos, drinking, running a stick shift on an old truck motor. Laughing, speeding up and slowing down.

JJ: Where else have you been arrested? Of course in L.A.

TW: L.A. many times, yeah. Once I was jumped by four plain-clothes policemen. They all looked like they were from Iowa, wearing corduroy Levi jackets, tennis shoes, off duty. Grabbed me and a buddy of mine, threw us into the back of a Toyota pickup with guns to our temples. Guy says, "Do you know what one of these things does to your head when you fire it at close range?" He said, "Your head will explode like a cantaloupe." I thought about that. I was very still. They marched us down to the car, threw us in the back. I thought they were going to take us out to a vacant lot and shoot us in the head. They took us to the station where we spent the night. We'd been kind of mouthing off. But they were real belligerent, they'd taken over the tables of some people that we knew at the restaurant. They'd bullied their way into a table. We let 'em know that we didn't think it was the kind of thing that we do around here, and they didn't like that. Now I'm trying to learn how to be invisible. I haven't been pulled over since I moved out of L.A. I think it is possible to be invisible, certainly more in an area like this than it is in Los Angeles or New York City.

JJ: Any other strange memories?

TW: Well, I bought some coke one night about four in the
      morning from a guy in an apartment building in Miami,
      real down apartment, and he had a gunshot wound in
      his chest and he was bleeding through the bandage, you
      know, and we were counting out the money on a glass
      table and he was, he kept (grabbing for his shoulder),
      and that was a really scary night. And the lighting in
      there was like whoa! God! All low light, desk light,
      nothing above the knees. The place was like a black
      swimming pool at night. This was some hellish scene.
      Somebody had a phone number, and it was after a con-
      cert, and we had to drive over there. Real gangster stuff.
      Y'know, with a gun on the table and everything. Bad
      scene: black guy with suspenders and a terrible wound.
      "No cops, no cops, no doctors. I'll ride it out." But you're
      burnin' up, you're runnin' a 106, it's off the map, I can't
      even record your fuckin' fever it's so high! "No cops."
      That could be the third scene in *They All Died Singing*.

TOM AND JIM TAKE A DRIVE

JJ: (Car interior) What's that instrument in your studio that
      looks like a vacuum cleaner with horns attached to it?

TW: Airhorn from a train.

JJ: It's one chord?

TW: One chord, yeah. I pick up junk when I find it. I wanna
      get a thing that I can do a stick sound with like eight

sticks mounted on a frame, almost like a pitchfork, only the forks would be wood, and on a spring base, so that when you hit it against the ground you get a flam, a stick flam of eight characters. You get the clack, clack, clack, but you'd be able to do it with just one stick, hitting the stick and hitting the sound of eight sticks. I dunno . . .

JJ: And that metal frame with the metal pieces on it that you were playing yesterday?

TW: The conundrum.

JJ: The conundrum? It's something you built?

TW: No, Serge Etienne, a guy that lives right here. (points out the car window)

JJ: In fact is that Serge right there?

TW: That's Serge.

JJ: The guy in the T-shirt?

TW: Yeah . . .

JJ: He's got some motorbikes back there, too.

TW: Yeah, he drives motorcycles. He created a car out of a motorbike. He built a car frame around a . . . motorcycle. Out of fiberglass and styrofoam, and it's very light. It looks like those cars that we saw at the carnival the other night going around on the little track.

JJ: And the conundrum . . . did you find those metal pieces and have him make it for you, or did he build the instrument himself?

TW: He built it and gave it to me as a gift. I said I need some sounds I can use in the studio that are just metal sounds, a variety and range of vibrations I can use. It really does sound like a jail door closing if you hit it right.

JJ: Yeah. It sounded amazing. So many different sounds out of it. You have several accordions.

TW: One that Roberto Benigni gave me. I don't really play accordion. I can play one-handed passages, with the left hand, but the button side is, uh, I'm lost.

JJ: It always seemed real complicated to me.

TW: Oh shit the car is smoking! It's on fire, Jim.

JJ: From the exhaust or from the engine?

TW: I don't know, we better pull over.

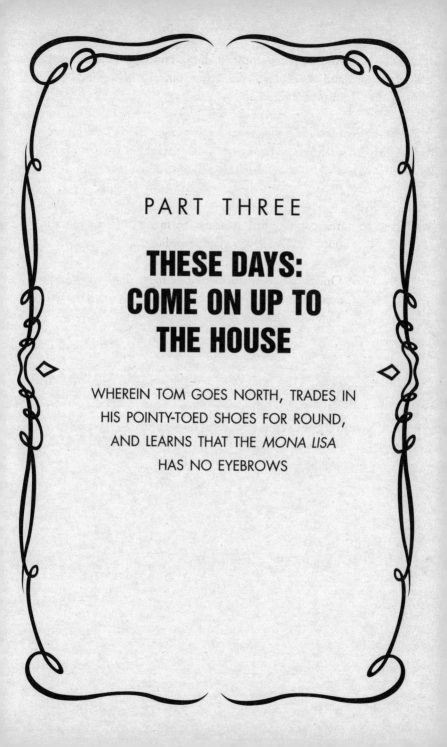

PART THREE

THESE DAYS:
COME ON UP TO
THE HOUSE

WHEREIN TOM GOES NORTH, TRADES IN
HIS POINTY-TOED SHOES FOR ROUND,
AND LEARNS THAT THE *MONA LISA*
HAS NO EYEBROWS

Tom Waits Joins Indie Epitaph for *Mule* Set

Billboard, March 20, 1999

Bradley Bambarger

For his first album of new songs in six years, Tom Waits wanted to avoid what he calls "the plantation system of the music business." To that end, he is putting out the beautifully ornery *Mule Variations* April 27 in league with the Los Angeles-based punk-rock specialist Epitaph.

It is fitting that Waits should partner with an indie-rock label after twenty-five years of near-legendary musicmaking. Full of piss and vinegar as ever, Waits is independent in ways befitting his iconic status. And the man still has more untamed rock 'n' roll spirit than a dozen MTV bands.

Regarding the personal connotations of his new album title, Waits explains, "My wife likes to say, 'I didn't marry a man, I married a mule.' And I've been going through a lot of changes, thus *Mule Variations.*"

Musically, *Mule Variations* melds backwoods blues, skewed gospel, and unruly art stomp into a sublime piece of junkyard sound sculpture. Fans of Waits's years as a bar stool bard on Asylum in the seventies should warm to the boxcar romance of the single "Hold On," while those enamored of the lunatic cabaret of his eighties Island tenure will have a field day with the album.

The woozy valentine "Black Market Baby" and spooky *sprech-stimme* of "What's He Building?" are prime latter-day Waits, as are a host of other numbers that sound like work songs bellowed down a Tin Pan Alley. Adding to his own raw-boned guitar and carnival keyboards, Waits tapped such veteran collaborators as saxist Ralph Carney, bassist Greg Cohen, and guitarist Marc Ribot, as well as aces in the hole like harpist Charlie Musselwhite.

With his live shows few and far between over the past decade, Waits's live debut of *Mule Variations* is something of an event. The first show will be March 20 in Austin, Texas, with a band featuring album contributors Larry Taylor on bass, Smokey Hormel on guitar, and Stephen Hodges on percussion. Five to ten dates in North America will follow (booked by Stuart Ross in Los Angeles), including late May shows in L.A. and San Francisco.

Also, in late May or early June, Waits will appear on VH1's *Storytellers,* a venue that should help introduce Waits to those fans who only know his classic "Downtown Train" as a big hit for Rod Stewart.

Going Indie

After his decade-long stay with the singer/songwriter-oriented Asylum, Waits transformed himself from Beat troubadour to art-house provocateur with 1983's *Swordfishtrombones.* That disc began a fertile six-album association with Chris Blackwell's Island Records, highlighted by 1992's Grammy-winning *Bone Machine* (and encapsulated on last year's anthology *Beautiful Maladies*). Now, as then, Waits has no truck with preconceptions.

"When people have a notion of who you are," Waits says, "they want you to stay that way. Asylum wouldn't release *Swordfishtrombones;* only a guy like Blackwell would put it out. People always like to have continuity in their products and services. But music isn't breakfast cereal, or at least it shouldn't be."

Waits was intrigued by Epitaph after reading about founder Brett Gurewitz's do-it-yourself ethos, and he settled on the label after getting to know the staff. "Epitaph is rare for being owned and operated by musicians," he says. "They have good taste and a load of enthusiasm, plus they're nice people. And they gave me a brand-new Cadillac, of course."

Epitaph president Andy Kaulkin says the label was "blown away that Tom would even consider us. We are huge fans. Actually, I consider myself the typical target customer for the new Tom Waits album, so at least I know how to reach people like me."

At its core, Epitaph is "a punk-rock label, and we always will be," Kaulkin adds. "But the company is small enough to be flexible, and we're great at niche marketing. In fact, our best-selling disc right now is a blues record [R. L. Burnside's *Come On In*]."

From mid-March to early April, Epitaph will host thirty *Mule Variations* listening parties in North America for fans and members of the trade. The RED-distributed label plans promotions with such chains as Tower Records and Border's Books & Music, as well as an extensive program with the seventy-six outlets of the Coalition of Independent Music Stores (CIMS).

Corby Harwell, indie buyer at CIMS retailer Waterloo Records in Austin, says, "We work well with Epitaph—they're really good at what they do. And the new Waits record is the logical next step for the punk rockers who have gotten into the Fat Possum stuff that Epitaph distributes, like R. L.

Burnside. But Tom does great here anyway. His sound is timeless—and a lot more universal than people think."

In a creative way of dealing with Waits's limited patience with promotional duties, Epitaph has produced an interview CD titled *Mule Conversations.* The disc will feature Waits in conversation with Jody Denberg of KGSR Austin, along with six album tracks and a radio edit of "Hold On." The interview disc ships to triple-A, alternative, and college radio in late March, shortly after a promo CD single with the edit of "Hold On" ships separately.

Quick on the draw as ever, Nic Harcourt, PD of KCRW Los Angeles and host of the station's *Morning Becomes Eclectic* program, leaked the lo-fi rocker "Big in Japan" (featuring members of Primus) in late February. "We got calls straightaway from excited fans—Tom has a real history with the station," he says. "I know it'll be a big record for us, and we should have him in to sing a few songs on the air."

"Big in Japan" was heard nationwide via KCRW's Internet site (www.kcrw.org), and the World Wide Web figures to be a key realm for promoting *Mule Variations* as a whole, according to Epitaph product manager Dave Hansen. The label is embarking on promotions with Internet retailers Amazon and CDnow. Several Internet sites will feature a streamable album track, with "Big in Japan" slated for brick-and-mortar sites like towerrecords.com.

Epitaph is also going to launch a comprehensive Tom Waits Internet site (www.officialtomwaits.com), covering his entire music and film career with rare photos, excerpts from *Mule Conversations,* and RealAudio for one of the new tracks. In addition, the label plans to Webcast one of his shows with Sonic.Net.

Waits manages himself with his wife and frequent co-writer/producer, Kathleen Brennan; his songs are published by Jalma Music (ASCAP). The deal with Epitaph is for one record, Waits says, "but keep your eyes open for coming attractions." He has given *Mule Variations* to Epitaph under a long-term lease.

"It's appropriate, since it isn't like we're investing in creating a career for him," Kaulkin says. "Someone of Tom's experience and stature really deserves to own his own work. After all, he has been doing this a lot longer than we have."

THE VARIATIONS OF TOM WAITS; OR: WHAT DO LIBERACE, RODNEY DANGERFIELD, AND A ONE-ARMED PIANIST HAVE IN COMMON?

Dallas Observer, May 6, 1999

Robert Wilonsky

E verything you are about to read is a lie. Well, perhaps that is an exaggeration, much like most of what comes out of Tom Waits's mouth. It's not as though he doesn't know the truth, it's just less fun to tell it. Every interview, and he has handed out only a handful in conjunction with the release of the brand-new *Mule Variations,* reads as though it were granted by a stand-up trying out new material, throwing out anything with the hope that at least some of it will shtick. Ask him what took so long between the release of 1992's *Bone Machine* and *Mule Variations,* and he's likely to respond that he's been in traffic school or breaking in other people's shoes. Today's response?

"Sheet rock, plumbing, and electrical."

His publicist had warned as much, hinting that there's no need to try to, ya know, interview the man. He will do and say as he pleases—ramble at length about something he's making up on the spot, filter "the truth" through a dozen fictions, even reuse his old tried-and-true jokes when all else fails. The result is an experience that seems at first excruciating and useless; it's only when listening to the interview again on tape that it all begins to make sense. It's not what he says; it's what he almost says, what he almost discloses. It's about the pauses, the shifts in tone, the revelations that blur into one-liners—the straight man who steps aside and lets the stand-up do his talking for him.

Only a few minutes into the conversation, Waits is discussing why, during a performance in March in Austin, he decided to perform so many of his older, better-known songs along with those from *Mule Variations*. Myriad times before, he insisted he hated hauling out those old numbers ("The Heart of Saturday Night," "Jockey Full of Bourbon," and "Downtown Train" among them), dusting them off for the ravenous crowd. He didn't want to become a lounge act doing his best-of monkey dance for tips.

That night was different: He sat at the piano or stood behind the microphone stand (which he gripped so tightly, it looked as though he would bend the metal) and performed each song, old and new, as though he had just discovered it at his door, a bow wrapped around its tiny, pink frame. He didn't merely play the old songs; he laid into them, turned dormant memories into flesh and blood. Waits explains that there was something about staying at the historic Driskill Hotel that made him want to go bravely into the past. That, and the fact that having gone so long without playing them made the songs feel brand-new in a way . . . maybe, he shrugs, because they are.

"Sometimes it seems appropriate," he says in a voice that sounds remarkably warm and inviting, like an old friend's handshake. "I mean, that's what songs do ideally—underscore something that's happening or allow you to revisit something."

He explains that songs begin to mean something different ten or fifteen years after they're first written. "Well, sometimes they start out like prayers, you know? Your own . . .

wish," he begins. "And sometimes, in a very ironic way, I guess they end up fulfilled and sometimes unfulfilled. Sometimes all you've got is the song."

He is asked if that's enough—to have only the song, nothing more or less.

"Gee, we're getting metaphysical here." He laughs, a quick and hoarse henh-henh-henh-henh. "Is that enough? That's one of those questions that doesn't have an answer. Ask Susan Hayward. She'll know the answer to that. Ask Sylvia Miles. Ask Warren Oates. He's out in the corral." He laughs again.

There are fifty-seven minutes more like that—deep talk cushioned by throwaway one-liners and the accompanying gruff laughter of a man who cracks himself up.

Perhaps that's just as well: All you need to know about Tom Waits is right there on each of his albums, beginning with 1973's *Closing Time,* on which a twenty-four-year-old kid from Southern California with a notebook full of Cole Porter melodies and Jack Kerouac lyrics introduced himself with songs about old cars and lost, long-distance loves. All you need to know is there on *The Heart of Saturday Night, Small Change, Foreign Affairs, Blue Valentine,* and *Heartattack and Vine*—the blue-note, jazzbo, boozy, bloozy records he made for Elektra/Asylum in the 1970s. All you need to know is there on *Swordfishtrombones, Rain Dogs, Frank's Wild Years, Bone Machine*—the salvage-yard symphonies made by the guy who wanted to see how out out-there really was and found what he was looking for when he started pounding on brake drums with Howlin' Wolf's bones.

And all you need to know is right there on *Mule Variations,* the record made by a forty-nine-year-old husband and father of three who ends the disc with the most beautiful, hopeful song of his entire career: "Take It with Me." For the first time in forever, Waits unabashedly sings. There is no growl to hide behind, no harsh barrier between maker and taker, only these simple, heartfelt words: "Children are playing at the end of the day / Strangers are singing on our lawn . . . All that you've loved is all you own / I'm gonna take it with me when I go."

Waits has made a career out of distancing himself from his songs, singing through a voice found at the bottom of an ashtray, but he's never been able to completely disappear. All those years spent living in his car, playing dead-end Hollywood dives even Raymond Chandler's characters would avoid, pretending he's Neal Cassady on the lam with Kerouac, turning raindrops into diamonds, giving voice to the voiceless—somewhere buried not too deep beneath all of that is the romantic, hopeful, sanguine Tom Waits of Pomona, California, the son of schoolteachers.

And he's a funny guy, that Tom. So what if he doesn't always go for deep and meaningful? Either you like the sound of a barking dog, or you buy yourself a cat.

They approached him as though he were a freak-show attraction, The Monkey Boy escaped from the circus. They were curious, amused, delighted at the sight of their hero sitting near the bar in the cozy confines of the venerable Driskill Hotel in downtown Austin. Waits could often be found downstairs in the Driskill, waiting alone or with wife, Kathleen Brennan. Hidden beneath his dusty brown hat, swathed in black denim, he looked as if he didn't want to be bothered.

But that never stopped them, the fans and the fetishists, from getting the bartender to send over their gallons of brown liquor—compliments of that young man over there, sir. They ordered up the most expensive bourbon in the joint, convinced that their hero—a man who once swam laps in the stuff—would be pleased.

Waits gracefully declined their offers, shooed away their gestures with a gruff but friendly no thanks. You see, he doesn't drink anymore, hasn't for years. He's a responsible father, a husband, a country gentleman who moved to the countryside north of San Francisco so he could piss in the great outdoors. That's about as licentious as he gets these days; Tom's wild years are well behind him, buried beneath the parking lot that used to be the Tropicana Hotel in Hollywood.

Still, to the fawning faithful, Waits exists now as he did two decades ago—as the Bowery Bum living in the dumpsters of Tin Pan Alley, as George Gershwin dolled up in Salvation Army drag. They see him now as they saw him then—in a cigarette-smoke haze with a Wild Turkey chaser, a dog-eared copy of *On the Road* in one hand and a still-smoldering, down-to-the-butt Viceroy in the other. They recall him as he appeared on the cover of 1976's *Small Change,* looking so beat that he can't even stand to gaze upon the stripper standing a few feet away. They see him as he appeared on the back of 1978's *Blue Valentine:* hovering over a woman (ex-girlfriend Rickie Lee Jones, actually) as she leans against the hood of his beat-ta-shit Fine American Roadster.

It's all so romantic, all so seedy, and all so tragic—the man with "a bad liver and a broken heart," as he groaned-moaned on *Small Change;* the man who "don't have a drinking problem 'cept when I can't get a drink." And maybe Waits is partly to blame for his fans' perception of him. No performer ever went so far out of his way to become his songs, to live in the worn-out skin of the broke-down sumbitch who has his mail forwarded to the corner of Pork and Beans.

"It's compulsive to create a mythology about others and to create a certain amount of mythology about oneself," he says. "You put a light on it, and if you take water out of the river, it's no longer a river—it's water in a can. You put a light on yourself and ya stand on stage, you're masking out a great deal. Same is true of songs that were extracted from a particular experience. There's a careful operation. It's like history. What you choose to ignore is part of the history as well."

Then, it's easy to forget that all myths were once children, that they had parents who loved them, that there are pictures somewhere of a baby-faced Tom Waits who spoke in a high voice and hadn't yet lit up his first cigarette. Waits was born into the middle class on December 7, 1949, the son of schoolteachers, Frank Waits (who taught Spanish) and Alma McMurray, who divorced when he was ten. He lived for a while in Whittier, California, then moved with his mom to National City, near the Mexican border; he would spend much time in Mexico, especially with his father.

He says now that it was during those trips to Mexico that he realized music was the job for him. Songs spoke to him, embraced him like an old friend. The child who had taped Bob Dylan lyrics to his walls, who taught himself how to play piano using the neighbor's instrument, found all he was looking for in a Mexican ballad. He can't remember the exact name—and if he could, he'd just make it up anyway—only that it was "probably a ranchera, you know, on the car radio with my dad." He sings a snippet of one in rasping, perfect Spanish. "Probably one of those."

But what was it about that song that made him realize he wasn't simply a fan, but someone who could write his own songs?

"That's when it's more important that music likes you," he explains. "Everybody loves music, but it's important that music likes you. Some people work good with animals—they really love animals—but what if the animals don't like them? A lot of it is in the hand. It's like medicine. Every procedure in medicine requires two hands. The same is true in music, for the most part. I mean, there aren't a lot of pieces written for one-armed piano players.

"In fact, I met a one-armed piano player in Chicago when I was on the road doin' clubs all the time. His name was Eddie Balchovsky. He was also a painter who had fought in the Spanish Civil War. He was excellent. And the song he played over and over again was called 'Without a Song.' You know that song? Bob Dylan quoted it one night at an awards ceremony: 'Without a song, the road will never bend / Without a song.' He would slam that hand down on the piano, and he'd do the low chords, and then he'd slam over and hit the octaves, then he'd get it in the middle there. It sounded huge. He sounded like Horowitz. He actually did have a nub on the end of his stump. It was like a little finger, so he could pick up a little bit with that. But it's . . . hmmmm. Where were we?"

No one could ever blame the audience for thinking that the man on stage was The Real Thing—the tramp who wandered in through the back door with a bottle of whiskey in his tattered coat pocket, his lyrics written in the mud beneath his fingernails. He inhabited the role too well for a while, drank too much and smoked too much and kept telling the same stories over and over. Waits, for a while, was the corner drunk trying to getcha t'c'merebuddy so he could exaggerate yesterday's lies.

But in the end, he is no less than a poet pounding out his tales on the keys of a piano. At his best, on songs such as "On the Nickel" (originally written for a documentary about homeless children) or "Christmas Card from a Hooker in Minneapolis" or "Small Change" or the brand-new "Georgia Lee," he allows you inside a world you tried to escape from or never wanted to visit. He noticed things others weren't even keen enough to ignore. The man was, and remains, all about the details—the little boys "who never comb their hair," the kid who "got rained on with his own .38," the man whose only dance partner is the broom he uses to clean up the pizza parlor, or twelve-year-old Georgia Lee Moses, murdered and forgotten till Waits came to tend to her grave. Waits knew about all those things, had worked the shitty job at Napoleone's Pizza House and read the tiny newspaper item about Georgia Lee, but it hardly matters where the stories came from. After all, no one ever asks a fiction writer if he's telling the truth.

"You use the word 'I' or 'me' in a song, and you're telling about some disparate tale, and people go, 'My God, is that autobiographical?' Novelists aren't performers. Novelists are chicken." He busts up. "No, no, I don't know what it is. It's solo work. People only got to go on what you give them. It's all show business.

"We have this thing about onstage and backstage. It's that keyhole mentality." His voice lowers. " 'What's goin' on back there?'

" 'Is he putting on stockings and a garter belt? What's going on back there? Who ordered the Yukon Jack?' Not me.

"I don't know. Uh, most of us have a limited perspective on the rest of us. You know three or four things about somebody, and ya put it together and make a story. I don't know.

"I do the same thing myself. I want to know more about Liberace, OK? I heard this story that he was bringing the dry-cleaning up to his room, and he fell asleep on his bed, and the fumes got to him, and he passed out and went to the hospital and eventually recovered. But is that what really happened? Or was he doin' crack out on Euclid Avenue? It's just our innate celebrity curiosity, I guess. It goes with the territory. The mind is only able to wrap itself around three or four little rough sketches of folks, and then . . . But, hey, that's the public."

He is referring now to those folks at the Driskill who kept sending him whiskey.

"That's not my family. Those aren't my friends. My friends and family don't relate to me like that. That's the ventriloquist act. I went to see Rodney Dangerfield, and imagine what happens to him. 'I get no respect . . . please.' I mean, you know by now he gets an inordinate amount of respect as a humorist, right, so how does he deal with the fact that he has to go out every night and say, 'I get no respect, no respect at all?' I asked him how he feels when people start doin' his act, and he says, 'It's like hittin' my kid.' " Waits laughs hysterically. "People are possessive about their act, because you're kinda like hangin' out there in the wind like you're Marcel Marceau or whoever you are."

He then pauses, long enough to allow for the comedian's beat.

"Marcel Marceau's got a new album out, by the way." He cackles. "They say you should listen to it very loud."

But if you need any further proof that the performer and the persona are interchangeable, you need look only at a handful of legal documents. Indeed, in 1990, Waits pocketed small change—and then some—when Dallas-based ad agency Tracy-Locke, Plano-based Frito-Lay, and a Denton musician appropriated nothing more than his sound for a Doritos advertisement.

In 1988, a Tracy-Locke exec began working on a campaign for SalsaRio Doritos and used as his inspiration Waits's 1976 song "Step Right Up" from *Small Change*—a tune for which Waits had adopted the voice of the sneering, leering huckster trying to sell perfume to old ladies and "smoke-damaged furniture you can drive away today." An engineer working on the radio-only Doritos commercial recommended Stephen Carter as a singer, since Carter's act included his double-take impersonation of Waits. Carter signed on, but with reservation; after all, he was an acolyte, and well aware of how much Waits despised commercials and musicians who sold their souls to pitch products, a sentiment Waits often repeated in interviews. As he sat down at the mike to render his gravel-and-Luckies impression, Carter worried: God, what's Tom gonna think?

Tracy-Locke execs, too, fretted over the impression, but that didn't stop the ad agency from running the radio spot in the fall of 1988. In the time it takes to turn off a radio, Waits was in a Los Angeles courthouse filing a federal suit against Frito-Lay, claiming voice misappropriation and false endorsement. Carter's worst fears had come true: He had betrayed his idol, the man whose records had once "saved my life," as Carter told the *Dallas Observer* several years ago.

When the case went before a jury in U.S. District Court in L.A. in April and May 1990, Waits testified that he was "very angry" when he first heard the spot; never would he sell out for a "corn-chip sermon." He told the jury that the ad "embarrassed me. I had to call all my friends, that if they hear this thing, please be informed this is not me. I was on the phone for days. I also had people calling me saying, 'Gee, Tom, I heard the new Doritos ad.' " He was afraid his friends thought him a hypocrite. After all, Waits said, "part of my character and personality and image that I have cultivated is that I do not endorse products."

On top of that, he was creeped out by how perfectly Carter had the impression down. "Somebody had studied me a little too closely," he testified. "It was the equivalent of all the scars, dimples, the lines all being in the same place." He told the jury the experience "was a little spooky."

At the trial, Carter sided with Waits. Frito's and Tracy-Locke's attorneys contended that the singer hadn't been hired to imitate Waits, but Carter testified in his hero's defense, admitting what was already obvious to jurors who hadn't ever even heard of Tom Waits. (One juror, a thirty-six-year-old car salesman from the L.A. suburbs, would later tell a reporter that when he first saw Waits walk into the courtroom, "I thought this was a criminal case and he was a criminal.") In the end, the jury awarded Waits $2.5 million in damages, which was knocked down to $2.375 million by the Ninth Circuit Court of Appeals. In January 1993, the U.S. Supreme Court let stand the lower court's ruling.

But Waits wasn't finished defending his right to keep his music out of ads. In the fall of 1996, the singer-songwriter was again in an L.A. courtroom, this time to keep his former music publisher—Third Story Music, with whom he signed while a struggling nobody living out of his car in 1971—from licensing his older material to foreign advertisers. He would win again. No one protects his children like Tom Waits.

Waits once made records that were opulent, sentimental, loaded with more strings than a week at Wimbledon. He says now he will never go there again—it's too sweet for him, too manipulative. He prefers instead the clang and twang of his post-*Swordfishtrombones* albums—the abstract dissonance obscuring pretty pop songs, the furor that gives way to the occasional meditative respite.

"I guess now I'd say I'm more in the salvage business," he explains. "I'm more eccentric I guess in that sense."

He says that were it not for Kathleen, his wife and collaborator since 1980, *Mule Variations* would undoubtedly feature fewer ballads and more up-tempo pieces—songs that "are a beat quicker than the heart," he explains. Nine such songs were discarded from the new record, and they may yet resurface again.

After a while, Waits begins to talk about the fact that every single one of his records is schizophrenic in a way, torn between chaos and solace—between the kerrang-and-bang dissonance of "Big in Japan" that kicks off *Mule Variations* and the mournful farewell of "Georgia Lee," a song that could well have been on his 1970s albums. He coughs slightly, then begins to explain the unexplainable.

"I have unreconcilable influences, I think, and I think that's what shows up on the record for me sometimes," Waits says. "You know, I end up with the Cuban and the Chinese, but it never really becomes Cuban-Chinese. Henh. I just kind of like accepted that, that I have the different sides to me— that I like Rachmaninoff and I also like the Contortions. So be it. Shoot me. Otherwise you feel at a certain point like you're wearing Bermuda shorts and a bathing cap and fishing boots and a necktie."

Is that a bad thing?

"I didn't say it was a bad thing, but at a certain point, when you're in your twenties, I think maybe you equate music . . . music is . . . um . . . some people are afraid . . . Uh, gee, I don't know how to put that. It's like Bob Dylan said, some people are afraid of the bomb, and some people are afraid of being seen with a *Modern Screen* magazine under their arm." He chuckles. "Right?"

After a moment, Waits is asked when he realized it was OK to have those irreconcilable influences. Perhaps it was *Heartattack and Vine* in 1980, or maybe it was 1983's *Swordfishtrombones,* the beginning of his "Frank's Wild Years" trilogy that sounded as though it were recorded at Fred Sanford's house. Waits is having none of it.

"There's a lot of intelligence in the hands," he explains. "When you pick up a shovel, the hands know what to do. The same thing's true of sitting at the piano—your hands just, after a while, kind of wrap themselves around certain structures and voicings. I think it's good to kind of surprise yourself sometimes. It's like, I've got a friend who's a painter who wears glasses. He goes out in the woods, takes off his glasses, and draws, you know, 'cause everything looks different.

"It's like, when I went down to Mexico, and I went into a sushi bar, and the guy asked me if I want that with or without cheese," he says, cracking himself up. "I said, 'Awright, this is a good thing.'"

And Waits keeps right on laughing.

GONE NORTH: TOM WAITS, UPCOUNTRY

LA Weekly, April 23, 1999

Robert Lloyd

―――――――――――――――

"I usually have a hard time talking about things directly, you know?"

— Tom Waits, not just whistling "Dixie"

I.

Morning. A truck-stop diner along Highway 101 near Santa Rosa, California, north of San Francisco. A horseshoe counter, tables, booths. Plain but clean. The focal point of the room is a large painting of an eighteen-wheeler on a country road, a painting that somehow speaks not of modern power but of classical repose: the Peterbilt as stag. The customers are mostly in their forties, fifties and sixties, dressed for hard work or unfashionable comfort, the men almost invariably bearded.

In a booth by a window sit two patrons: One of them, Most Obviously Not From Around Here, is me. The other is Tom Waits, a musician and occasional actor. (His next film,

Mystery Men, a superhero comedy, is due out this summer.)
Formerly of Los Angeles, he has lived in the area several years
with his wife (and co-writer and -producer), Kathleen
Brennan, and their three children, and has taken on something of the local coloration. He wears unprefaded denims
and big boots, and the only remaining emblem of his erst-
while cloth-cap-and-pointed-shoes flophouse-jazzbo neoboho
fingersnappin' self is the Dizzy G. soul patch parked subtly
beneath his lower lip. The towering monolith, or towering
inferno, that was famously his hair has collapsed into something more like a brushfire.

Born on the eighth anniversary of the bombing of Pearl
Harbor, Waits will celebrate fifty years on Earth three weeks
before the end of the century. But like some other people who
do not punch clocks, unless it's to stop them from ringing, he
seems to exist outside of conventional time, and—judging at
least by the person on his records, which range from his
folkish 1973 debut, *Closing Time,* to the bop prosody of
Small Change and *Foreign Affairs,* to the taxonomically confounding vaudeville of *Swordfishtrombones* and *Rain Dogs*
and the stone-age blues of *Bone Machine*—even to have
lived backward, from premature middle age into middle-aged
youth, from (apparent) sophistication to (deceptive) sim-
plicity. His first new album in six years, *Mule Variations,*
which incorporates, refines and extends these previous
researches into something at once fresh and familiar, is set for
release April 27. And it was in this very diner that he sealed
his new surprising-yet-not-really-when-you-think-about-it
deal with Epitaph Records, the Los Angeles-based independent best known for the punk pop of Pennywise and
Rancid, and founded by Brett Gurewitz, formerly of Bad
Religion. Though he can claim Jackson Browne as a onetime
labelmate and has been covered by the Eagles and Rod

Stewart, Waits is by persuasion an outsider. "I think they're all great," he'll say later of Epitaph's young, enthusiastic and musically inclined staff. "I came from the whole period where record guys, it's like meeting guys from DuPont—they start looking at you like they want to lift up a part of you and look underneath, you feel like they're smelling meat."

Tom leaning forward confidentially: The Washington Monument sinks six inches each year. Six inches.

Me: You brought notes?

Tom: You don't think I'd come unprepared, do you? I'll tell you what's good here: specials. If you're hungry go for the specials. It's like your grandma. They got borscht here. They got turkey loaf. This place hasn't really been discovered yet. (Indicates the truck painting.) That's the table I usually try to get. Just to be near the painting. It's kind of like the *Mona Lisa*. The *Mona Lisa* has no eyebrows—you ever notice that?

Me: Maybe that's the secret of that painting, more than the smile.

Tom: The shaved eyebrows. That's what I go for . . . When I was a kid, I had a friend whose dad was a truck driver. His name was Gale Storm. We had moved to National City, and his dad was coming through town, and he picked me up and he took me back up to L.A., to Whittier, to stay for a weekend. And I rode in the truck all the way up there. I was just like, "I'm gonna—I don't know what I'm gonna do, but I'm changed."

Me: How did you end up in this neighborhood?

Tom: It just seemed a good place to go—north. You live in L.A., you go south, there's more L.A. We bought a house here several years ago right along the railroad tracks. And it was one of those things, they show you the house and you sit on the porch, and as you sit down on the porch there's a train going by, right? And the engineer waves to you. And then a cardinal comes and sits down right near your shoulder, and you hear the train whistle blowing, and the sun is going down, you have a nice glass of red wine. You think, "This is it." You buy the place, and the next day they say, "That was the last time that train ran. No cardinals have ever been seen around here. It must have been some freak thing." Then you quit drinking, and you're stuck with a house on a busy road, and the traffic noise is deafening. That was my introduction to the area. Now I live out. Way out.

Me: You must be well-established here by now.

Tom: I'm not well-established at all—but I'm here.

Me: You ever go down to San Francisco?

Tom: I go down sometimes—in for a weekend of excitement. Watch women's wrestling, or mud wrestling. Midget female mud wrestling. It's big there—it's huge. It's bigger than the opera—in fact, they call it "The Little Opera."

Me: And have you been playing music in the time between records?

Tom: The standard answer? I've been in traffic school.

Me: You know, you can get through that in a day.

Tom: They wanted to make an example out of me. I didn't have a good lawyer, and I just said, "Look, I'll do the time."

Me: Traffic school is hard.

Tom: It is hard. People don't really give it the weight it deserves.

Me: To get something out of it.

Tom: Exactly. More than just a diploma. I feel better as a person. I graduated vaya cum laude . . . Actually, I've been breaking in other people's shoes. Just on the side. Just to stay busy. You get 'em new, you're unhappy with them—I wear 'em four or five weeks and mail 'em back to you. No obligation necessary. But just 'cause you're not fishin' doesn't mean there aren't fish out there. You can go out there when you want, when you're ready to do it . . . We've got a piano called a Fisher. And that's what we use to catch the big ones.

Me: Could you stop playing music and still be happy?

Tom: I thought about that. I don't know. I'd probably end up gluing bottlecaps onto a piece of plywood. I don't know how long I'm going to last. Until I get sick of it. Sick of myself. I get a lot of weird mail. I get letters from guys that say, "My wife and I ran a hotel for many years, and we've sold it. The folks that took it over are a nice couple, and if you're ever in town, you should go visit them. Tell them that you spoke to us." And I don't know those people. They've already told me some people that they know that I should go and talk to and tell 'em that I know these people that I don't know. And then they tell me about the fact that he had bypass surgery and he has two blood clots, and his wife had a fourteen-pound hairball removed from her and then they mounted it, you know, on a . . . globe. You know there's a device that they invented during World War II that could print 4,000 words on a surface the size of a piece of rice?

Me: I did not.

Tom: That's what I'm here for. Here's something else: Now, I hope you never have to use this, but if you're ever pursued by a crocodile, run in a zigzag fashion. They have little or no ability to make sudden changes in direction. But they're fast, they're very fast. In fact, there are probably more people that are killed by crocodiles than there are by . . . anything. More than heart disease. And I hear they're headed west.

Waitress returning: You're not going to eat? Not yet?

Tom: Still nothing.

Waitress: Nothing from nothing is nothing. You want more coffee? He nods. She refills the cups and moves on.

Tom: You can sit here as long as you want. A pause, as he consults his notes. A mole can dig a tunnel three hundred feet long in one night. A grasshopper can jump over obstacles five hundred times its height. You know what creature has the largest brain in relation to the size of its body? The ant. An ostrich's eyeball is larger than its brain. You put those two things together and . . . I don't know what that means. I'm not going anywhere with that.

Me: Where do you pick this stuff up?

Tom: Just livin' . . . The Ringling Brothers at one point were exhibiting Einstein's eyes, Napoleon's penis and Galileo's finger bones, all on the same bill. Different tents. 'Course I missed that. You ever hear of Johnny Eck? He was a Ringling act. The Man Born Without a Body. Johnny Eck had his own orchestra and was an excellent pianist and he'd stand on his hands and wear a tuxedo. I used to take the bus to the Troubadour and stand out front at nine o'clock in the morning on a Monday and wait all day to get up and do fifteen minutes onstage . . . 'Cause you know, you never had confidence, you have absolutely no self-esteem, but you have this mad wish to do something public at the same time. You're sitting all day next to a guy with a silver trumpet who's on acid, you're sharing cigarettes and drinking Tabs. And then like a whole Mexican family with nine kids comes in in matching vests and pants and studs and hats, from ages nineteen down to four, and they get up and do "Guadalajara," "Eres Tu?"—remember that? Break your heart, just break your heart . . . I saw Miles Davis there. Professor Irwin Corey. They swing a spotlight around right by the cigarette machine to pick you up: And nowwww, ladies and gentlemen, the Troubadour is proud to present . . . And they'd say your name, and they'd walk you up to the stage in the spotlight. I used to watch other acts do that, and I'd be in the audience with my coffee, and I said, "That's it. That's it for me." You know this group called That Mean Old Man Next Door? They've got a record called *Tijuana Moon*.

Me: I like the name.

Tom: I just made it up.

Me: Did you?

Tom: Could be the other way. Could be a group called Tijuana Moon.

Me: Could be. It's confusing sometimes.

Tom: You ever try to get a sandwich made for you in England? It'll just make you crazy. "Put a little more sauce on that." And it's your sandwich, you're gonna pay for it and you're gonna eat it. But they look at you like snooty voice, "I won't do it." "Put a little more lettuce on that for me." "I can't do it." "And don't cut the crust." "I have to cut it off." I used to get in arguments. I used to end up going over the counter. I'd say, "Gimme that bread, goddamn it. Let me have that thing. I'll show you how to make a goddamn sandwich." I was young. I was rude. But there was something real and sincere about my reaction.

The waitress approaches with a coffee pot.

Tom: You got a decaf? I got to calm down.

II.

Driving me back to my hotel in the big black Silverado he calls (today, at least) Old Reliable, Waits detours to a flower-bedecked makeshift roadside shrine dedicated to the memory of twelve-year-old Georgia Lee Moses, the subject of "Georgia Lee," a lilting Irishy lullaby on *Mule Variations*.

"It's a good spot," he says as we pull over to a grassy plot of trees and brush by a freeway on ramp. "She'd run away from home, been missing for like a week. I guess this is where they found the body." He takes a plastic point-and-click camera from his pocket and shoots a picture. "Not to make it a racial matter, but it was one of those things where, you know, she's a black kid, and when it comes to missing children and unsolved crimes, a lot of it has to do with timing, or publicity . . . and there was this whole Polly Klaas Foundation up here, while Georgia Lee did not get any real attention. And I wanted to write a song about it. At one point I wasn't going to put it on the record, there were too many songs. But my daughter said, 'Gee, that would really be sad—she gets killed and not remembered and somebody writes a song about it and doesn't put it on the record.' I didn't want to be a part of that."

Waits recorded twenty-five tracks for the sixteen-song *Mule Variations*, which takes its title from the fact that "Get Behind the Mule," a low-slung gospel blues more or less about persistence, had been attempted in several styles; but the mule is an apt enough totem for the record, stubbornly itself and not as pretty as a horse. Like Bob Dylan's *Time Out of Mind*, it's a mature work that trades away a young man's flash effects for an older one's plain speaking—a step forward that can sound like a step back—and like that record, it alternates between mutant blues and bravely sentimental ballads. ("It's got a lot of ballads," he says, "which I was nervous about at first," but which makes the album more immediately accessible than the elemental *Bone Machine* or the troll-cabaret *The Black Rider*.) While he has not abandoned his familiar lyrical complement of drifters, town-edge dwellers and sideshow freaks (like the "not conventionally handsome" "Eyeball Kid," whom the singer gives his own birth date), his subject here overwhelmingly is Home. (He will say no more about it than "You write about what you go through.") Waits—who moved several times as a child, and conceived a fondness as an adult (in what might be termed his Bukowski phase) for flophouses and fleabag hostelries, living notoriously for a spell in West Hollywood's Tropicana Motel—was formerly a poet of transients, and of transience; *Mule Variations,* a family man's album, is by contrast founded primarily upon household images: "Evelyn's kitchen," "Beulah's porch." "Never let the weeds get higher / than the garden," he advises in "Get Behind the Mule," while at the "House Where Nobody Lives," "the weeds had grown up / just as high as the drawers," and the unsavory neighbor of "What's He Building?" "has no dog and he has no friends and his lawn is dying." "I hope my pony knows the way home," sings the weary traveler of "Pony." "Picture in a Frame" provides a swell little metaphor for commitment and the civilizing influence of small gestures. "Filipino Box Spring Hog" concerns a barbecue. And in the breathtakingly intimate "Take It with Me," perhaps the most beautiful and most beautifully sung song in his canon, domestic pleasure inspires a vision of transcendent permanence:

> *Children are playing*
> *at the end of the day*
> *Strangers are singing*
> *on our lawn*
> *It's got to be more*
> *than flesh and bone*
> *All that you've loved*
> *is all you own*
> *. . . I'm gonna take it*
> *with me when I go*

"Come on Up to the House," the raucous hymn that follows, appropriately caps the album with a general offer of refuge.

What makes Tom Waits most valuable, and continually attractive to succeeding generations of listeners looking for something . . . nonstandard, is—apart from his heart and his humor—his restlessness, his perfect willingness to destroy the lab for the sake of the experiment. (He's the kid you knew who made models just to blow them up.) Except for *Closing Time*, a singer-songwriter album in an age of singer-songwriters, he's gone his own way, often too far from the pack even to be called out of step, but he's been influential around the significant fringes. (Beck, Sparklehorse, Nick Cave, Giant Sand, and Los Lobos all owe him something.) Most important, he has never—as pop stars so often do in their middle years—equated quality with either technique or technology; if anything, he's a bit of a Luddite, standing for the "junkyard choir," the real room sound, the unplannable accident. He'd far sooner hit something with a stick than plug something in. There is an element of cultural bravery in all this, even if unintended, and Waits has become a kind of hero to the pop discontent. His appearance last month at the South By Southwest music conference in Austin was the weekend's hot ticket.

Because it gets relatively little airplay—being too strange for the stations that play his chronological contemporaries and altogether unrelated to the business of modern rock radio—Waits's music is spread most often, like a seditionary pamphlet, from friend to friend, lover to lover, parent to child, teacher to student—a conspiracy of Tom. On the Internet one finds testaments from fans who first heard him . . .

. . . in the fifth or sixth grade when my science teacher listened to *Bone Machine* every day before we students arrived . . . from my ex-boyfriend, and I am certain that it was the best thing he gave me at all . . . from a Swedish girl driving through Omaha with my cousin . . . in my AP history class . . . in Trondheim, Norway, as an exchange student . . . in my dad's record collection . . . via a girl I fell in love with during my early years as a poor starving acting student in a small Miami art college—she was a dancer who ultimately stepped on my heart and squashed it into the cheap beige carpet that covered the floor in my dorm room. Thank god for her, anyway . . .

They are every last one of them hoping he will come to their town, now that he has a record to promote. But Waits, who has scant patience for touring ("I like to come home before I get angry"), will likely make only a few appearances in a handful of "major markets."

"You don't feel the need to get up in front of a crowd and play, obviously?" I ask as we drive along a frontage road.

Tom: Not unless I can wear a leotard and a bathing cap and some fishing boots. That's what I'm looking for, some new channel, so you don't feel like you're doing a medley of your hits—not that I've had hits. I'm just saying that after a while you sit down at the piano and start feeling like a lounge act. Everybody wants to hear this song or that song . . . This used to be all fruit stands, eucalyptus trees, used-car lots. There's an old Buick right there. Is that a Buick or an Olds? See the one I'm talking about? The four-door?

Me: It's the only one you could be talking about.

Tom: It's an Olds . . . fifteen hundred dollars—Jee-sus. My first car cost me fifty dollars. It was a '55 Buick Special.

Me: Did it run?

Tom: Oh God yes. Swing low, sweet chariot. It was just a . . . boat.

Me: Do you have other cars than this?

Tom: I got an old Caddy. I got a '72 white Suburban that no one in the family will ride in. My vehicles have always been humiliating for the kids. This one, it's like a motel, and they even complain about this. I say, "You're nuts. You could live in this car."

Me: A family of five.

Tom: Comfort. Roadability. Reliability—hence the name "Old Reliable." Smoked windows. For anonymity. 'Cause there's times when you just want to sneak in, do your business and sneak out.

III.

Later that same day. An old roadhouse Italian restaurant forty minutes out into the countryside, amid the green hills and spotted cows. "It's got the largest Elvis Presley decanter collection in the West," Waits had said. "That's something you gotta see. And they also have this tilted floor, and glasses fly out of your hand. I was gonna suggest perhaps later this afternoon meeting me there to see if we could get a glass to fly out of our hands. It's very chic. Big line around the block. Guy wears a uniform at the door. Little band. Very chichi. I don't even know if you can get in the way you're dressed . . . I never go anywhere without a tuxedo. At least the upper half of a tuxedo. Might be able to get away with your own pants, if you stay seated. In fact, you might want to bring a chair that you're already in, and just sort of scoot towards the door."

No one is at the door, in a uniform or in line. The interior is strictly red checks and paneled walls. There's no band, but there is an old upright piano, an enormous rack of antlers, a collection of dusty paintings, including one of John Wayne, "the patron saint," says Waits, "of all Italian restaurants." And in wall-mounted glass cases, dozens of decanters of varying shapes and sizes—nary an Elvis, however.

Me: Do you feel isolated out here?

Tom: I guess I used to, but I don't really anymore. I think what happens is that when people move to the sticks, they still want all their products and services, and they get out here and then gradually the place they thought was bucolic and serene starts looking like all the places that they left, because they brought with them all the things that made the place they used to live in look so . . . crappy. And they have to keep moving further away, but they're really bringing it all with them. When I went back to Los Angeles after having not been there for a while, I was surprised at how many words you see when you're driving. It's shocking. Every square inch of space that you can see from your windshield there are words. Hundreds and hundreds of words. In places you never would imagine. And I found myself unable to drive safely. Even after seven years of traffic school, I was having problems with focus and attention. I was going to lose my diploma. There was an earthquake in 1812 in the Midwest that changed the direction of the Mississippi River. Did you know that? Church bells rang as far away as Philadelphia.

Me: From the earthquake?

Tom: I don't mean it was Sunday.

Me: Is this how you spend your time?

Tom: I can't finish a book, you know, but I snack on information. The origin of pumpernickel bread, for example. Napoleon's horse ate the best bread. All the soldiers were livid. What they really wanted was to eat as well as Napoleon's horse ate. And he ate pumpernickel. His horse's name was Nikolai. Nikolai . . . pumpernickel.

Me: I think of that as a German word, and yet it's apparently from the French.

Tom: And yet. And yet. It's just one of those things that . . . gives you a reason to live.

Me: Keeps you mystified.

Tom: Like this place. Notice the plastic pitcher. The plastic tumbler. It was at one time glass. You know how the nicer restaurants have a piece of glass? They finally just said . . .

Me: Flew off the table too many times.

Tom: The overhead was just amazing.

A waiter approaches. Waiter noticing the tape recorder: You're not going to tape me, are you?

Tom: No. We're going to listen to music. But only we can hear it. We're dogs.

Waiter: Well, crank it up.

Tom: It is cranked up. What do you mean, crank it up? A puzzled pause. After which Waits orders lasagna.

Waiter: And some soup?

Tom: I'll have some soup. In preparation for my lasagna.

The waiter withdraws.

Me: You're really putting on the feed bag this evening.

Tom: It's a matter of being polite. If you don't eat, they'll get you later. "Well, why'd you come in here? To laugh at us? To laugh at our decanters? Our crooked floor?"

Me: When you were living in Hollywood twenty years ago, did you ever imagine you'd wind up a country squire?

Tom: Then, no. Now, neither. You do get addicted to noise living in the city. There's a great deal you have to recover from if you leave. When I first came out to a small town, there's a guy with a dustpan and a whisk broom, a policeman, in the middle of the street, sweeping up glass. And then I ordered a coffee in a little café—the waitress says sweetly, "Hi, how are you?" "I don't think that's any of your business, how I am. I'm just drinking my coffee." Took me a while.

Me: You had the shell on. The protective coating.

Tom: It's a little drop of Retsin. That outer candy shell that seals in the freshness.

Me: Do you feel countrified yet?

Tom: I don't know. I hope I'm becoming more eccentric. More room, you know. More room in the brain.

Me: Did you feel limited by Hollywood or New York?

Tom: Well, gee, after a while, it just gets . . . change is good. I can go there if I want. They didn't get rid of it.

Me: No, they did. It's gone.

Tom: I was afraid that might happen if I left. But I have film; I have a lot of it on film . . . Western Avenue, you know, is the longest street in the world. I hear it runs down to Ensenada.

Me: Tierra del Fuego.

Tom: La Paz. You get on Western and you just keep driving and it's pretty unbelievable. A lot of hair-care places. I think there's probably more hair-care places on Western than there are in Hollywood. You think of Hollywood as obsessed with its hair, but folks who live way out on Western are just as interested in hair care and hair-care products.

The waiter brings soup.

Tom: What was that big high-speed chase that came through here in the thirties—remember that?

Waiter: Gosh, I forgot about that.

Tom: There was a bank robbery in the city, and it was like a . . .

Waiter: You're talking about the thirties or the seventies?

Tom: The thirties. There was a shoot-out at the creamery—you know the creamery? Big shoot-out. Three guys dead. The car was on fire, the whole place.

Waiter: I missed out on that one.

Tom: I thought maybe you'd heard something recently about it. It's all in the Library of Congress.

Waiter: That's the first time I heard it.

The waiter withdraws.

Tom: They don't like to talk about it here—afraid they're

gonna lose business. I think they stole like half a million dollars. On back roads from Petaluma. Like a Bogart movie. There was a dairy right behind here, and that's where they had this big shoot-out . . . And afterwards they all came here. And they all made up.

Me: They sat down together.

Tom: You gotta eat. You have to stop a minute and just . . . eat. My stepfather's mom dated Al Capone.

Me: Really?

Tom: Went out on a few dates.

Me: Nothing serious.

Tom: I don't know.

Me: Could have turned into something.

Tom: Could have developed. Who knows? How much of what really happened do you tell? The reason that history is so distorted is 'cause most people aren't talking. Most people really don't want you to know the truth.

The waiter returns with lasagna.

Waiter: Tom, you ready for that lasagna?

Tom: Um, yeah . . . I was going to ask you about the Elvis decanters. Was there an abundance of Elvis decanters here for a while? Or did I just create that, out of a desire to see more of them?

Waiter: Well, that may have been. The bartender at one time, who was married to Dolores, who's bartending now, he was an impersonator of Elvis. Maybe you saw him.

Tom: No, I could have sworn I saw . . .

Waiter: I think there's a couple in the bar.

Tom: There's got to be.

Waiter: He may have taken them when he left.

Tom: There it is, you see.

Waiter: The thirties, though.

Tom: The thirties. A high-speed chase. Big bank job. A

shoot-out. All along the Shoreline Highway. Ended up at the creamery. Three guys dead. And afterwards they came over here. It's in the library. Now I've got to ask a question. Those stories about the glassware. I'm surprised you brought a glass. You set a glass down on a table here. There are certain places here where a glass will fly off the table and hit the wall?

Waiter: I've heard that. (Pointing over there.)

Tom: Is that why there's no glassware on that particular table? First thing I noticed—that you'd gone with the plastic cups. A safety feature. What else has happened over there?

Waiter: Pictures.

Tom: Pictures have fallen?

Waiter: Fallen off the wall. That one . . .

Tom: I just saw it move.

Waiter (concerned): Do you want your check now?

Tom: No. I came for that.

The waiter withdraws.

Tom: You notice on trash day how somebody's going through the trash, you stick your head out the window and say, "What the hell you doing in there?" And then they leave and you start going through your own trash. You start re-evaluating the quality of your own trash, wondering if you made some terrible mistake, if you've thrown out something that is now going to be essential to your life.

Kathleen and I came up with this idea of doing music that's surrural—it's surreal and it's rural, it's surrural. (Sings) *Everybody's doin' it doin' it doin' it.* Surrural. She'll start kind of talking in tongues, and I take it all down. She goes places . . . I can't get to those places. Too, I don't know . . . pragmatic. She's the egret of the family. I'm the mule. I write mostly from the world, the news, and what I really see from the counter, or hear. She's more impressionistic. She dreams like Hieronymus Bosch. She's been a lot of things. She drove a truck for a while. Had her own pilot's license. Worked as a soda jerk. Ran a big hotel in Miami. She was going to be a nun. When I met her, she was at the corner of nun or ruin. So together it's you wash, I'll dry. It works.

She's exposing me to all kinds of things I'd never listen to. It's kind of like trying on hats. "Is that me?" You have to kind of let it all down and not worry about what's hip and what's cool. I guess I'd been trying to find some music that's my own music—it's like home cooking, you know? Of course if I'm making something just for me, I'm not very picky, I might just pour some sugar in my ear, suck on a piece of dirt in my mouth, light my hair on fire. I'm fine with that.

What I did for a long time was put my head on other people's bodies. You look for your own niche. How have all these things synthesized in you? You take your Elmer Bernstein and you take your seven inches of throbbing pink Jesus and you put it together and you try to make some sense out of it. Melt it, crush it, saw it, solder it. I've always had diverse influences, and I never know how to reconcile them. There was a point where I wasn't sure whether I was a lounge act or . . .

Me: A main-room act.

Tom: Yeah. "Am I too hip for the room?" I don't know. "I'm not hip enough for the room." Or am I just, like, you know, a garage sale? It's an ongoing dilemma. Where are you, what are you? In popular music, the key word is "popular," and popular usually connects something very temporary—once popular, then they call you once-popular.

Me: Ninety-five percent of everything is temporary.

Tom: I'm okay with that . . . But it's nice to think that when you're making your music and you bring it out, someone's going to pick it up. And who knows when or where? I listen to stuff that's fifty years old or older than that and bring it into myself. And so you are in a way having communion and fellowship with folks you have yet to meet, who will someday hopefully bring your record home and—you know, they're running a little lingerie shop down on Magnolia —and put it on, and bring it together with the sounds that they hear in their own head. It's nice to be part of the dismemberment of linear time.

The meal is finished, the check paid. On the way out, half a dozen decanters representing Elvis Presley in the several stages of his fine, fine, superfine career are discovered in the bar. Outside, a red Corvette is parked. Waits hands me his camera, and I take his picture posing proprietorially by the car. For a second, he looks about seventeen. Then he climbs into his hulking black Silverado and drives away, into the cow-covered hills, back to the family, as night falls on the countryside.

ROMANCE IN TALL TALES OF
DRIFTERS AND DRUNKS

New York Times, September 27, 1999

Jon Pareles

Tom Waits brought his own dust to the Beacon Theater on Thursday night. He sang from a podium that had a pile of powder on it, and every so often he'd kick up a little cloud. There's dust in his songs, too: the dust of back alleys and back rooms, run-down bars and cheap motels. But Mr. Waits had also brought silvery glitter, tossing handfuls of it into the stage lights as if, like his songs, it could spawn beauty from desperation and sleaze.

It was the first of four sold-out concerts by Mr. Waits, who has not toured since 1987. Since he began making albums in the early 1970s, he has been depicting low-life Americana with an exacting eye and ear, joining a long line of American artists and writers who find romance and bitter honesty in the gutter. By now he has conjured his own realm within rock. He looks back to an era before strip malls and multinational branding, when hobos rode the rails and pitchmen set up on street corners instead of Web sites. In his songs he spins tall tales of hustlers, drunks, crackpots, and drifters who are never far from love or death.

Mr. Waits turns himself into a caucus of bit players from

1930s movies: the paranoid neighbor, the carnival tout, the codger who hides a sentimental heart behind grouchy bluster. He has survived in the music business because a few of his songs, like "Downtown Train" and "Ol' 55," have been kindly enough to be recorded by Rod Stewart and the Eagles. But most of his narrators are antiheroes and casual philosophers who rasp out maxims like "Time's not your friend" and "You must risk something that matters."

Onstage, wearing a dark suit and a stingy-brim fedora, Mr. Waits stayed in character: joking in a nasal cackle, gesticulating like a backwoods preacher, dancing with his microphone stand. He sang in a deep, phlegmy bellow or a hungover whisper, with phrasing that shambled around the beat. But he's not one of his narrators. He's as familiar with Edward Hopper, Charles Bukowski, Louis Armstrong, and Kurt Weill as he is with sideshows and jalopies, and he orchestrates his songs to sound meticulously dilapidated.

With his 1983 album *Swordfishtrombones* (Island) Mr. Waits reinvented his music, trading pop-folk arrangements for lurching, clattering backups that are as unkempt as his voice. His touring band—Smokey Hormel on guitar, Danny McGough on keyboards, Larry Taylor on bass, and Andrew Borger on drums—invoked blues, parlor songs, gospel, country, and New Orleans rhythm-and-blues, but all with rusty parts and loosened screws.

The old bar-band styles were slowed down and fractured, with empty spaces and shards of dissonance. "Eyeball Kid" was barked over the steady, dissonant plinking of a percussion menagerie—marimba, slit drum, glockenspiel—while "What's He Building?" was whispered amid random twangs and rumbles. And when Mr. Waits played hymnlike, tenderhearted songs on an upright piano, his voice turned even rougher, lest he sound too sensitive.

In a generous set, the songs ran to extremes, full of contradictory impulses: the ghoulish visions of "The Black Rider," the obstinate faith of "Jesus Gonna Be Here," the surreal slapstick of "Filipino Box Spring Hog," the cad's confessions in "Tango Till They're Sore," the lover's devotion in "I'll Shoot the Moon." The final juxtaposition was "I Don't Wanna Grow Up," a vow not to be trapped by responsibilities, and "Pony," about a wanderer's homesickness.

To ramble or stake a place: it's the old American dilemma, and Mr. Waits doesn't try to resolve it, only to find its creaky, disheveled, dusty epiphanies.

SEWERS OF BUDAPEST

Village Voice, May 12, 1999

Luc Sante

I t seems like a long time since old Pop Waits last came around here with his swaybacked horse and his peddler's wagon, brightly colored gewgaws hanging off the sides, pots and pans clanging away, baskets crammed with novelty items, labor-saving devices, and sentimental ballads. On his last trip he was ranting in a German accent, trying to sell us horsehair underpants and cast-iron nosegays, and while that (*The Black Rider*, 1993) was interesting, it will reassure his steady customers to know that *Mule Variations* conforms to the product line they've come to know and love.

That would be product line B, inaugurated in 1983 with *Swordfishtrombones*. Line A, the original bill of goods, which covered the previous decade, featured the inevitable-seeming confluence of several archetypal streams (shoot the piano player, spontaneous bop prosody, America drinks and goes home, etc.), brownishly tinged with the period's Elektra-Asylum singer-songwriter shellac. *Swordfishtrombones* yanked the lounge shtick and the drunk jokes and opened up the territory with found percussion, surrealism, and a deeper range of Americana. The move may not have been quite as radical a shift as his record companies (before or after) seemed to believe, but among other accomplishments it brought Waits to the attention of listeners who (like your reviewer) ordinarily experience sinus problems when within range of a singer-songwriter.

In retrospect, you can see how Waits had to change gears just then. The Waits of the seventies would have fit the eighties all too well. The booze, the suits, the tail-fin Cadillacs with which he thumbed his nose at patchouli-infested California would a decade later attach themselves to an unforeseen regiment of Harry Connick Juniors marching forth from the frat houses to restore normalcy. This is not to say that Waits calculated his move; he just located and fleshed out his inner eccentric, taking as his patron saint the mid-century composer Harry Partch, who was an avant-gardist *and* a hobo, and who with his spectacularly oddball homemade instruments represents the grandest effusion of the American DIY ethos. Maybe Partch's example showed Waits how contrariness could be a complete aesthetic, not limited to reacting against the current mood.

In any event, Waits blossomed in the mid 1980s. The trilogy of *Swordfishtrombones, Rain Dogs* (1985), and *Frank's Wild Years* (1987) worked as sonic landscape, as theater, as narrative, and as a great bunch of songs. Waits seems to have set out, compass in hand, to find and stake the cardinal points of his personal terrain, in the process collecting and scrambling together what seems like every sort of music ever played in a bar in the twentieth century. Country and western mated with French chantoozie stuff, which crossed with New Orleans jazz, which intersected with sea chanteys, and so on—this was all adult music; Waits's jukebox never carried much youth culture. The surrealist mix 'n' match produced results that were occasionally literal ("9th and Hennepin" merely superimposes Partch's "The Street" on model-A Waits's "Christmas Card from a Hooker in Minneapolis"), sometimes anthemically mainstream (such cover-version generators as "Downtown Train" and "Blind Love"), and often enough irreducible ("Tango Till They're Sore," for example, which sounded immediately familiar without being reminiscent of anything specific).

All the above examples come from *Rain Dogs,* an album that in some parallel world could have spun off seven or eight singles, but which recedes somewhat amid the torrent of greatest non-hits from 1983 through 1993 surveyed last year on *Beautiful Maladies.* It's an anthology full of syncopation, oompah, metal pipes, underwater noises, hurdy-gurdyish sonorities, perplexed nostalgia, rueful sentimentalism, battle-scarred innocence. Every song is a little movie triangulated from musical, lyrical, and atmospheric allusions all heading off in different directions. "Sixteen Shells from a Thirty-Ought Six," for example, marries a prison-farm work song to lyrics that could be the work of some backwoods Hart Crane, with percussive hooks supplied by various auto parts; "Temptation" suggests a hybrid of "Suspicion" and the cartoon-snake-charmer standard "In a Persian Garden" warbled by an apostate muezzin in the drunk tank; "Jockey Full of Bourbon" stirs together nursery rhymes, surf guitar, bullwhip percussion, and the ghost of "Hernando's Hideaway." Waits is an uncanny pastiche artist, even in a time when you can't spit in a major city without hitting a pastiche artist. "Strange Weather" is the most convincing fake Kurt Weill song not written by Hanns Eisler; "Innocent When You Dream" makes you want to hear the version that must have been recorded by the immortal Irish tenor John McCormack on an Edison cylinder in 1912.

The collection also delineates the 1001 uses to which Waits has put his patented gravel throat. It's a bit like watching a really acrobatic fat man: you can't quite believe that an attribute that ought to be a handicap can manage such agility. He can shout and moan and leer with it, but he can equally well use it to croon and trill and sigh, and his rare falsetto ("Temptation") raises the fur on my dog's neck. Over the years he's put together a repertory company of supporting musicians that can apparently produce any sort of texture; tell them "Christmas in the sewers of Budapest after the Martian invasion of 1962" and they're there. Marc Ribot, Ralph Carney, et al. could probably sound like the Longines Symphonette if they set their minds to it.

An innovation on *Mule Variations* is the employment of a turntable artist, who as it turns out is so discreet you hardly notice, except on "Eyeball Kid," which makes brilliantly apposite use of a sampled gospel choir and Balinese ketjak chanters (one of whom sounds remarkably like a tobacco auctioneer). Another innovation is a major paring-down of lyrics. Where formerly Waits might knot together strings of lexemes ("Put a hi ball in the crank case / Nail a crow to the door / Get a bottle for the jockey / gimme a 294 / There's a 750 Norton bustin' out January's door . . .") that could sound like the collected dialogue from a dozen American International pictures passed through a Vegematic, there's a new restraint and purposefulness here that is perhaps attributable to the growing collaborative presence of Kathleen Brennan, Waits's wife, who cowrote twelve out of the eighteen songs. After all, she's responsible for the chorus of "Black Market Baby": "She's a diamond that wants to stay coal"—the single best line on the disc.

Mule Variations finds Waits in a more rural mood than he's previously been, although you wouldn't exactly call it mellow.

The change is subtle, in any case, because there are as many crazed rants and dream sequences and paranoid vignettes as ever—there's just a more tangible smell of soil. It's always hard to review a new Waits record hot off the truck, because the kick-in time of its component songs can be so delayed that the tune you barely notice now may turn out to be your favorite in 2007. (Kick-in time has not received its due from popular-music scholars; for purposes of comparison, my all-time champ is Love's *Forever Changes,* whose songs didn't finish kicking in until twenty-three years after purchase.) The current leading contenders on this item are the aforementioned "Eyeball Kid," "Georgia Lee" (a murder ballad that sounds like an illegitimate offspring of the Irish Christmas carol "The Holly and the Ivy"), "Hold On" (a cover magnet in the grand tradition), "Come on Up to the House" (a natural for gospel outfits, who however will have to omit the line "Come down off the cross / We can use the wood"), and "Cold Water" (might have been dictated by Leadbelly via Ouija board). Right now, *Mule Variations* sounds like a rock-solid Waits outing with less angst and more roots and few huge surprises, but that last phrase is subject to change.

THE RESURRECTION OF TOM WAITS

Rolling Stone, June 24, 1999

David Fricke

> For *Mule Variations,* his first record in six years, Tom
> Waits rounded his multiple personalities—barfly poet,
> avant-garde storyteller, family guy—and came up with
> the biggest hit of his career

"You know what I'm big on? Strange and unusual facts,"
Tom Waits says, flipping through the pages of a crumpled
notebook filled with bursts of serpentine scrawl that he has pulled
from his back pocket. Waits should be gabbing about *Mule
Variations,* his first album of new songs since 1993 and his debut,
after long spells with Elektra and Island Records, on the independent Epitaph label. Instead, the forty-nine-year-old singer
and composer—dressed in ranch-hand denim, with brown dirt
encrusted on the left shoulder of his jacket—takes a moment to
decode his handwriting, then looks up with a lopsided grin.

"Did you know there are more insects in one square mile
of rural earth than there are human beings on the whole
planet?" Waits asks in the warm, lumpy growl that, with a few
extra notes, doubles as his singing voice. "Most dangerous

job? Sanitation worker. There are thirty-five million digestive glands in the human stomach." Waits turns to the blackboard menu in Washoe House, a nineteenth-century roadhouse that is a short drive from Waits's home in the verdant California farmland north of San Francisco. "What did you order—the club sandwich? You're gonna need all those glands."

When he finally starts talking about the fantastical blues and spectral ballads on *Mule Variations*—about his songwriting and the autobiography embedded in his stories—Waits still sounds like he's reading weird-science entries from his notebook. Take, for example, "Chocolate Jesus," a hobo-string-band stomp about religious icons that literally melt in your mouth.

"My father-in-law has, over the years, tried to get me interested in certain business propositions," he says. "One of them was Testamints: These lozenges, they got a little cross on 'em and a Bible saying stamped on the back. Unable to worship? Have a Testamint," Waits says, his face so deadpan you're tempted to ask for a stock prospectus. "So Kathleen and I"—referring to his wife, co-songwriter and coproducer, Kathleen Brennan—"just took it out: 'What is he trying to get us involved in? What's next? A chocolate Jesus?' "

The riotous field holler "Filipino Box Spring Hog" is, Waits claims, based on the queer cuisine and mad guests ("Rattlesnake piccata with grapes and figs / Old brown Betty with a yellow wig") at rent parties he used to attend. And the vacant piece of real estate in "House Where Nobody Lives"— a country-soul weeper about how love, not decor, makes a home—was inspired by a place not far from Washoe House.

"It had busted windows, weeds, junk mail on the porch," Waits says. "It seems like everywhere I've ever lived there was always a house like that. And what happens at Christmas? Everybody else puts their lights up. Then it looks even more like a bad tooth on the smile of the street.

"This place in particular," he goes on, "everybody on the block felt so bad, they all put some Christmas lights on the house, even though nobody lived there."

Waits stops for a gulp of his split-pea soup. "I'm just like everybody else," he admits. "I'm nosy. If I know three things about my neighbor, I take those, and that's enough for me to go on." And what he doesn't know doesn't stop him: "Everybody mixes truth and fiction. If you're stuck for a place for a story to go, you make up the part you need."

Waits wags his notebook in the air as if to suggest that his most outrageous *Mule* inventions—"Eyeball Kid," a guy who is all cornea and smarm; the mystery recluse in the creepy spoken-word piece "What's He Building?" ("He has no dog, and he has no friends, and his lawn is dying. . . . And what about all those packages he sends?")—are only as twisted as life itself. Songwriting, he says, "is not a deposition."

Waits is standing in a record store down the road a piece from Washoe House holding a Japanese import CD by Rage Against the Machine that he's just bought for his thirteen-year-old son, Casey. "He'll think I'm really cool for getting him this," Waits says proudly.

He looks at the store racks packed with CDs. "It's gotta be hard for someone starting out now," Waits remarks, a bit sadly. "All the business you have to go through, making the videos, all this competition." He waves a hand at the mass of music in front of him. "I thought it was bad when I started out."

That was in 1973, the year Waits issued his debut album, *Closing Time*—a collection of hard-luck and bruised-love songs, soaked in Johnny Walker Red and Johnny Mercer chord changes, released in the thick of glitter rock and arena boogie. "I'm on the wrong end of the wheelbarrow every time," Waits notes with a gritty laugh.

Waits has spent much of the nineties disengaging himself

from the grind of what he drolly calls "this business we call show." His last major tour was more than ten years ago, documented on the 1988 live record *Big Time*. You can count the albums he's issued since then on one hand: 1992's *Bone Machine* and the soundtrack to the Jim Jarmusch film *Night on Earth;* Waits's score for *The Black Rider,* his 1993 theatrical collaboration with Robert Wilson and the late William S. Burroughs; the anthology *Beautiful Maladies: The Island Years.*

"I see what you mean," Waits concedes. "It's like looking for your waitress. People get like that with artists. We are a product-oriented society. We want it now, and we want an abundance of it in reserve.

"But there are limits to what you can do. One is not a tree that constantly blooms in the spring; the fruit falls and you put it in a basket."

As an Epitaph artist, Waits is no further from the mainstream than he was as a major-label act. Of the fifteen records he made for Elektra and Island, only *Small Change* (1976) and *Heartattack and Vine* (1980) cracked the Top 100. Waits's deal with Epitaph, the indie-punk imprint founded by ex-Bad Religion guitarist Brett Gurewitz, only covers *Mule Variations.* But Waits says he already plans to re-sign: "They're easier to be around than folks from DuPont. Not to generalize about large record companies, but if you're not going platinum, you're not going anywhere."

Ironically, *Mule Variations*—which debuted at number thirty on the Billboard 200—is Waits's most commercially accessible record in years. It is actually three records in one, a vibrant survey of a restless talent often compartmentalized on concept albums, "Big in Japan," "Get Behind the Mule," and "Chocolate Jesus" are all cut from the Brecht-does-Leadbelly crust of Waits's mid-eighties classics, *Swordfishtrombones* and *Rain Dogs.* The deathbed dada of *Bone Machine* is cranked up to comic effect in the guitar-and-toolbox clatter of "Eyeball Kid" and "Filipino Box Spring Hog."

And in "Hold On" and "House Where Nobody Lives," Waits returns to the Gin Pan Alley romanticism of *Closing Time, Small Change,* and his cult breakthrough LP, 1974's *The Heart of Saturday Night.* "I wasn't very adventurous," Waits says, explaining why he ditched the genteel-beatnik act in the eighties. "Most people, when they start out, are much more adventurous. As they get older, they get more complacent. I started out complacent and got more adventurous."

But Waits's early, barroom-piano diamonds—"Ol' 55," "(Looking for) The Heart of Saturday Night," "Drunk on the Moon"—were the product of sincere research. Born December 7, 1949, in Pomona, California, the son of a Spanish-language teacher, Waits has, since adolescence, been fascinated with the surreal properties of real life. "When I was fourteen," he says, "I worked in an Italian restaurant in a sailor town. Across the street was a Chinese place, and we'd trade food. I'd take a pizza to Wong's, they'd give me Chinese food to bring back. Sometimes Wong would tell me to sit in the kitchen, where he's making all this food up. It was the strangest galley: the sounds, the steam, he's screaming at his coworkers. I felt like I'd been shanghaied. I used to love going there."

Later, when he started touring, Waits made a point of avoiding standard rock-star hotels. "I'd get into a cab at the train station," he says, "and pick an American president. I'd tell the driver, 'Take me to the Cleveland.' Invariably, there would be a Cleveland.

"I would wind up in these very strange places—these rooms with stains on the wallpaper, foggy voices down the hall, sharing a bathroom with a guy with a hernia. I'd watch TV with old men in the lobby. I knew there was music in those places—and stories. That's what I was looking for."

By the end of the seventies, Waits had burned out on the stew-bum-bard routine. "I felt like one of those guys playing the organs in a hotel lobby," he says, making the *boom-chicka-chicka* sound of a cheesy rhythm machine for emphasis. "I'd bring the music in like carpet, and I'd walk on it. My wife, she's the one who pushed me. Finding a new way of thinking—that came from her."

Waits and Brennan met in 1980. He was in a small office at Francis Ford Coppola's Zoetrope studios, working on the score for *One from the Heart.* She was a script editor at Zoetrope. He was listening to Captain Beefheart, Howlin' Wolf, and Ethiopian music. She encouraged him to take more risks in his writing—to, Waits says, "distort the world." After they were married, Waits made *Swordfishtrombones.* "It was interesting," he says. "My life was getting more settled. I was staying out of the bars. But my work was becoming more scary."

Brennan declined to be interviewed for this story. Waits, too, is privacy-conscious; he is politely sketchy about his personal life, the location of his home and the couple's three children, Casey, Kellesimone, and Sullivan. But he talks about how he and Brennan work together—with a rented piano in a local hotel room—and describes cowriting as "a sack race. You learn to move forward together." Example: Brennan had some lines—"I got the style / But not the grace / I got the clothes / But not the face." Waits had an old tape he'd made of himself beating a jungle-telegraph rhythm on a chest of drawers. The result: "Big in Japan."

"Fish in the Jailhouse," written for but not included on *Mule Variations,* came from a dream Brennan had one night: that she was in prison and an inmate was singing about how he could open any jail door with a fish bone. "It kind of became a swing tune, with a big backbeat," Waits explains, then belts out a verse in his gale-force howl: "Peoria Johnson told Doug Low Joe / 'I can break out of any old jail, you know / The bars are iron, the walls are stone / And all I need me is an old fish bone' / Servin' fish in the jailhouse tonight.

"I went through a period where I was embarrassed by vulnerability as a writer—things you see, experience, and feel, and you go, 'I can't sing something like that. This is too tender.' Maybe I'm finding a way of reconciling that," he says of *Mule Variations*. "I'm married, I got kids. It opens up your world. But I still go back and forth—between deeply sentimental, then very mad and decapitated." Waits grins. "I live with a bipolar disorder."

If you can't understand why Waits has stayed off the road for the last eleven years, only giving sporadic concerts and appearing at benefit shows, consider this list: Redd Foxx, Blue Oyster Cult, Richard Pryor, Big Mama Thornton, Bette Midler, Fishbone, Link Wray, the Persuasions, Frank Zappa, and Howdy Doody. Those are just a few of the acts Waits opened for in his character-building travels in the mid-seventies.

"Zappa—that was my first experience of rodeos and hockey arenas," he says, shaking his head. "The constant foot stomping and hand clapping: 'We! Want! Frank!' It was like *Frankenstein*, with the torches, the whole thing."

The gig with fifties TV star Buffalo Bob and his marionette, Howdy Doody, was a double whammy: at 10 a.m., in front of housewives and kids. "I wanted to kill my agent. And no jury would have convicted me," Waits says, only half-kidding. "Bob and I didn't get along. He called me Tommy. And I distinctly remember candy coming out of the piano as I played.

"Jesus," he sighs. "That's when you need the old expression, 'You gotta love the business.'"

Waits feels no great need to "love the business" anymore. He will give a few concerts to promote *Mule Variations;* he taped an edition of VH1's *Storytellers*. But Waits will not tour.

"Every night, you sing the songs," he muses. "How do you do that without feeling you're hitting them real hard with a hammer, until they're flat?"

He is quite happy with the shadowy, personalized space he inhabits in popular music, way off Celebrity Highway. Waits's work is critically respected; his songs have been covered by Rod Stewart, Bruce Springsteen, and the Ramones, among others. He participates in outside projects of exquisite taste and eccentricity: a tribute album to the late Moby Grape singer and guitarist Skip Spence; the recent experimental-music collection *Orbitones, Spoon Harps & Bellowphones,* to which Waits contributed "Babbachichuija," a composition for squeaky doors, a 1982 Singer sewing machine, and a washer set on spin cycle. "I'm the kind of bandleader," says Waits, a keen student and collector of bizarre instruments, "who when he says, 'Don't forget to bring the Fender,' I mean the fender from the Dodge."

Waits also has a burgeoning second career, as a character actor, playing the same kind of colorful nuts and drifters who pass through his songs. He recently finished work on *Mystery Men,* a comedy starring William H. Macy, Ben Stiller, and Geoffrey Rush, in which he portrays a weapons designer for a gang of hapless superheroes. "I make something called a Blamethrower," Waits explains. "You aim it at people and they start blaming each other. 'It's your fault!' 'No, it's your fault!' It's a nutty movie.

"There's something to be said for longevity," Waits says of his career. "For some people, being in pop music is like running for office. They court the press in a very conscientious fashion. They kiss babies. No matter how black their vision is, their approach is the same.

"I'm more in charge of my own destiny," he insists. And the music, the stories, the weird shit he writes in his notebook for future reference—they're always there, waiting for him, no matter how long he goes between records. "The songs are coming all the time," he says. "Just because you didn't go fishing today doesn't mean there aren't any fish out there.

"So you don't want to fish for a couple of weeks, a couple of years?" Waits adds with a subterranean cackle. "The fish will get along fine without you."

HOLDING ON: A CONVERSATION
WITH TOM WAITS

Newsweek, April 23, 1999

Karen Schoemer

─────────────

We are at Jerry's, a greasy spoon in Monte Rio, California, with red-checkered tablecloths and Betty Boop decorations on the wall. At first we sit at a table, but Waits is more comfortable at the counter. He takes the seat closest to the pass-through window to the kitchen—"so I can keep an eye on the cook," he says. Waits brings journalists to places like Jerry's because his family (wife Kathleen and three kids) won't let him choose restaurants anymore. "Everybody wants nutrition," he bemoans. "No one wants atmosphere."

Tom Waits [looking at menu]: I'd say a place like this, the safest thing is breakfast.

Karen Schoemer: I brought you a present. I hope you like it. You might not, and if you don't it's okay, you can throw it away.

TW: [opens it] Oh no, it's beautiful. Wow.

KS: It's a cigar box.

TW: With Chinese lettering on it. Well, that's very nice of you. Well, there. It's a great box. It still smells like cigars.

KS: Does it? I didn't smell it.

TW: Oh yeah. Very distinctive. That's great. I appreciate it. I bet I could put cassettes in there. Or CDs. Or I could put record albums in there, but I'd have to fold them. Well thanks. I gave up smoking. But I remember it fondly.

KS: You did? All kinds of smoking? [blush] That was a little more loaded than I meant it to be.

TW: It was loaded. Sometimes I burn leaves in the yard and stand over them. "What are you doing, Tom!" "Oh, nothing!"

KS: I'm interested that you're on Epitaph.

TW: Well, it's just one of those things. I don't want to say anything bad about large record labels. But you try to find someplace that's somehow suited for where you are right now.

KS: Were you done with Island when you went to Epitaph?

TW: I was, yeah. I left my contract, my last record for them was *The Black Rider*. The big fish ate the little fish, which happens invariably. But Epitaph, they're forward-thinking people. They're definitely not old school—old school being "Ten for me and one for you, ten for me and one for you." They kind of describe themselves as more like a service organization. "If you don't want to tour, fine, we can work with that." They don't give you a list of things they expect from you. In fact, they have a group on the label that was hell-bent on getting its record off the radio, for God's sake. I mean, most people spend their life trying to get on the radio. This group was getting airplay, and they were pissed! And they sued! And the record company was 100 percent behind them. "We'll get you off the radio!" They brought in the big guns and they went down to the station and said, "Listen, we hear you're playing this group and we want them off of there!" So I thought that was pretty good. I thought that showed a kind of madness and flexibility.

KS: Did they come after you?

TW: They did. And the fact that they're musicians, that helps too. You go to the company office [in Los Angeles], there's a big engine, a car engine in the lobby, right at the desk.

KS: Right, and I think that building used to be a taxidermy shop.

TW: It was, and before that it was Red Car [the L.A. trolley service]. I used to go by that building all the time. I used to live in that neighborhood. And I remember when it was a taxidermist. And there was an enormous stuffed bear and a couple of decomposing reindeer that for years I used to remark on as I went by. The fact that it's now Epitaph is real Los Angeles, for it to be one thing for a while and then be something else. So yeah, it's a good feeling.

KS: I have this image of the corporate Christmas party and you socializing with all the punk rock bands. Have you done any interaction with the other bands?

TW: A little bit, a little bit. I haven't met everybody on the label. There are a lot of groups on the label. I'm sure over time we'll, you know, [obnoxious voice] "see ya at the softball game." I don't know how it works. But it's a good feeling. They like the record a lot. They like blues. They've got a room with a piano over there. They seem to really genuinely, sincerely love music. I can't say that's true everywhere you go. There are a lot of companies that might be better suited for selling appliances.

KS: There's a lot of appliance-type salesmanship in the music industry right now.

TW: Lenny Bruce said you'll never go broke underestimating the taste of the American public. People have built fortunes on it! But we had the Monkees. There's always something. Teenybopper music. It comes and it goes. It's like decals. It's like ice cream. "We had ice cream, and it's gone." "We had a balloon, and it popped." So what. You'll get another one. We seemed to be geared toward that—so you drop it into the water, and everyone's drinking it, and you get real silly, and then it wears off, and then you wake up and move on. It seems like that's part of the rhythm and cycle of American merchandising and promotion. You just have to know what's right for you and what's not. Other people are lining up to watch a guy in a leotard and a blond wig blow into a piece of wood. It comes and it goes, right?

KS: I know you didn't really go away but I kind of had that feeling.

TW: My standard answer? Where was I? Traffic school. I had all these tickets and I had to go back to traffic school.

KS: Were you working? I mean, between *The Black Rider* and now, you must have been working on things—

TW: Well—um—I dug a big hole in the yard. I don't know. I'm going to go look for that annoying answer. The news around here is pretty remarkable, the newspapers. —Could I have a refill on that coffee?—A couple of days ago a man choked to death on a pocket Bible. It was a 287-page Bible. He felt like he was full of the devil and he wanted to get that Bible down in there. And he choked to death. What folks are up to. Thank God there's a newspaper, or we wouldn't know what any of us are up to! [flipping pages] They arrested a man for having twenty-one pigeons stuffed into his pants. He was wearing these loose-fitting pants, and he went down to the park and he put a pigeon in his pants and just liked the way it felt. He said, "I'm not hurting anybody." All the animal rights groups got on him and they nailed him! A man in Occidental fainted while robbing a bank with a toy pistol. He'd locked his keys in the car. He wouldn't have been able to get out anyway. And he had this little squirt gun, and he was delirious at the counter.

KS: Did you read all this in the newspaper?

TW: In the local paper here. I'm not kidding you. Anyway. So what was the question, now? Where have I been? Reading the paper.

KS: When you're writing with Kathleen, do you write together or separately?

TW: Sometimes we write separately and bring it together. It's different every time. You know, "You wash, I'll dry." You find a way to work. "You wring its neck, I'll take all the feathers off him." "You boil the water, I'll build the fire." You find a way. Sometimes you got a line, nothing more than a line and you don't know where to go with it. It might have been something thrown away and Kathleen says, "Oh, no, hang onto that, we can make something out of that." She'll say, "I can cook that up." Writing together's been really good.

KS: Does she like being the silent partner?

TW: She doesn't like the limelight. But she sincerely has an incandescent contribution. We've been working together since *Swordfishtrombones*. We go back that far. We got married in '80, we've been married eighteen years.

KS: How old are your kids?

TW: I've got two teenagers. Help. My daughter's fifteen and a half, and I have a boy thirteen and a boy five. So we've been together since '80. We were married in an all-night wedding chapel in Watts.

KS: Did you know her for a long time before you got married?

TW: I knew her a week.

KS: Really?

TW: A week. Ha ha ha! Oh, I did not. I knew her a month. Four weeks.

KS: Really?

TW: Two months. Then we got married. [raspy laugh] It's true, two months. But I like one week better. You just met, and then—bang!

KS: Whose idea was it to get married?

TW: My idea. Kathleen was really the one that encouraged me to start producing my own records. At that point I had done all my records with a producer. I kind of got stuck. I needed something to kick me. I needed some kind of car wreck or something. She was the one that started playing bizarre music. She said, "You can take this and this and put all this together. There's a place where all these things overlap. Field recordings and Caruso and tribal music and Lithuanian language records and Leadbelly. You can put that in a pot. No one's going to tell you you can't. You like James Brown and you also like Mabel Mercer. There's nothing wrong with that." We're all that way. We all have disparate influences. And we all know people that don't know each other! Right? I mean, some people are afraid to have parties and invite them all.

KS: I am.

TW: You know what I mean? It's like bringing a rabid dog to a birthday party. We all try to reconcile those things in music. We all have facets of ourselves.

KS: I'm so amazed that there's this loud, chaotic stuff, but then in the middle there's these perfect pop songs. Like "Hold On." I guess what I'm trying to say is that it's amazing that you have the capacity to do this rough stuff, and then you can do these songs that are big and universal and pretty to hear on the radio.

TW: Well, I got it all in me. I love melody. I also like dissonance and factory noise. But melody's a big part of my life. It's just a matter of trying to find a way to fit all those things together, so you put them on a record together. They're facets of you.

KS: "Hold On" reminds me of "Downtown Train." It could be a big hit for Rod Stewart.

TW: "Hold on"—I thought that was a good thing to say in a song. Hold on. We're all holding onto something. None of us want to come out of the ground. Weeds are holding on. Everything's holding on. I thought that was a real positive thing to say. It was an optimistic song. Take my hand, stand right here, hold on. We wrote that together, Kathleen and I, and that felt good. Two people who are in love writing a song like that about being in love. That was good.

KS: Using music to sell something [bothers you, doesn't it]? I guess I'm thinking about the Fritos thing, when you sued over their use of a voice like yours in an ad.

TW: Well, that was more a case of voice impersonation. Intellectual property, being in that we took the position that that was my voice that they lifted and ran off with it. We won.

KS: I know, you got a lot of money.

TW: Two and a half million bucks. Spent it all on candy. My mom told me I was foolish. I've always been foolish when it comes to money . . . You asked me about fame, and I wrote a poem about it. 'Cause I really didn't know how I felt about it, and then I realized how I felt about it. Here's how it goes:

> *I want a sink and a drain*
> *And a faucet for my fame.*

It's a haiku about fame. That's all it is. I could expand on that, but right now that's all I've got. I think that's what everybody wants. Anyway, that's all. Those are my thoughts on fame.

KS: Thank you. I like that.

TW: Well, when you haven't recorded in a while people want to know what you've been doing. They want a very specific answer. Like, why were you late for school? The teacher wants a real answer. If you're going to make a note, get it signed. The dog ate my homework. And the dog had to be operated on, we had to get the homework and dry it, and the dog is recuperating.

KS: Did you just kind of wait till you had something to say?

TW: Yeah. You know, songs are out there all the time. Some of them only live two weeks. They're like houseflies. So if you don't get them, that's it. I got all these old songs. So it's good to have new songs to sing. And the new ones, you send them out there and you say, "Go my beauties, go! Bring Dad home some money! Come back with money!" Ahhh, that's not really how I feel about it.

KS: What was Whittier like [when you were growing up]?

TW: Lot of orange groves. A lot of vacant lots. Open space, vacant lots.

KS: What was your house like?

TW: My dad built the house. He used to stop at a vacant lot and he'd take a shovel out and dig up a tree or a plant and bring it home and plant it in our yard. We had errant, illegal foliage at our house. I was a tree guy. I was always into trees, growing up. If your cat was trapped in a tree, you'd go get Tom. Tom would get in the tree and get the cat out.

KS: Really!

TW: [shifty] Yeah. It was just a way of showing off for me. And I ate spinach so I could get stronger, so I could beat up the bullies. Ate a whole can of spinach once and got in a big fight. I was really surprised that spinach wouldn't actually pop out of the can. I was really embarrassed that I had to open it with a can opener.

KS: You brought it with you to the fight?

TW: No, I kind of hid the can opener and opened it very slowly, and then when the top was off I threw it in my mouth. I had this big wad of spinach flying toward my mouth. And then I crushed the can together. I was concerned with image from a very young age.

KS: Do you like spinach now?

TW: You know, that's a good question. I only use it in times of need. When I'm low, feeling kind of down. I'll buy a can of spinach. I got one out in the car. It's like a little first-aid kit. What is the significance of all that, I don't know.

WAITS: GUTHRIE'S HEIR?

The Nation, May 24, 1999

Gene Santoro

Tom Waits is an imaginary hobo. He cruises the oddball corners of American pop culture, collecting the deft and moving and loopy short takes he sees and imagines there. Back in 1973 *Closing Time* first caught Waits's grizzled voice on disc, growling about unguarded moments in real lives. Unlike that era's Me Generation singer-songwriter crop, Waits made you feel other people, because he did. He was ironic or direct, caustic or unabashedly torn open by loss and hope and love and fear—the pivotal emotions that daily face folks who don't live inside recording and movie and TV studios, ivory towers, newspaper and magazine offices, the Beltway or their own swollen heads.

When Tom Waits's death-and-sound-obsessed 1992 disc *Bone Machine* won him his first Grammy, *Rolling Stone,* by way of yuppified praise, summarized his output to date this way: "For more than twenty years, Tom Waits has chronicled the grotesque losers of the seedy underworld." More revealing and to the point, Bruce Springsteen covered Waits's "Jersey Girl"—one master chronicler's homage to another.

Waits's long career falls into two congruent pieces. For his first ten years and eight recordings, the SoCal boho (remember Rickie Lee Jones?) collected noirish pictures for his outsider's album of Americana. Meanwhile, he started acting in 1978, with a small part in Sylvester Stallone's *Paradise Alley*. He's notched four Coppola flicks, Robert Altman's *Short Cuts,* plus a half-dozen others since, but his most telling performance was in Jim Jarmusch's *Down by Law* (1986). That offbeat prison-break movie teamed him with a downtown-music leader named John Lurie and a then-little-known Italian comic named Roberto Benigni.

What led Waits to outsider auteurs like Jarmusch and Robert Wilson (Waits's last album was 1993's *The Black Rider,* his music for the folktale-based opera Wilson directed) was a switch thrown by his eccentric muse. With *Swordfishtrombones* (1983), Waits hopped a creative freight train into the New York music scene—sound-scramblers like Lurie and John Zorn and Laurie Anderson and Run-D.M.C., all with their own ideas about recombining and recycling ideas. *Swordfishtrombones* ditched hi-fi recording and noir song-writing for impressionistic soundscapes dreamed in rude facilities—bathroom echo chambers, a concrete-and-wood bunker-studio on a chicken farm, a Mexican hotel room where he battered a dresser to pieces while screaming into a cheap cassette recorder. Waits amassed an eighteen-wheeler's worth of weird instruments—calliopes, Balinese metal aunglongs, glass harmonicas, bowed saw, pump organ, accordion, Mellotron, bass boo-bams, brake drums, parade drums, even one he built called a conundrum. No big surprise that Waits wrote the foreword for *Gravikords, Whirlies, and Pyrophones* (Ellipsis Arts), an interesting book-plus-CD pack about strange soundmakers.

Hanging out with all those grotesques over the decades has

helped Waits grow into an American original, a wonderfully gifted miniaturist with a romantic's touch and bruised ironies, like Sherwood Anderson.

Mule Variations (Epitaph) is Waits's first album since 1993, but it's unmistakably the sound of him opening up his outsider scrapbook again. A sharp pal who's a fan heard the advance CD and said to me, "Good, huh?" He paused, a shade defensive. "A lot like the last two." Another beat. "But that's who he is." Exactly.

It's hard not to be yourself when you're as much who you are as Waits is. With cowriter/producer and wife Kathleen Brennan, he covers so much stylistic and dramatic ground, you could call him a musical avant-archivist. *Mule Variations* naturally catalogs a lot of American music. There's gospel ("Come on Up to the House"), parlor songs and Civil War ballads ("Take It with Me," "Pony," "Georgia Lee"), jazz noir ("Black Market Baby"), Stax-Volt soul ("House Where Nobody Lives"), jungle-funk ("Big in Japan"), gently buoyant Tex-Mex ("Hold On"). There's even electroblues surrealism straight out of Captain Beefheart ("Eyeball Kid," "Filipino Box Spring Hog"). And in "Chocolate Jesus" (whose chorus runs: "When the weather gets rough / and it's whiskey in the shade / it's best to wrap your savior / up in cellophane / He flows like the big muddy / but that's ok / Pour him over ice cream / for a nice parfait") there's more than a hint of Weill and Brecht.

An old-blues hound, Waits now makes his own. "Lowside of the Road" rides a lo-fi sonic rumble made by instruments with names like Optigan and Chumbus and Dousengoni. The booze-soaked raunch called "Cold Water" stumbles along like an imaginary hobo who's hooked down some LSD with his hooch; Marc Ribot's bitingly thick-tongued guitar is hilarious. "Get Behind the Mule" uses delta-blues doggedness, a saying attributed to Robert Johnson's father and Chicago blues veteran Charlie Musselwhite's lurking harmonica to set jabbing vignettes of murder and fear that finish with a simple moral: "Pin your ear to the wisdom post / Pin your eye to the line / Never let the weeds get higher / than the garden / Always keep a sapphire in your mind / Always keep a diamond in your mind."

Our imaginary hobo ain't churchgoing, but he believes that how you live matters. "This world is not my home / I'm just passin' thru," Waits bellows in "Come on Up to the House," a few lines after wisecracking, "Come down off the cross / We can use the wood." That's characteristic. He holds nothing sacred, but like most of the people he meets, he has a code of ethics. And so the lyrics put old queries in moving ways and aren't embarrassed about exploring how most folks understand their lives: "If there's love in a house / It's a palace for sure / Without love . . . / It ain't nothin but a house / A house where nobody lives"; "You been whipped by the forces that are inside you"; or "sometimes there's nothin left to do / You gotta hold on, hold on, take my hand, I'm standing right here, you gotta hold on." Of course, the tunes also regularly turn maxims inside out. "Take It with Me" undercuts the cliché with a list of impressions and memories and the love of another, the things that survive. "Black Market Baby" is about ". . . a diamond that / Wants to stay coal." But Waits never lets hipster cool mask genuine heartbreak. Take the story of "Georgia Lee," in which the chorus returns over and over to the unadorned, chilling question, "Why wasn't God watching?"

Waits has a smashed foghorn of a voice, somewhere between Beefheart's and Howlin' Wolf's, and he uses it to ruminate and yelp and scream and croon and plead and threaten. It can be a blunt, heavy instrument, but he wields it with incongruous dexterity—even, at times, lightness. The ways he can ask "Why wasn't God watching?" make your pulse heat up. His clashing vocal overtones can surround a note the way a clot forms around a gash.

You can't make a hobo, even an imaginary one, flinch easily, and Waits's scrapbook is full of things we'd mostly rather sidle past or turn our backs on.

As in "What's He Building?": Musique-concrete clanging, hissing and feedback set spoken lyrics that start like this: "What's he building in there? / What the hell is he building / In there? / He has subscriptions to those / Magazines . . . He never / waves when he goes by / He's hiding something from / the rest of us . . . He's all / to himself . . . I think I know / why . . ." It ends starkly, "We have a right to know . . ."

With all these snapshots rolled into his knapsack, Waits is an American *bricoleur*. Before you grab a brick to heave at me, let's say that just means he's one of our very own cranks from a very long line, the yowling and yawping sort of romantic barbarian seer who gets tossed into the tank by bored cops and takes in the turned backs and locked doors as he passes through town, sympathizes with the pregnant women and Vietnam vets begging on the freeways, steps into the cool and still graveyard for a nap, and then hunkers down with an old stray dog in front of the furniture-store window to catch a little TV. In fact, you probably don't want a guy like him hanging out in your neighborhood, even if he is named Walt Whitman or Harry Partch or Kenneth Burke, Woody Guthrie or Charlie Mingus or Allen Ginsberg. You're thinking 911 if he's named Howlin' Wolf or Lenny Bruce or Captain Beefheart or Richard Pryor. Why put up with Tom Waits?

Here's one reason: He can show you what you already know and make you believe it again.

THE POOR SOLDIER GETS THOSE PROLETARIAN LOVESICK BLUES

Independent, November 19, 2000

Robert Wilson and Peter Laugesen

The singer Tom Waits and Robert Wilson, the renowned director, are collaborating on a production of Buchner's classic drama *Woyzeck.* Where? Denmark. Why? Over to them . . .

ROBERT WILSON: To me, one of the attractions of *Woyzeck* is that it's not dated. I mean, who would ever think that this was a play from the nineteenth century? It's much more contemporary than most modern plays. All of the contemporary playwrights I can think of are nowhere near as modern as this. Five hundred years from now this'll still be interesting because there's no shit, there's no garbage. And at the same time it's about the mysteries of life. He must have been a genius of his age to construct these few works that he did.

TOM WAITS: It deals with madness and children, obsession and murder—all the things that we care about, as much now as we did then. It's wild, sexy, and curious: it catches your imagination. And it makes you reflect on your own life.

The first thing that you realize—and it's widely talked about—is that it's a proletariat story: a story about a poor soldier who is manipulated by the government, has no money, is used to experiment on and slowly becomes mad. I guess if they had antidepressants in those days they could have straightened him right out . . .

I first met Bob in New York in 1983. My wife and I had written a play called *Frank's Wild Years*. We asked Bob if he would direct the play, and one thing led to another. We didn't actually do that project, but we went on ultimately to do two other projects together.

RW: I think my responsibility is to provide a space where I can hear Tom's music. Can I make a picture, a colour, or setting where we can listen to this music? Often, when I go to the theatre, I find it very difficult to listen: the stage is too busy or things are moving around too much and I lose my concentration. If I really want to concentrate deep, I have to close my eyes to hear. I try to make a space where we can really hear something: what we see is important because it helps us to hear.

The thing that's great about Tom is that he of course writes songs for himself, but he's able to write music and other people can sing it. I think that was a great test for Tom: that he came in as a composer and could find a voice for other people whose voices are very different to his. In that sense he's a real composer.

TW: Yeah, it's a challenge. I was wondering if I was going to be up to it. Sometimes I was real cold, but it's ultimately very satisfying. It's hard sometimes when somebody else is doing your song. What I like about Bob is that if he's telling somebody how to move on stage he'll come on up and he'll show them how to move: he'll do this most spontaneous and mystical physical movement. Then he'll ask them to try the same movements. They're never completely the same, but they break eggs for the cast each time he does that. And sometimes you can do that with the songs as well—you can sing it for them.

Technique is not important—emotional telegraphing and truth are what is important. As to how many notes you can hear, or how fast you can get there, it doesn't really matter. That's what everybody wants to do when they come to the theatre—they want to connect.

RW: Theatre is something plastic: make this quicker or make this slower or deeper. You can tell if the actors are thinking too much, if they're forcing an idea. Often you feel like it's blocked in the head: you have to open up, receive, let it come to you.

TW: I told someone the other day that the song doesn't begin at the beginning of the song. You don't want to feel the sense of stopping and then planting your feet, looking up to the balcony, throwing your head back and starting a song. You really do want to create a condition of music that starts at the beginning of the play, or in the lobby.

It's hard to describe how you do what you do. I collaborate on the music with my wife, Kathleen Brennan. I guess starting really is the hard part. I didn't know the story and had to find out all about it. In some ways it's like writing music for a murder mystery and a children's story at the same time. You don't really start at the beginning: you start somewhere in the middle and split off, and half of you goes down this way back to the beginning and the other half of you goes off toward the end.

Sometimes we start with titles: the title itself stimulates ideas. And a lot of times we come here to the theatre. We're sitting out in the dark and Bob's doing something on stage . . . an idea for a song will come if you're in the right condition for it. And with Bob you always have to be ready to improvise, which is a really great muscle to develop, something that a lot of people stop doing when they grow up. The good part about working here is that you stay in shape using your imagination all the time. Bob will say, "Give me something here, we need some music right now."

RW: We don't talk a lot about it beforehand. Often I find if I talk too much about a piece beforehand I go to rehearsal and I am trying to make what I've been talking about instead of letting the piece talk to me. Martha Graham said that for her all theatre was dance and in some ways I feel the same way: we're always dancing, it's always movement. So I usually start with the body first, with movement, and later let the other things come.

TW: You have to have kind of an innocent bravery trying to get started looking for songs. Kathleen said, "Well it's a circus story really. It starts with the Ferris wheel and this gal Marie is a Coney Island baby." And so we started there. She had this beautiful melody on the piano—it was like the way a kid would play the piano—and I hung on to it, put it on a tape recorder and carried it around. And now it's the opening melody in the story. It's the first thing you hear—what sounds like a child's piano lesson—and it really works. Sometimes you scratch and scratch and you can't find any seeds and a moment later there isn't enough pots and pans to catch it in. The beauty of that is that it could be a very ordinary thing that you get an idea from. Something falls, a pigeon flies in or you hear a siren. The other night when we were playing in here, a siren went by the theatre and I thought for a moment it must be part of the sound department. But of course it was just something that happened. That type of thing happens all the time and that's what I love about doing this—that there is a place where life overlaps . . .

RW: *Woyzeck* is also a very strange love story. I haven't figured out how to do it and don't know how successful we'll be. There's Marie and Woyzeck standing there, both looking straight ahead. They are somehow separate and together.

TW: No more writing songs for other singers. My voice is going to be the voice of the monkey at this point.

RW: I've got a little monkey in this play—and that's Tom.

IN THE WORDS OF WAITS

Weekend Australian, March 27, 2004

Steve Packer

On August 1, 1977, Tom Waits appeared, very much as himself, on the American satirical talk show *Fernwood2Night,* set in a fictional town in Ohio.

The story was that Waits, already a cult figure for albums including *Closing Time* and *The Heart of Saturday Night,* had been driving by when his car had broken down, stranding him. He had little money—he sponged twenty dollars on the show—and only the thrift-shop suit he was sitting down in.

He faced hosts, role-playing comedians Martin Mull and Jerry Hubard, with a trademark Kent burning in his lips and pulled a bottle of booze out from under his jacket. The hosts regarded him as some kind of lowlife curiosity.

Hubard: Tom, where do you hail from professionally? Is it the Big Apple, as they call New York, or is it Hollywood?

Waits: I live at Bedlam and Squalor. It's thataway (pointing over his shoulder).

Mull: I think we all lived there at one time. It's kind of strange to have a guy sitting here with a bottle in front of him, ha, ha.

Waits: Well, I'd rather have a bottle in front of me than a frontal lobotomy.

The line got the night's biggest laugh and earned the show a footnote in television history. The "frontal lobotomy episode" had other memorable lines.

Waits: I was out last night. I went to the "Shoes and Socks" restaurant.

Mull: You mean the Cup and Sup?

Waits: A buck ninety-nine for all you can stand.

But "frontal lobotomy" entered the culture. It was soon being scrawled on walls and repeated by, and accredited to, other people. In Sphere's 1984 *Handbook of 20th Century Quotations,* it was "graffito quoted on BBC Radio 4" and expanded, nonsensically, to "I'd rather have a full bottle in front of me than a full-frontal lobotomy." William Gaddis slipped the line into his 1985 novel *Carpenter's Gothic* (now a Penguin Twentieth-Century Classic) and it is on lists of favourite quotations all over the Internet.

Although often accredited to "anon," its lineage seems secure enough to ensure the Waits name is attached when it inevitably appears in future editions of quotation dictionaries, with other great drinking quips such as "I always keep a supply of stimulant handy in case I see a snake—which I also keep handy" (W. C. Fields) and "You are not drunk if you can lie on the floor without holding on" (Dean Martin).

With dubious originality, Waits has also used the lobotomy-like line "Champagne for my real friends and real pain for my sham friends" and widely gets the credit for it.

But many other, certifiable Waits quotes stand a chance of making posterity's cut. In fact, he is sure to end up being one of the most quoted figures in rock music, out-worded perhaps only by Bob Dylan and Lennon/McCartney/Beatles. He may well be remembered less as a musician and songwriter than as a wit and raconteur whose life and art were a seamless, larger-than-life creation, in the fashion of those other demon quotemeisters Oscar Wilde and Noël Coward.

The comparison might seem flattering, but the evidence is stacking up. Like Wilde and Coward, Waits's lines flow from both his public conversation and a variety of creative output, and the division is blurring as it becomes irrelevant with time. "The piano has been drinking, not me" and "There ain't no devil, it's just God when he's drunk" will exceed their birthright as lyrics the way "mad dogs and Englishmen go out in the midday sun" and "mad about the boy" did for Coward.

Or consider Coward's "Certain women should be struck regularly like gongs," from the play *Private Lives,* against the opening of the Waits song/monologue *Frank's Wild Years* (which he expanded into avant-garde theatre): "Frank settled down in the Valley and hung his wild years on a nail that he drove through his wife's forehead." Which isn't to imply that Waits is simply a misogynist drunk. It's all part of his loser-sinner shtick, wrapped up in a character as elusive and flexible as Wilde's charming cynic or Coward's camp cad.

Inherent in the ruse is a roguishness that has allowed Waits, like his flamboyant predecessors, to constantly bend the truth, exaggerate, plagiarize, and obscure and reinvent his past. He has long claimed he was born in a yellow taxi, with numerous elaborations—"parked in a loading zone," "with the meter running," "I shouted 'Times Square, and step on it!' " He has also claimed he was born on the day legendary black American folk musician Leadbelly died, "and I like to think we passed in the hall." In fact, he was born the day after, but who's counting?

It can all be elevated to a literary level where Waits is the purveyor of a place at once as historical and mythical as the Wild West. In his realm a century later, he's as big as Clint Eastwood and John Wayne combined, and he never gets down off his horse. For three decades, the man born Thomas Alan Waits, on December 7, 1949, in Pomona, California, has been riding laden with Americana that isn't so much nostalgic as peopled by contemporary characters stuck in the past.

"Remember me? I ordered the blonde, the Firebird . . . somebody's made a terrible mistake!" was a line worked into interviews for a while. So was: "I stay in a place called 'Rooms.' There's a whole chain of them." That would be in a place like Putnam County where "if somebody gets shot on a Saturday night, the Sunday papers just say they died of natural causes." His idea of a good time—at least, before he got married and rich and moved to rural northern California to raise his three children—was "a Tuesday evening at the Manhattan Club in Tijuana." (In a 1992 interview Waits told of visiting Graceland in Memphis where his apparently chip-off-the-block son, aged eight or nine, suggested loudly in the souvenir shop that they dig up Elvis and make a necklace out of his teeth.)

In U.S. *Vogue*, Mick Brown wrote that Waits "trafficked in a particularly American kind of sadness, using his vignettes as platforms for wry and truthful observations about the cavity of desperation and disillusionment beneath the bravura of American life." In British magazine *Uncut*, Gavin Martin wrote of his "phantasmagorical American dreamscape" of bars, dime stores, carnivals, and B-movie scenarios. Francis Ford Coppola called him "the prince of melancholy." Critics have compared his work to writers including William Faulkner, Jack Kerouac, William Burroughs, and Raymond Carver.

Waits might scratch his goatee or wink. More his style is Coward's "Strange how potent cheap music is." He plays a Common Man for anyone who grew up expecting more out of life than it delivered, and might be willing to at least partly blame themself.

His movie roles (*Rumble Fish, The Cotton Club, Down by Law, Short Cuts*) play the same hand in spades. Asked if he was worried about becoming stereotyped, he said, "I'm not an actor. I don't care." Making movies was "like working up fifty pounds of dough to make one biscuit," although he has conceded that "the beauty of show business is that it's the only business you can still have a career in after you're dead."

His fascination for the underdog extends to the under-belly—the misfits, freaks and fringe-dwellers of society. Since *Swordfishtrombones* in 1983, he has been extending his sym-pathies to rampant eccentricity and genuine weirdness ("If you want to join the madness, you'll have to wait in line"). For a while there, he was clanking and bellowing from cav-erns of suburbia beyond the reach of even a camera-on-shoulder Michael Moore. The likes of the title track to *Frank's Wild Years* and the hilarious circle of paranoia in "What's He Building?" on the *Mule Variations* album come from deep in Unabomber territory, and the narrator's voice is not that of a visitor. " 'Cause there's nothing strange about an axe with bloodstains in the barn / There's always some killing you got to do around the farm," from 1992's *Bone Machine,* also cap-tures the tone.

The real wonder is that he has been able to transcend the void with a rich and philosophical romanticism. It was encap-sulated in early lyrics like "I lost my St. Christopher now that I kissed her" and "How can the angels get to sleep when the devil leaves the porch light on?" It was distilled to its skid-row essentials in a monologue from the 1993 album and theatre production *The Black Rider:* "Now when I was a boy, my daddy sat me on his knee and he told me many things / And he said, son, there's a lot of things in this world you're gonna have no use for / And when you get blue and you've lost all your dreams / There's nothing like a campfire and a can of beans."

Half the impact is in how he says it. Asked on radio how he achieved his unique vocal style, he replied: "I drink my own urine." English singer and comedian Vivian Stanshall said the shock of first hearing Waits was "like being handed a saveloy, blindfolded, at a gay party."

On *Late Night with David Letterman* a few years ago, the cantankerous host asked Waits: "Some of your critics wrote that your new album sounded like something that came out of the belly of a wounded sick animal. Is that what you intended?" Waits: "I'm surprised they caught it."

He has already won two Grammys (best alternative album for *Bone Machine* and best contemporary folk album for *Mule Variations*), but his nomination for best rock vocal performance of 2003 was an eyebrow-raiser. Just as oddball was the fact that it was for his version of the Ramones' "The Return of Jackie and Judy" on a tribute album. As it turned out, the award went to Dave Matthews.

A decade ago, Waits said: "To be honest, I've always been afraid that I was gonna spend years and years tapping the world on the shoulder, and then everybody was gonna turn around and I'd forget what it was I had to say." He needn't have worried. Not long after, a court was determining what the mere sound of his voice was worth after a corn chip company had someone copy it in radio commercials without his permission. Waits got $2.4 million.

But it's better that the last word go to Boston singer Eileen

Rose, from her song "Tom Waits Crooning": "Angel falls in the water, wets his wings / He can't fly for a while, it's one of those things / He spends the downtime singing."

No Tom Like the Present

Entertainment Weekly, June 21, 2002

Rob Brunner

Tom Waits serves up a double shot of his strange brew
with a pair of high-proof albums.

Three hours late for a scheduled interview, Tom Waits
finally rolls up at the wheel of a lime green '52 Chevy
pickup, a Chesterfield dangling from his lips, and a Mickey's
Big Mouth sloshing in his hand, a midget in a sombrero
perched atop a truck bed full of tangled antique implements
of indeterminate function. "Pleasure to make your acquain-
tance," he croaks.

Or that's what you'd expect if you've immersed yourself in
the carnivalesque demimonde depicted in most of Waits's
eighteen-plus albums (including the new, simultaneously
released *Alice* and *Blood Money*). In reality, Waits, fifty-two, is
perfectly punctual and navigating a cavernous but conventional Suburban. "Come on in," he says, steering toward the
China Light restaurant, a favorite haunt in downtown Santa
Rosa, California, not far from where he lives with his wife and
two of his three kids (the third is in college). "Do you like the
new Wu-Tang Clan album?"

It's soon clear that Waits is a guy who knows things. He knows how to find lodging in a strange town ("I'd ask a taxi driver if they have any hotels named after presidents. 'We have a Taft . . .' I'd say, 'Well, that's where I'm going, then. I'm going to the Taft' "). He knows which room in your hotel is haunted and that the night bellhop, Valentin, is a clairvoyant who used to work for Mario Lanza. He knows that if you turn the volume WAY up at the end of Buddy Holly and the Crickets' "I'm Gonna Love You Too," you'll hear . . . chirping crickets.

He also knows how to maintain his own mystique. Take Waits's murky description of his key musical collaborator, wife Kathleen Brennan, who, according to Waits, once worked as a Hollywood newscaster, a Cadillac dealership service manager, and a chauffeur; can fix motorcycles and fly airplanes; is "a leading authority on African violets"; and was, he claims, on the verge of becoming a nun when they met in the early eighties. "I don't actually have a family," he jokes (probably) at one point. "I'm like the guy in *A Beautiful Mind*. I talk about them, but they don't exist. I live alone, I eat here [at China Light]. I have a rooming house across the street."

But why get distracted by reality when Waits's albums are, in both senses of the word, so fantastic? *Alice* and *Blood Money*—the former a new recording of his music for a 1992 Robert Wilson opera about Lewis Carroll, the latter inspired by Wilson's adaptation of the famously odd play *Woyzeck*—are classic Waits, full of unfathomable sadness and infused with Weill, Armstrong, and Bukowski. "I like beautiful melodies telling you terrible things," he says, slurping wonton soup. "I don't know why. It's a curse. After a while it becomes a steady companion. It's not something you distinguish. Is it my thorny, dark, oozing side, or is it just the way I see the world?

"Most people in show business are mining the strangeness that's inside of them," he says. "I tried for a long time to be like everybody else. You know, there's only seven haircuts available at the barbershop and a certain limited supply of shoes. But at some point, if you do have things about you that are irreconcilable, you say to yourself, 'Maybe I can make some money out of this.' You join the circus. That's what music is. So that's what I did."

After lunch, Waits climbs into the Suburban, cranks up a dementedly lovely recording of William S. Burroughs choking out Marlene Dietrich's "Falling in Love Again," and heads back to his family. Or, perhaps, the rooming house, the Taft Hotel, or whatever unpredictable place the circus happens to have pitched its tent in this week.

THE MAN WHO HOWLED WOLF

Magnet, June–July 1999

Jonathan Valania

> *Note: The following two interviews ran five years apart*
> in Magnet—*the magazine sent the same writer to meet*
> *Waits in the same spot. One interview occurred a*
> *couple years before September 11, 2001, the other a*
> *few years after.*

The Astro is a broken-down, drunk motel located about an hour north of San Francisco in Santa Rosa, near the arid, wine-growing region of the Sonoma Valley. It's Tom Waits country—he lives somewhere around here, although exactly where remains a closely guarded secret. *Magnet* booked a room at the Astro because the price is right, but upon closer inspection, it's the ideal setting to await an audience with the man who elevates the down-and-out in song. The bard of boardinghouse madrigals. The man who reads the lines in people's faces like a palmist, uttering the stories behind the wheelchair smiles and motel miles that map the crazy countenances of the characters that haunt his songs.

Our room, as Waits puts it in the song "9th and Hennepin," is "filled with bitters and blue ruin." It's a stomped-out cigarette butt of a place. The ventilator is broken, and it's clear the oxygen has left this room years ago. There's mold on the ceiling and a hint of urine in the air. A brick holds up the short leg of the bed, which is dotted with cigarette burns and mysterious stains. The faucet won't stop dripping, and there's a pubic hair clinging to the rim of the bathtub like a garnish. The swimming pool is filled with dirt and weeds. There is, however, free HBO. The only other guest amenity is the comfort of knowing that the woman who checks you in also minds the cash register at the liquor store around back. It's ten A.M. and the residents are getting an early start, stocking up on their daily allotment of vodka, brandy, and cigarettes. A little girl stands out front mimicking the happy-hour wobble of a drunk ambling down the sunstroked street. "He bumped into a wall and now he's skipping," she says to nobody in particular. There are two kinds of guests at the Astro: those who are only staying for an hour and those who will never leave.

File our stay under "Accidental Tourism," a random touchstone to Waits's boozy, flophouse residency at the Tropicana Motel in the endless, doomed summer of Los Angeles in the seventies. It was a simpler time then. A piano served as furniture, and down the hall lived Waits's partner in grime, Chuck E. Weiss, "the kind of guy that would sell you a rat's ass for a wedding ring," joked Waits to an interviewer at the time. Weiss brought around Rickie Lee Jones, with whom Waits shared a brief creative and romantic dalliance. It was at the Tropicana that Waits forged the image that would stick with him through the years: a rumpled, bourbon-fed balladeer, holding up a drunk piano, eyes-closed, eighty-proof chords dancing the tarantella with his bullfrog croak of a voice, pirouetting in the halo of smoke and stubble ringing the low-slung, tweed dude cap.

Between regular tours opening for acts like Frank Zappa and the Rolling Stones, Waits would record the seven albums that would mark his early incarnation as a crushed romantic huffing the last remaining fumes of the Beat and jazz eras. On albums like *The Heart of Saturday Night, Small Change,* and *Nighthawks at the Diner,* Waits hung his weary, gonna-drink-the-lights-out persona on a dancing skeleton of upright bass and plaintive piano chords. It was a Tin Pan Alley full of hoboes and drifters, dancing girls and desperate characters, barroom wit and gutter poetry. Waits was the guy playing piano in the corner of the coffee shop in Edward Hopper's painting *Nighthawks.* Unfortunately, it's the corner that you can't see.

Waits checked out of the Tropicana life years ago, though the image still clings to him like the stink of the cigarettes he doesn't smoke anymore or the scent of the bourbon he no longer drinks. In 1980, Waits married Kathleen Brennan (then a script reader for Francis Ford Coppola's Zoetrope Studios), whom he met while working on the score to Coppola's *One from the Heart.* Brennan, who doesn't care to be interviewed or photographed, has been his collaborator and muse—not to mention the mother of their three children—ever since. "She saved my life," Waits says. It was Brennan who helped steer his musical direction into the deep left field of what has become known as the Island Years. Albums like *Swordfishtrombones, Rain Dogs,* and *Frank's Wild Years* play like a series of disembodied ham-radio broadcasts colored with otherworld instrumentation, clanking percussion and surreal street reportage. With all bare ruined choirs, Beef-heartian sea chanteys, and clubfoot klezmer orchestras wandering in and out, these records have that Barton Fink feeling in spades. The only element that remains from Waits's seventies singer-songwriter days is his voice. A voice that sounds like he was born old, born smoking.

An outsider amidst the facile pomp of eighties pop, Waits stuck to the margins, striking up vital creative friendships with people like filmmaker Jim Jarmusch, downtown-NYC scenester John Lurie, and Marc Ribot, whose impressionistic guitar playing has been a fixture on Waits's recordings since *Rain Dogs*. In 1985, Waits acted alongside Lurie and Roberto Benigni in Jarmusch's excellent prison-break buddy saga *Down by Law*, effectively establishing an impressive acting career. "I wrote that movie with Tom and John in mind," says Jarmusch. "There's a lot of Tom in his character. That whole bit about kicking out the window of a police car—I think Tom has had some experience with that."

In all, Waits has appeared in more than twenty films, including Robert Altman's *Short Cuts*, Coppola's *Bram Stoker's Dracula* and *Ironweed* (a co-star billing with Jack Nicholson). Waits also tried his hand at theater, staging *Frank's Wild Years* at Chicago's Steppenwolf Theater in 1986. Recently, he reunited with Lurie for a highly amusing episode of cable-TV's *Fishing with John*.

By the early nineties, Waits had moved his family to northern California and released *Bone Machine*, a dark blast of rustic surrealism, apocalyptic blues braying, and killing-field hollers that won him a Grammy for Best Alternative Music Performance in 1992. ("He flipped out when he got the Grammy," says Jarmusch. "He hated that. 'Alternative to what?! What the hell does that mean?!' ") During this period, Waits also scored two Robert Wilson operas, *The Black Rider* (which features William Burroughs) and *Alice in Wonderland*, as well as Jarmusch's 1992 film *Night on Earth*. A six-year hermitage followed, presumably spent pursuing his own brand of rural domestic bliss and exploring his fascination with rare and experimental musical instruments. He penned the foreword to *Gravikords, Whirlies & Pyrophones*, Bart Hopkin's study of obscure and often homemade instruments, and contributed to Hopkin's follow-up, *Orbitones, Spoon Harps & Bellowphones*. Waits and Brennan also supplied the music for *Bunny,* an animated short that won an Academy Award this year. Recently, Waits collaborated with Mark Linkous on a track called "Bloody, Hands" that's slated to appear on the next Sparklehorse album. He also produced, co-wrote, and performed on Weiss's *Extremely Cool.*

In a surprise move, Waits left Island Records last year and signed a one-off deal with the punk-rock Epitaph label. *Mule Variations,* his first album in several years and possibly his best, finds him moving full circle. The cubist blues of his Island records is still there, along with the American primitivism of *Bone Machine* and the grainy flicker of his soundtrack work. Waits can still make the piano weep with just his voice, as he does on "The House Where Nobody Lives" and "Take It with Me When I Go." And he can still kick like a mule, as "Big in Japan" and "Filipino Box Spring Hog" can attest. *Mule* is hardly Frank's Mild Years. Some may complain that there are no great surprises here, but when you reinvent the wheel, well, sometimes you've just gotta ride on it awhile. This music is built to last. Who else is making recordings this harsh and masterful twenty-five years into a career?

Arriving at the Astro, Waits pulls up in a 1985 Suburban, an unlikely ride for a man known for driving cars made before Kennedy was assassinated. "I refuse to call it a Suburban—I call it a Bourbon," he says, and compliments *Magnet* on its taste in accommodations with a wry smile. He's dressed head to toe in dark blue denim, a lived-in pair of boots, and his trademark porkpie hat—a rabbit-fur Stetson he bought in Austin while in town for a rare live performance at the recent South by Southwest festival. We head over to the nearby Mission Café, an unassuming greasy spoon, for eggs and sausage. Still a bit morning groggy, his voice sounds an even rougher grit of sandpaper than on record. Laughing easily with a chesty wheeze, a pair of reading glasses perched low on the bridge of his nose, Waits looks almost fatherly as he dispenses bits of folk wisdom, oddball factoids, and good old-fashioned horse sense from a beat-up notebook he brought with him. Though the camera tends to add a few miles to his face, catching the shadows in the lines, in person Waits looks younger than his forty-nine years. The advantage of being born an old soul is that you never really seem to age. You just become a classic.

Tom Waits: When I was comin' down here, I was thinkin', of all the cars I had in my life, I'm drivin' this '85 Suburban, kind of a *Men in Black* car. I started thinking about it because I got a letter from the daughter of my neighbor, who sold me my first car, a '55 Buick Special. From there, I got a '55 Buick Roadmaster. I had a '56 Ford Wagon, beige. Somewhere in there I had a '59 Volvo.

Magnet: You don't strike me as a Volvo guy.

No, it wasn't me, but somebody was trying to get rid of it, and he wanted $5,100 for it. And he was a cop, so I said, "I'll take it." Had that sloped back, that scoliosis back. I had four Buicks: a Special, a Century, and a Roadmaster and a '65 T-bird. Had a '59 Dodge wagon; it was gorgeous. A '56 Mercury convertible, a '54 Caddie, black—they said it was in *The Godfather,* and I think I paid more for it because of that. *Godfather* prices, that's what they said. Had two Caddies, a '54 Coupe DeVille and a '52 Caddie, blue and white. A '64 Cadillac, champagne color—bought it in Montana. My wife drove it back out, no air conditioning, it was 120 degrees. She's still mad about that. [Reading from his notebook] Most American auto horns beep in the key of what?

Key of C?

You cheated! You were looking at my notebook! The key of F. [Reading from his notebook] You know, more steel is produced for the manufacture of bottlecaps than auto bodies. There's a national thirst going on here. When gentlemen in medieval Japan wished to seal an agreement, they would urinate together and crisscross the streams—that was an early contract . . . Recently, a Korean fisherman was arrested for feeding his wife to a school of sharks after getting into a heated argument; it's still against the law to use your wife as bait in Korea.

Let's talk about shoes.

All I wear now is engineer boots. Before that, I only wore pointy shoes and I destroyed my feet. My feet are now in the shape of a pointed shoe. I have a lot of room on either side in these boots, and I have to put newspaper in there. But I lived to see the pointed shoe once again emerge as a footgear leader. That was exciting. When I started looking for pointed shoes, I used to go to Fairfax on Orchard Street in New York City, one of those little pushcart guys. I'd say, "You got any pointy shoes?" They would go way, way in the back and come back with a dusty box, blow the dust off the top, and say, "What do you want with these things? Give me twenty bucks. Go on, get outta here!" And that was the beginning. From there, I saw it grow into a burgeoning industry, a pointy industry. The ultimate was the pointy toe and Cuban heel. But I was younger then. Now, I go for comfort and roadability.

What about suits?

I still don't pay more than seven dollars for a suit. When I first went on the road, I was very superstitious; I would wear the same suits onstage as I wore off. A lot of times, we would leave early in the morning. I hated the whole ritual of getting dressed, so a lot of times I would just lay down on the bed in my suit and my shoes, ready to get up at any time. I would just put the blanket over me and sleep in my clothes, I did that for many years. I stopped after I got married. My wife just won't have it. Whenever she goes away for a couple of days, I put on a suit and get in bed but she can always tell.

Speaking of the road, are you going to tour for this record?

[Assumes mock belligerence] I'm not gonna tour. I want to be set up with a theater like those guys in Missouri, and people come to me. The Wayne Newton Theater. The Trini Lopez Theater. I want my own, a little tin shack with a marquee and a work light, six chairs and a dirt floor. I can see it—I know exactly what it looks like. I'll play six nights a week. You come to see me. [Paging through his notebook] I got some things for you—you'll like this. You ever hear of a bombardier beetle? A bombardier beetle, when disturbed, defends itself by a series of explosions. Actually five individual reports from his rear end, in rapid succession, they are accompanied by a cloud of reddish-colored, vile-smelling fluid.

I'll have to be careful. Do you still smoke?

Gave it up. I'm like everybody else, quit a hundred times. It's a companion and a friend. I would smoke anything in the end. I would take a pack of cigarettes and dig a hole in the backyard and piss on them and bury 'em. Dig 'em up an hour later, dry them in the oven and smoke. That's how bad I had it.

Do you still drink?

Now, is this of interest to your readers? We talked about the pointed shoes, the smoking—I have a feeling you're trying to steer me into the bars . . . I just got an image of one of those emergency-wall things that says "Break In Case of Emergency," and inside is the beverage . . . I gave it up, gave it up. I haven't had a drink in six years.

You have a new movie coming out called Mystery Men. *What's the premise?*

It's about low-rent superheroes. There's a guy named the Shoveler. And there's the Bowler, who has the skull of her famous bowler father sealed in this polyurethane bowling ball. There's the Blue Raja; they make their own costumes and never get a chance to save the day. I play Dr. Heller, a weapons scientist they come to for firepower. Sounds like a blockbuster.

Who's in it?

Ben Stiller, Janeane Garofalo, Hank Azaria, Paul Reubens, William Macy, Eddie Izzard, Geoffrey Rush. Directed by Kinka Usher, who was a prince. I don't know why I agreed to do this except he made the whole thing sound like a softball game.

By the way, great English accent as Renfield in Bram Stoker's Dracula.

They say I should be doing Shakespeare instead of all this pop music crap.

How did you meet up with Jim Jarmusch?

Met him around the time of *Rain Dogs*. He stuck out. His movies were like Russian films, like nothing anyone had ever seen before. For me, they were like the hair in the gate. You know when you used to go to the movies and a big hair would get stuck in the projector, and you would sit there and watch that piece of hair? You would lose the whole plot for a while. So, he was the hair in the gate.

The episode of Fishing with John *is a hoot. How did you hook up with John Lurie?*

John's an unusual guy. Met him in New York around the time of *Rain Dogs*. I did [*Fishing*] because of John. But once I got down there, I wanted to kill him. He knows this. It was pretty pathetic. A fishing show. High concept—the idea is that it doesn't matter if we catch anything, which is the whole idea of fishing, anyway, getting out in the woods and being together. Just an excuse to hold something in your hand and look off into the distance and talk about life. We caught nothing, which is embarrassing. It got to the point where we bought fish from fishermen in a passing boat, which was humiliating. And I got seasick and sunstroke—I was an unhappy guy for most of it. But it turned out to be funny anyway. John is an excellent composer and musician, can pick up anything and play it. We'll be walking along and he'll pick up a piece of irrigation pipe and very seriously ask you to hold one end of it while he tries to get a sound out of it. He's like a kid, a cross between a kid and a wizard—a kizzard. Great nose, too.

Let's talk about the new record. You told journalist Rip Rense that the title comes from something your wife says when you're being stubborn: "I didn't marry a man—I married a mule."

And the fact that you were going through some "changes." What changes?

Electrolysis. I had a lot of unwanted hair removed. Went through aromatherapy. I'm third-year medical school now—love it!

The first song on Mule Variations *that struck me was "What's He Building?" I got kind of a Unabomber image. We seem to be living in a time when the guy next door may be building a fertilizer bomb in his basement.*

Guess it's the rat theory: There's too many of us, and we're going crazy because of the proliferation of the human manifestation. You go down the freeway, and all of a sudden there are 350,000 new homes where there used to be wilderness. They all have to go to the bathroom somewhere, they all want toys for their kids, they all want eggs and bacon and a nice little car and a place to vacation. When the rats get too plentiful, they turn on each other.

In the song you mention a town called Mayors Income, Tennessee.

Came to me in a dream. Two towns. The other one, same dream, Miner's Prayer, West Virginia.

You collaborated with Kathleen on most of the songs on Mule Variations. *Can you describe how you two write together? Is she a musician?*

Excellent pianist, plays contrabassoon, classically trained. Used to play recitals with all the relatives around, and she would start the nocturne and then go off and everybody would cock their ears like the RCA dog: "That ain't Beethoven anymore." She's free-floating. She doesn't seem to be pulled in any one direction. You see, we all like music, but what we really want is for music to like us, because it really is a language and some people are linguists and speak seven languages fluently, can do contracts in Chinese and tell jokes in Hungarian.

Getting back to the names of places, St. Louis seems to pop up a lot, in "Hold On" from the new record and "Time" from Rain Dogs *and you've mentioned it a lot in interviews. Ever live there?*

No, never lived there. It's a good name to stick in a song. Every song needs to be anatomically correct: You need weather, you need the name of the town, something to eat—every song needs certain ingredients to be balanced. You're writing a song and you need a town, and you look out the window and you see "St. Louis Cardinals" on some kid's T-shirt. And you say, "Oh, we'll use that." [Paging through his notebook] There is still a law on the books in Kentucky that says you have to take a bath at least once a year, so we left Kentucky. They were too pushy.

I understand that you cover the walls of the studio with maps when you record.

Makes it more like an expedition.

Where is "The House Where Nobody Lives"?

That was the house I used to go by when I would drive my kids to school, abandoned and the weeds were literally as tall as the trees. At Christmastime, all the neighbors in the area kicked in and bought some lights for it. It was kind of touching. It was like the bad tooth in that smile of a neighborhood.

What about "Big in Japan"? How big are you in Japan?

Haven't played there in a long time. Last time I was there, I was on a bullet train, had my little porkpie hat, my pointed shoes, and my skinny tie. There was a whole car of Japanese gangsters dressed like Al Capone and Cagney, really zooted. Everyone says, "Don't go in there, don't go in there," but it was the only place with seats—everybody else was huddled together like cattle. And they are in this huge air-conditioned car, with tea and little cookies and six guys sitting around talking with cigars. I said, "Fuck, I'm gonna go in there and sit down." And I did. It was like this big, heavy standoff, then they all started laughing, we all tipped our hats and did that little bow. It was pretty funny. Then I brought my guys in and we all sat down, my mob with the Japanese mob. They always want me to do ads for underwear and cigarettes, but I never did them. I did one and I'll never do it again. I used to see celebrities doing ads and my first reaction was, "Aw, gee he must have needed the money. That's tough." When somebody was on the slide, they would do an ad.

You successfully sued Frito-Lay for doing a commercial with a guy who sounds and acts just like you.

This guy from Texas got paid three hundred bucks to do me. That was his specialty, anyway, that he does this perfect imper-sonation of me. And they did this whole thing around "Step Right Up," and every now and then they would say "Fritos" or whatever. And afterward, the guy felt so bad, he came out as our star witness. We won $2.5 million. David beats Goliath.

Let's talk about some of the characters in the songs on Mule Vari-ations. *Who is Big Jack Earl?*

Tallest man in the world. Was with Barnum & Bailey. If you see old archival photographs, they used to put him next to some guy that was like a foot tall. Big hat, tall boots. That's why "Big Jack Earl was eight-foot-one and stood in the road and he cried." Imagine a guy eight-foot-one standing in the middle of the road crying. It breaks your heart.

What about Birdie Joe Hoaks?

I read in the newspaper about this gal, twelve years old, who had swindled Greyhound. She ran away from home and told Greyhound this whole story about her parents and meeting them in San Francisco. She had this whole Holden Caulfield thing, and she got an unlimited ticket and criss-crossed the U.S. And she got nabbed.

What did they do to her?

They took her bus pass, for starters. I don't think she did hard time. Me and my wife read the paper and we clip hundreds of articles, and then we read the paper that way, without all the other stuff. It's our own paper. There is a lot of filler in the paper and the rest is advertising. If you just condense it down to the essential stories, like the story about the one-eyed fish they found in Lake Michigan with three tails, you can renew your whole relationship with the paper.

There's a line in "What's He Building?": "You'll never guess what Mr. Sticcha saw."

Mr. Sticcha was my neighbor when I was a kid. He didn't like kids and he didn't like noise. All the kids would go past his house yellin' and making noise, and you would see his fist out the window and he'd threaten to call the cops. His wife used to say, "You're gonna give him a heart attack if you keep this up." And he finally had a heart attack and he died, and his wife told us that it was our fault, that we had killed him as a group. We all had to distribute that guilt and live with it, and it was upsetting: "Sticcha died and we killed him." We might just as well have plotted his murder.

"Cold Water" is a kind of a hobo anthem. You ever sleep in a graveyard or ride the rails?

I have slept in a graveyard and I have rode the rails. When I was a kid, I used to hitchhike all the time from California to Arizona with a buddy named Sam Jones. We would just see how far we could go in three days, on a weekend, see if we could get back by Monday. I remember one night in a fog, we got lost on this side road and didn't know where we were exactly. And the fog came in and we were really lost then and it was very cold. We dug a big ditch in a dry riverbed and we both laid in there and pulled all this dirt and leaves over us like a blanket. We're shivering in this ditch all night, and we woke up in the morning and the fog had cleared and right across from us was a diner; we couldn't see it through the fog. We went in and had a great breakfast, still my high-water mark for a great breakfast. The phantom diner.

In "Black Market Baby," you call the baby in question a "Bonsai Aphrodite." Great line.

Kathleen came up with that. We know this little gal who's just a gorgeous chick, but she's about four-foot-ten, looks like she's been bound, like the Chinese do with feet. Kathleen said, "She's a Bonsai Aphrodite." It was Patricia Arquette. We told her about that, she said, "I love that, I'm gonna open up a flower shop and call it Bonsai Aphrodite," which she did. But, apparently, it didn't last, went under.

There's a great line in "Picture in a Frame": "I'm gonna love you 'till the wheels come off."

That's prison slang. Means until the end of the world.

I notice that the Eyeball Kid has the same birth date as you.

Just a coincidence. The Eyeball Kid is a comic-book character. Actually, it was Nic Cage that reintroduced me to comic books. I hadn't thought about comic books since I was a little kid, but he seemed to carry that mythology with him. It was inspiring to see him keep alive some of those principles that we associate with childhood, to the point where he named himself after Cage, the comic-book hero. But I was trying to imagine what it would be like for a person with an enormous eyeball for a head to be in show business. If Barnum & Bailey were still around, I imagine he would have thrown in with them.

The tour would be sponsored by Visine or Bausch & Lomb.

It's a metaphor for people that get into show business, because they usually have some kind of family disturbance or are damaged in some way or another. I had a manager when I was a kid, I threw in with a guy named Herbie Cohen, who worked with Zappa. I wanted a big bruiser, the tough guy in the neighborhood, and I got it.

A knee-breaker?

You said that, not me. I got to be careful what I say about Herbie. I'll wind up in . . . court.

Speaking of the business end of things, why did you leave Island Records?

It started changing a lot. [Former owner Chris] Blackwell's gone. For me, it's about relationships. And when Blackwell pulled out and started his own company, I lost interest.

What do you think of all the consolidation that has been going on with the major labels, cutting staff and artists?

I think you should fight for your independence and freedom at all costs. I mean, it's a plantation system. All a record company is is a bank, and they loan you a little money to make a record and then they own you for the rest of your life. You don't even own your own work. Most people only have a small piece of their publishing. Most people are so happy to be recording, which I was—you like the way your name looks on the contract, so you start signing. I got myself tied up in a lot of knots when I was a kid.

Your deal with Epitaph is for one record, where you license the record to the label for a limited time and then ownership reverts back to you. I don't know how aware you are of the Internet, but there is this technology called MP3 that basically allows artists to put songs on the Net and people can download them and burn their own CDs, essentially cutting the record companies out of the equation.

I don't know what I think about that. I don't know about the Internet. I'm not on that. I'm way behind. I have a rotary phone.

Progress is compulsive and obsessive, I guess. I get the feeling that people aren't leaving their homes. They are sitting in front of their computer desks and everything comes to them from their screens. That's what the whole nation really wants, but anything that is that popular or easily accessible is usually not good for you. It's like tap water is not good for you; it's recycled piss and chemicals, that's all. There is a reason that a bottle of water costs more than a gallon of gas. And what's the biggest enemy of computers? Water. And the computers are trying to eliminate all the water. I don't know where I'm going with this. I guess we're in the middle of a revolution and nobody knows where the rocks are going to fall. The record companies are terrified. But I don't want to be a record company. Too much paperwork, and I get too many calls already. Plus, I have two teenagers, and if I was a record company, you would never be able to get through.

Mule Variations *is your first record in six years. There were rumors floating around that you weren't putting out records or performing because you were sick.*

No, I'm not sick, but it's interesting that rumors of that nature would circulate. Rumors of my death were greatly exaggerated, as they say. The rumor was that I had throat cancer.

Bone Machine *had a lot of death in it. And there's that song on* Mule *called "Take It with Me." Beautiful song. This is an absurd question, but I'll ask it anyway: Are you afraid of dying?*

[With mock bravado] Who me? Naw, bring it on! Come on! Who me? I don't wanna go. I gotta rake the leaves first. I got a lot of things to do. I'm like that guy who said on his deathbed, "Either that wallpaper goes or I do." Famous last words. My favorite epitaph is the town hypochondriac's: "I told you I was sick."

In 1976, you were quoted in Newsweek *as saying, "There's a common loneliness that just sprawls from coast to coast. It's like a common disjointed identity crisis. It's the dark, warm narcotic American night. I just hope I'm able to touch that feeling before I find myself one of these days parked on Easy Street." Twenty-three years later, here you are with a wife and kids and a house in the country, a tidy nest egg from Frito-Lay—Easy Street by most any standard—and still you seem to be at the height of your creative powers and popularity. Your career strikes me as a model for how to do it the right way in a business cluttered with bad examples.*

OK, thank you. I'm just improvising, like everybody else . . . I never thought I would live out in the sticks. But now I'm the mean old man next door. Voila. I'm Mr. Sticcha. I got a whole collection of baseballs that have been hit into my yard, and I'm not giving them up for nothing.

It's Last Call Somewhere in the World

Magnet, October–November 2004

Jonathan Valania

> In the midst of a national hangover mired in war and
> division, Tom Waits offers stories of happier hours and
> sobering realities.

When Batman takes someone other than Robin back to
the Batcave, usually to extract some crucial information via one of his super-scientific mind-reading devices, he
knocks them out with Batgas so as to keep the exact location
of his lair a secret.

Something similar happens when you go to interview Tom
Waits. You find yourself in some sleepy town north of San
Francisco. He pulls up in his hearse-black, old-model Chevy
Suburban, then takes you to some Waits-appropriate location—
a greasy spoon, a truck-stop cafeteria—for a Q&A session that
ends promptly when the check arrives. He is, without fail,
charming, witty, odd, poetic and often profound. Then he
drives you back to your hotel, tips his porkpie hat and asks you
to turn around. Before you can look back, he's gone, back to
that someplace in the rolling pastures and pines of Sonoma

County, where he lives with Kathleen Brennan, his wife, collaborator, muse and mother of his three teenage children.

I first interviewed Waits for *Magnet* in 1999 in Santa Rosa. I had a room at the Astro, a broken-down welfare motel straight out of one of the bourbon-fed boarding house madrigals Waits used to pound the horse teeth to in the seventies. This time it's the Metro Hotel & Café, a quaint bed and breakfast in Petaluma recommended by Waits. With its beguilingly appointed rooms—a blend of vintage-store Victoriana, bohemian bric-a-brac and faintly Wiccan aura (if Stevie Nicks were a hotel, it would be the Metro)—it seems fitting of Tom Waits circa now. He's gone from the flophouse to the big house in the woods with the mysterious wife, three kids, the dogs, the garden and a lot of funny ideas about what sounds good.

Upon arriving at the Metro, I check in with the *Magnet* office back in Philadelphia. It's a sunny, immaculate northern California day, but the news on the line is cloudy at best. I'm warned that Waits is in a "weird" mood today. Not to worry, his publicist assures me, Waits is just a little nervous because this is the first interview he's doing for his new album, *Real Gone*.

The man has nothing to be nervous about. *Real Gone* is Waits at the top of his game, another brilliant late-period canvas from an American master. It picks up where 1999's *Mule Variations*— with its perfect blend of what Waits calls "creepers and weepers"—left off, reflecting the midnight mood of the times. In 2002, Waits released *Blood Money* and *Alice,* two separate scores for theatrical productions by frequent collaborator and acclaimed avant-garde dramatist Robert Wilson. While those albums are prime examples of Waits's mastery of Brechtian burlesque and carny surrealism, they're more akin to 1993's *The Black Rider,* another Wilson theatrical score. As good as they are, you come away from *Blood Money* and *Alice* with the distinct feeling you kind of had to be there, with "there" being the Thalia

Theater in Hamburg, Germany, where the pieces were staged. Unlike those scores, *Real Gone* isn't the soundtrack to some far-away show; it is the show, with all the drama and pageantry unfolding right between your ears. As ever, the music is other-worldly and full of dustbowl sadness, somehow managing to sound both as old as an Alan Lomax field recording and as modern as tailfins on a '59 Caddy.

But where most Waits records seem hermetically sealed off from the world that does backflips over *American Idol*, *Real Gone* ripples in the same troubled waters we all find ourselves bobbing in these days. Waits directs a fair share of his hobo magic-realism at current affairs: rigged politics, imperial blood sport, humanity tattered under the grinding wheels of war and the greed and hate that keeps them spinning without mercy. All of this is reflected in the sometimes somber and wistful conversation I have with Waits, a stark contrast to the left-field whimsy of the talk I had with him five years ago. But, as a wise man once said, those were different times.

Which isn't to suggest anyone will confuse *Real Gone* with *Sandinista!* The socio-political commentary is tinted with Waits's patented sepia tones, lending it both a currency and timelessness that manage to blend seamlessly with the standard Waitsian themes of love, dreams, circus freaks and murder in the red barn. Nor is this *Mule Variations* part two. Piano, long a fixture of most Waits recordings, is nowhere to be heard. While there is, as per usual, plenty of bloozy abstraction, sad-eyed balladry and organ-grinder-monkey dance music punctuated with odd conks of percussion, most of the songs are built around "mouth rhythms" Waits created by huffing and puffing into a tape recorder in his bathroom.

It's not for everyone. In fact, you can tell a lot about people from what they make of Tom Waits. His career is a musical Rorschach test: Some just see spilled ink, others see fantastic chimeras. He's one of those love-'em-or-hate-'em artists, and the great divide between us and them is invariably Waits's worn-out shoe of a voice. If you like your singers to sound like a shiny new sneaker, well, there's always *American Idol*. Waits's frogman croak is a far more versatile instrument than he's given credit for, capable of morphing from lupine howl to grainy, heart-warming purr, from a devil-horned carnival barker to a three-pack-a-day Romeo wheezing sweet nothings that are, upon closer inspection, about everything. Everything that matters, anyway: life and death, love and hope, sex and dreams. And the infinite spaces in between that God fills.

It's hard to say where the public Tom Waits begins and the private one ends, and vice versa. Which is just how he wants it. It's how he maintains his aura. When Waits finally pulls up to the Metro in his Suburban, he's dressed exactly as he was for his last conversation with *Magnet*—rumpled porkpie hat, head to toe in ranch-hand denim—but he seems a little on edge. Chalk it up to opening-night jitters for a veteran performer pulling his public persona out of mothballs for the first time in a couple of years. The suit still fits, but it's a little stiff from the hanger.

Yet the same old tics—the "walking Spanish down the hall" body language, the pretzeling of the arms—don't seem like affectations. There's something Lenny Bruce-raised-by-wolves about the way Waits carries himself: part wolfman, part Wolfman Jack. It's really not difficult to imagine Waits out in the backyard around midnight, howling at a full moon. At one point, he's talking on his cell phone to Brennan, leaning with one arm against the trunk of his publicist's rental car like an old man urinating or a chain-gang member getting patted down before being shipped back to the prison farm. Like the man's art, this moment seems at once highly theatrical and utterly natural.

Waits wants to go to his favorite Chinese restaurant in Petaluma, but he has some difficulty finding it. We pull up one street, and Waits looks around dumbfounded, like they'd moved the joint. Then he remembers that it is, in fact, located in a nearby strip mall. Charmless and anti-septic under a drop ceiling and fluorescent lights—not to mention completely devoid of other customers—the place has none of the Oriental opium-den vibe you can't help but imagine when Waits says, "We're goin' for Chinese." But he has a way of lending color and character to any room he walks into. Studying the menu, Waits makes a point of ordering some steamed vegetables. "If I don't eat something green, my wife will be very upset with me." When the food arrives, Waits seems more comfortable in his own skin. Full of green tea and sympathy, he shares jokes and fears, dreams and memories, does some sound effects, even sings a little Ray Charles.

And then he's gone again. Like, real gone.

JV: I'm noticing you have the words "diapers" and "fire-works" written on the back of your hand in magic marker. Would it be impolite to ask you why?

TW: Shopping list. Fireworks and diapers is all anyone ever needs. Life is what happens between fireworks and diapers.

JV: With age supposedly comes wisdom. What do you know at fifty-four that you didn't when you were younger?

TW: I've learned a lot. Most of the big things I've learned in the last ten years. Of course, I've been sober for twelve years. Let's see, what have I learned? As a nation, we are addicted to cigarettes and underwear. And it's getting harder and harder to find a bad cup of coffee.

JV: Let's go back to ancient history for a second.

TW: OK, don't go back too far. I get lost back there.

JV: When you were a teenager, you worked as a doorman at a nightclub in San Diego. What do you remember about that time?

TW: I don't know. I got paid eight dollars a night, and I got to hear a lot of great music.

JV: I've read that when you were young, you heard sounds the way van Gogh saw colors. Even everyday sounds took on these hyper-iridescent tone colors.

TW: I went through a period like being colorblind with regard to your hearing. Or astigmatism of the ears.

JV: Then you would recite these little incantations that made it go away?

TW: [Goes into chant, which sounds like "gila-monster-killa-monster-chilla-monster-boom," while tapping on a water glass with a spoon.]

JV: Do you still do that?

TW: I just did it.

JV: No, I mean do you still have those kind of experiences with sound?

TW: I write music that way. It's sort of like automatic

writing. Wouldn't you love to go into a darkened room with a piece of paper and a pen and just start drawing circles and wind up writing the great American novel? Recording for me is like photographing ghosts.

JV: How did you first encounter Captain Beefheart?

TW: We had the same manager back in 1975–76.

JV: You weren't acquainted with his music in the sixties?

TW: Nope. I became more acquainted with him when I got married. My wife had all his records.

JV: It's interesting you came to Beefheart so late considering how often critics compare you to him.

TW: Anything you absorb you will ultimately secrete. It's inevitable. Most of us are original paintings, and it's a mystery as to what is learned and what is borrowed, what is stolen and what is born, what you came in with and what you found while you were here.

JV: What do you know about this Waitstock thing in Poughkeepsie, New York, each year? What do they do?

TW: Incantations, speak in tongues, wake up at six in the morning and have whiskey and eggs, walk around in their undershirts. I don't know; it's just what I imagine. It's just some attempt at a worshipful homage.

JV: Do you still spend time scavenging in junkyards?

TW: I practically live at Costco. I am still a bit of a scavenger. I bring home useless things.

JV: Are you one of those guys who has a front yard full of car parts, old birdbaths and lawn jockeys?

TW: If I could find a lawn jockey, I would pay good money for it. As for my yard, I will leave that up to you to imagine because if I told you, you wouldn't believe me. Mostly medical supplies and Venus flytraps.

JV: I was surprised to learn *Mule Variations* sold a million copies worldwide. How does that feel?

TW: I guess it feels good. Isn't that supposed to feel good?

JV: But what does that mean when an artist like Tom Waits can sell a million copies of an album at a time when the music business is basically saying nothing but easy-sell artists are worth bothering with?

TW: I don't know what it means. If they were lawn chairs, what would it mean? If they were potted plants, what would it mean? If they were little poodles, what would it mean? It's America: free enterprise.

JV: There's no piano on *Real Gone,* was that intentional?

TW: No. I moved the piano into the studio, and we never touched it. We put drinks on it. I put my coat on it. Before you know it, I couldn't even see it. It just became an end table. Most of it was written a cappella. I started with these mouth rhythms, making my own cycles and playing along with them. That's fairly new. Sometimes when you just do sounds into the tape recorder, you don't realize it, but you're channeling something, like incantations or talking in tongues.

JV: Was this a real old, vintage tape recorder?

TW: No, a Fostex four-track with a Shure SM-58 [microphone] in a really small bathroom with about a four-second delay and overload the hell out of it . . . I'll tell you what else is new. There's an instructional dance number on there. When was the last time you heard an instructional dance number on a record?

JV: Which one is that?

TW: "Metropolitan Glide." It has instructions [in the lyrics] on how to do the dance. And it also has lots of other dances on there that the gentleman is able to do. It's a real dance. They used to do it in the twenties. It's kind of a revival.

JV: You sometimes use an instrument called the "bastarda." What the hell is that?

TW: That's something Les [Claypool] played. It's like an electric stick with four strings, like a bass without a body. *Real Gone* is definitely not a record filled with bizarre, left-wing sound sources. The idea was to go in and do something that was going to be bread and water, skin and bones, three-legged tables, rudimentary three-minute songs. That was the idea.

JV: When did you start working on the album?

TW: Gee, I don't know. A few months ago.

JV: Is that a new thing for you, writing and recording so quickly?

TW: We wanted to get it done before the summer began. When the kids are out of school, it's a whole new paradigm shift at home. They're everywhere.

JV: Where did you record it?

TW: It got misconstrued. It was recorded in the Delta, and everybody thought we were working in Mississippi. It was the Sacramento Delta.

JV: A lot of great bluesmen came out of the tar-paper shacks of Sacramento.

TW: I'm not pulling your leg. There really is a Sacramento Delta. We recorded in an abandoned schoolhouse. I don't like the politics of a studio. It's used as a studio all year long, and then you come in. I was looking for a place that might have an unusual sound.

JV: Let's talk about some of these obscure references in the lyrics on *Real Gone*. On "Sins of my Father," you mention a "Tyburn Jig."

TW: When someone was being hung, the dance they would do at the end of the rope was called the Tyburn Jig. It was also called "the dance upon nothing"; that kind of explains itself. The reason theaters traditionally have no performances on Monday night is because Monday night was

Hanging Night, and nobody could compete with Hanging Night. To this day, theaters are dark on Mondays.

JV: I think most people would be surprised how recently there were public hangings in this country.

TW: Well, we still do it today. It's just a little more civilized: lethal injection. How long after the discovery of electricity do you think somebody invented the electric chair? Probably the next day. How long do you think after they invented these picture phones that somebody put it in their pants? Less than a day. Crime is always way ahead of technology, waiting for it to catch up.

JV: What about some of these characters on the new album? There's the line "Jesus of Nazareth told Mike of the weeds."

TW: Well, if there is a Jesus of Nazareth, there had to be a Mike of the weeds and a Bob of the parking lot, Jim of the river, Steve of the backyard.

JV: Was Weeds the next town over from Nazareth?

TW: No, Mike lived in the weeds. Jesus lived in Nazareth. They corresponded.

JV: There was a guy back in Jesus's time named Mike?

TW: I don't know if they pronounced it like that.

JV: Who is Knocky Parker?

TW: Old Delta-blues guy.

JV: Bowlegged Sal?

TW: Singer. I think from St. Louis. Sorry, Bo. [Laughs.]

JV: Who's Joel Tornabene?

TW: He's in the concrete business. [Laughs.] Mob guy. He was the grandson of Sam Giancana from Chicago. He did some yard work for me, and I hung out with him most of the time. He died in Mexico about five years ago. He was a good friend of [producer/composer] Hal Wilner's, and he was a good guy. He had an errant—I don't know how to put this—he used to go around, and when he saw something he liked in somebody's yard, he would go back that night with a shovel, dig it up and plant it in your yard. We used to get a kick out of that. So I stopped saying, "I really like that rosebush, I really like that banana tree, I really like that palm." Because I knew what it meant. He came over once with twelve chickens as a gift. My wife said, "Joel, don't even turn the car off. Turn that car around and take those chickens back where you found them." He was a good friend, one of the wildest guys I've ever known.

JV: I love the line "I want to know the same thing everyone wants to know: how's it going to end."

TW: What's it gonna be? A heart attack at a dance? An egg that went down the wrong pipe? Wild bullet from a conflict two miles away that ricochets off the lamppost and goes through the windshield and pierces your forehead like a diamond? Who knows? Look at Robert Mitchum. He died in his sleep. That's pretty good for a guy like Robert Mitchum.

JV: How about "My baby's so fine, even her car looks good from behind"?

TW: [Laughs.] I was following my wife home once, and I said, "I don't know where I am, baby." She said, "Follow me." And I remarked to myself, "My baby's so fine, even the back of her car looks fine." How about Ray Charles? What a shame.

JV: Did you ever meet him?

TW: I met Ray in an airport, and he had all his handlers around him like he was Muhammad Ali. And I knew I could never get through unless I looked really stupid, like I didn't know any better.

JV: It blows my mind what he overcame to get to where he was. To be a black man in America at that time, blind and a junkie.

TW: Well, *Brother Ray* is an excellent autobiography if you want to get all the dirt on Ray. The most commonly told story about Ray was about [his back-up singers] the Raylettes. If you wanted to be a Raylette, you had to let Ray . . . [Laughs.] My favorite image of Ray is this wonderful story of him touring north Carolina in the fifties as a rhythm 'n' blues act, playing empty tobacco warehouses. They would just call a dance and put out notices, and the place would fill up. People were dancing so hard that the dust from the floorboards made it so smoky in there that after a while you couldn't even see who you were dancing with, and Ray would just be howling . . . You know, showbiz is the only place where you can actually make money after you're dead. And he'll also live on. You put those records on and he's here; it's really like a hologram of your spirit.

JV: If you go back through history, the rich and powerful would strive for immortality by building monuments so they would always be remembered. To a certain extent, there was some permanence, but only in that one place. You would have to travel to see it. A Ray Charles record is everywhere.

TW: And it's just as fresh as the day it was recorded. When I listen to old field recordings, maybe you'll hear a dog barking way off in the background. You realize the house it was recorded in is torn down, the dog is dead, the tape recorder is broken, the guy who made the recording died in Texas, the car out front has four flat tires, even the dirt that the house sat on is gone—probably a parking lot—but we still have this song. Takes me out when I listen to those old recordings. I put on my stuff in the house, which is always those old Alan Lomax recordings. My son Casey started doing his turntable stuff; he's upstairs listening to Aesop Rock, El-P., Sage Francis, and all those kind of guys. So I get exposed to a lot at home, and then, you know, I weave it all together.

JV: Have you ever thought about messing around with electronics more, maybe deconstructing some of your old stuff?

TW: I don't know if that's my culture. Maybe it's more of your culture. You're younger than me. I don't want to get a weird haircut just because I saw it at the mall.

JV: Does Kathleen do the woman's voice on "Trampled Rose"?

TW: No, that's me. That's my female voice. I got a big girl in me. Don't you?

JV: Probably. Don't take this the wrong way, but on "Misery Is the River of the World" [from *Blood Money*], you sound like one of those Swiss Alps rescue dogs that got into the brandy.

TW: [Laughs.] Sometimes my kids will listen to something I did and say, "Were you going for a Cookie Monster-in-love thing on that, Dad?"

JV: You have a daughter who's in college.

TW: It was inevitable. I have a son who's eighteen, played turntables on *Real Gone*. As far as my kids go, it's the family business. If I was a farmer, I would have them out there on a tractor. If I was a ballet dancer, I would have them in tutus.

JV: What do they make of what you do?

TW: I'm their dad, that's really the extent of it. They are not fans of mine. Your kids are not your fans, they're your kids. The trick is to have a career and have a family. It's like having two dogs that hate each other and you have to take them for a walk every night.

JV: There's a line on *Real Gone* about "She was a middle-class girl . . . Thought she could stand up in the deep end," which struck me as something a father would come up with. Am I off base?

TW: No, but not consciously. It's one of those things when you're a dad. When I see these pictures of these kids coming home from Iraq, they're my son's age: eighteen, nineteen years old. That's who's over there.

JV: Let's get to that. I'm hearing a lot of echoes of life post-9/11 on *Real Gone*.

TW: Well, "Sins of My Father" is political. "Hoist That Rag" is. There's a bunch of soldier songs.

JV: "Sins of My Father": Are you talking about George W. Bush?

TW: I'm talking about my father, I'm talking about your father, I'm talking about his father. The sins of the father will be visited upon the son. Everybody knows that.

JV: On "Day After Tomorrow," which sounds like a soldier's letter home to his family, you mention Rockford [Illinois], near the Wisconsin border.

TW: I read an article about a soldier who died and was from Rockford. A lot of these soldiers come from the South and the Midwest. And these ads for the Army? They're ridiculous. They all play rock 'n' roll, and it's turned up full blast; they all look so cool in their equipment.

326

JV: On that song, there's a line that goes, "I'm not fighting for justice, I'm not fighting for freedom, I'm fighting for my life."

TW: All the guys who come home on leave say that. That's why when you ask them why they just don't stay home now that they're safe, they say, "Because I've got buddies over there, and they need me. I'm not going over there for the government." Because in the end, it's just you and your rifle and your friends. They really are just gravel on the road. Do you think that a senator sleeping in a nice warm bed looks at a soldier as anything more than a spent shell casing? Nothing more. That's why we need more ammo, and the ammo is these children.

JV: How do you think the election is going to go?

TW: I don't know. I hope he gets voted out. I pray that we will be mobilized and it will be a landslide and everybody who's ever believed in these ideals that we're talking about will vote the bastard out. But now it's all done on computer, and there's probably somebody who's rigging the whole thing. It's such a huge thing. We're the United States of the World. It's not just a country; we're talking about world domination. Most of us aren't ready to absorb the truth about what's really going on.

JV: I don't know if you know about this, but there's a company called Diebold that makes the electronic voting machines used in Florida. One of these machines in Volusia County registered sixteen thousand negative votes for Gore in 2000. Here's the kicker: The CEO of Diebold

[Walden O'Dell] is a major fund-raiser for the Bush–Cheney campaign.

TW: [Sarcastically] No connection.

JV: These machines can be hacked into and manipulated very easily; this is all well-documented. Each vote is just a digital blip, really. There's this movement to make these machines print out a receipt of your vote, so if you wanted to have a re-count, everybody could turn in their slip of paper. And Diebold goes, "That's just not possible." Well, you know what other machines Diebold makes? ATMs.

TW: Please. I'm thinking that this is the last of our civilization. I think we are all going into the crapper, waiting to be flushed. It just feels like the whole world's on fire right now.

JV: You could last a long time out here in the woods when it goes police state.

TW: It will get to the point where the only food you can trust is what's grown in your backyard.

JV: Are you against irradiated food?

TW: Oh, God yeah. I got a big garden in my backyard.

JV: What do you grow?

TW: Tomatoes, corn, eggplant, squash, beans, pumpkins.

JV: So how does it work with you and Kathleen writing songs together?

TW: We just throw out lines, it's like dreaming out loud. When we're writing, we kinda go into a trance.

JV: Kathleen goes into the studio with you, right?

TW: Oh, yeah. She and I produced the record. It's like she's tying a rope around my waist and lowering me down into the well, hollering, "A little more to the left, a little more to the left."

JV: "Circus" is the kind of William S. Burroughs hurdy-gurdy narrative you've been honing to perfection your entire career. A lot of your albums have some great spoken-word pieces—"Shore Leave," "9th and Hennepin," "What's He Building?"—but I think "Circus" is the best. You've got Horse Face Ethel. You've got one-eyed Myra in her Roy Orbison T-shirt bottle-feeding an orangutan named Tripod. Is that because he's three-limbed?

TW: [Laughs.] Naw, naw. I think he got his name because he always had an erection.

JV: You've got Yodeling Elaine, the Queen of the Air with the tiny bubble of spittle around her nostril and a little rusty tear. And then over by the frozen tractor—I really love this phrase—"the music was like electric sugar."

TW: It's a daydream. We were just sort of dreaming of the place I'd like to work. If I was a kid and wanted to run away to the circus, this is the circus I would want to run away to.

JV: What about Poodle Murphy?

TW: She's a girl from Funeral Wells's knife act who was strapped to the spinning board. I don't know if I would want to work for a guy named Funeral Wells, especially if he threw knives.

JV: Another great line: "Damn good address for a rat."

TW: [Laughs.] Well, that's any ship, you know. They grab each other's tails when they cross the river, hundreds and hundreds of them. They're omnivorous. They'll eat anything. You put them in a room with an empty can, and they will eat the can, the label, the top and they'll digest and shit it out. The myth about rats is that they have to eat constantly or their teeth would grow too long and the bottoms would come out of the top of their heads like horns.

JV: That's not true?

TW: I don't know. I haven't spent that much time with rats.

JV: Let's talk about your scene with Iggy Pop in Jim Jarmusch's *Coffee and Cigarettes*. It was filmed a while ago.

TW: Ten years ago.

JV: I thought you were a natural. I love Iggy, but I think he made the right career choice going into rock 'n' roll instead of acting.

TW: Well, you know, they were vignettes. It wasn't an actors' thing; it was more like situation comedy. Jarmusch has been doing those a long time. When he's working on a project, he'll try and get people to go into the alley or the Italian restaurant and try and do something spontaneous. He really wants it to be like Beckett plays.

JV: Have you talked with him about doing another full-length feature along the lines of *Down by Law?*

TW: Acting is not something that I really pursue. I like to say that I'm not really an actor, but I do a little acting. I'm not really looking for something, but if something came along that I really loved, I would do it.

JV: Why don't you tour anymore? Is it just the stress and drudgery and "who needs it"?

TW: Exactly. Just the physics alone of going into a new hall every night. I'm a grumpy old guy. It doesn't take much to tick me off, I'm like an old hooker, you know.

JV: Why did you title the album *Real Gone?*

TW: That's Kathleen's title. I was going to call it *Clang, Boom and Steam.* She said everyone's going or really gone, and there's a lot of leaving on the record. It's almost hard to get laughs these days; we are living in such a dark place.

JV: I don't want to sound like one of those people who whines about 9/11, but up until then, I was generally an optimistic person. There was that bubble of peace, hope and endless possibility after the Cold War ended, that all of our energies as a civilization could be directed toward making the world a better place instead of just shooting at each other. But after 9/11, it occurred to me that I'll probably never see a time like that again, that there'll just be endless war.

TW: That's all you read about in the paper anymore.

JV: Well, that's why I think if you had to distill the essence of *Real Gone* down to one line, it's where you say, "I want to believe in the mercy of the world again." I think so many people feel that way right now.

TW: Do you know who said that? Bob Dylan. He didn't say it in a song; he said it in an interview. He was just talking about the state of the world, so I threw that in there.

JV: I was reading an interview you did with [director] Terry Gilliam, and at one point you said to him, "I feel like there is a battle going on all the time between light and dark, and I wonder sometimes if the dark has one more spear."

TW: Do you know who said that to me? Fred Gwynne.

JV: Herman Munster?

TW: Yeah. A good friend of mine. We worked together on *The Cotton Club*. We used to talk all the time, very deep guy. We rode to work every day in a van; we'd hang out for hours and hours. Sweet guy. Head bigger than a horse. I don't think they added any plaster when they made him up as Herman. But getting back to that bit about light and dark: I do believe that. But I also believe that when you do something really good, it goes into an account and other folks can write checks against it. I really believe that.

PLAY IT LIKE YOUR HAIR'S ON FIRE

GQ, June 2002

Elizabeth Gilbert

Tom Waits would be America's Springsteen—if America
were a strange dispossessed land of circus freaks.

He never looked quite right as a child. He was small, thin,
pale. He stood funny. He had a trick knee, psoriasis,
postnasal drip. There was no comb, lotion, or prayer in this
world that would get his hair to lie down flat. He read too
many books. He was unduly fascinated by carnivals, buried
treasure, and mariachi music.

When he grew nervous, he rocked back and forth like a
rabbi deep in prayer. He was often nervous.

Moreover, there was something kind of wrong with him
(maybe, he thinks now, some minor brush with autism) that
made him almost painfully obsessed with sound. He heard
noises the way van Gogh saw colors—exaggerated, beautiful,
shimmering, scary. There were sounds all around him that
made his hair stand on end, sounds nobody else seemed to
hear. Cars driving by under his bedroom window roared
louder than trains. If he waved his arm near his head, he heard
a sharp whistle in his ear like the whipping of a fishing line.

If he ran his hand across his bedsheets, he heard a harsh scrape, rougher than sandpaper. Engulfed by these noises, he'd be compelled to clear his head by reciting rhythmic nonsense syllables aloud (*shack-a-bone, shack-a-bone, shack-a-bone, shack-a-bone* . . .) until he could think straight again.

When he was eleven years old, his father—a Spanish teacher who used to drive his boy out of San Diego and over the Mexican border for haircuts—left the family. So now the child didn't have a dad around anymore. He became fixated on dads as a result. He would visit the houses of his friends and neighbors, not to hang out with his buddies but to hang out with his buddies' dads.

While the other kids were outside playing kickball in the sun, he would slip into the darkened den and sit there with somebody's father for the entire afternoon, listening to Sinatra records and talking about home insurance. He'd pretend to be a much older man, maybe even a father himself. Kicked back in some grown man's Barcalounger, this skinny little kid would clear his throat, lean forward and say, "So. How long you been with Aetna, Bob?"

He wanted to be old so bad it drove him nuts. He couldn't wait to shave. At eleven, he wore his grandfather's hat and cane. And he loved the music that old men loved. Music with some grizzled hair on its chest. Music whose day was long over. Dead music. Dad music.

"How 'bout that brass section, Bob?" he'd say to somebody's father while listening to the hi-fi on a quiet afternoon. "Can't find players like that anymore, can you, Bob?"

This was back when he was in, like, sixth grade.

So, yes, in case you were wondering—Tom Waits was *always* different.

* * *

I'm waiting for Tom Waits on the porch of the Washoe House—one of California's oldest inns. It's in the middle of the grassy countryside of Sonoma County, across the street from a vineyard, next to a dairy farm, and somewhat near the mysterious, secret rural location where Tom Waits lives. It was his decision to meet here. No mystery why he likes this place. The sloping wooden floors, the sticky-keyed piano in the bar, the yellowing dollar bills thumbtacked to the ceiling, the weary waitresses who look like they've been on the business end of some real hard love their whole lives—every story in the house is a true one.

So I'm waiting for Tom Waits when a homeless man wanders up to me. Thin as a knife, weathered skin, clean and faded clothes. Eyes so pale he might be blind. He's dragging behind him a wagon, decorated with balloons and feathers and signs announcing that the world is coming to an end. This man is, I learn, walking all the way to Roswell, New Mexico. For the apocalypse. Which will be happening later this spring. I ask his name. He tells me that he was christened Roger but that God calls him by another name. ("For years I hear God talkin' to me, but he kept calling me Peter, so I thought he had the wrong guy. Then I realized Peter must be my real name. So now I listen.")

With no special alarm, Roger-Peter informs me that this whole planet will be destroyed within a few short months. Pandemonium unleashed. Madness and death everywhere. Everybody burned to cinders. He points to the passing cars and says calmly, "These people like their comfortable lives now. But they won't like it one bit when the animals get loose."

Appropriately enough, this is the exact moment when Tom Waits shows up. He wanders over to the porch. Thin as a knife, weathered skin, clean and faded clothes.

"Tom Waits," I say, "meet Roger-Peter."

They shake hands. They look alike. You wouldn't know at first, necessarily, which one was the eccentric musical genius and which one was the derelict wandering doomsayer. There are some differences, of course. Roger-Peter has crazier eyes. But Tom Waits has a crazier voice.

Waits, immediately comfortable with Roger-Peter, says, "You know, I saw you around here just the other night, walking down the middle of the highway."

"God redirects traffic around me so I don't get hit," replies Roger-Peter.

"I don't doubt that. I like your wagon. Tell me about all these signs you wrote. What are they all about?"

"I'm finished talking now," Roger-Peter says, not impolitely but firmly.

He stands up, gives us a Bible as a parting gift, takes hold of his wagon, and heads east to meet the total destruction of the universe. Waits watches him go, and as we head inside, he tells me that he recently saw another hobo with apocalyptic signs walking down the same road. "He offered to sell me a donkey. A pregnant donkey. I had to go home and ask everyone if we could invest in a pregnant donkey. But they decided, no, that would be too much trouble."

For the past thirty years, Tom Waits has had a musical career in this country unlike anybody else's. His was not a meteoric rise to fame. He just appeared—a rough, tender, melancholic, thoroughly experimental, lounge-singing, piano-playing, reclusive hobo in a seven-dollar suit and an old man's hat—and that is what he has remained. Although he tinkers endlessly with his music (since his first album, 1973's *Closing Time,* he has given us tragic blues, narcotic jazz, sinister German opera, and delirious, drunken carnival mambos, to name just a few styles), he has never once tinkered with his image, and that's how you know it isn't an "image."

You don't see much of Tom Waits in public, although he's not a total hermit. He does go on tour every now and again, he has performed on *The Tonight Show,* and he shows up in the occasional movie (*The Cotton Club,* Francis Ford Coppola's *Dracula,* Robert Altman's *Short Cuts*) as a brilliant, scene-stealing character actor. Still, he prefers his privacy. He agreed to meet me today only because he has a new album coming out and he guesses he should probably promote it. Actually, he has two albums. (One is called *Alice,* the other is called *Blood Money,* and their single complexity and dark beauty shall be discussed at a later point in this article, so please hold tight.)

Tom Waits is, famously, not the easiest interview out there. Reporters often get frustrated with him because he speaks inaudibly or "won't give straight answers." (When asked once why he had allowed six long years to pass between albums, Waits replied stonily, "I was stuck in traffic.") He's notorious for telling make-believe stories about himself. Not out of malice, mind you. Mostly just to pass the time. He quite enjoys the lies that have been printed about him over the years. ("My father was a knife-thrower," he has said. "And my mother was a trapeze artist. So we were a show-business family.")

He's not the most marketable guy out there, either. He doesn't have the conventional good looks or a very nice voice. He has been called "gravelly voiced" so many times over the decades, you'd think journalists were required by law to describe him this way. Tom Waits has grown a bit weary of this description. He prefers other metaphors. A little Midwestern girl once wrote him a letter saying that his voice reminded her of a cherry bomb and a clown, to which he replied, "You got it, babe. Thanks for listening."

As a songwriter, he has an unerring instinct for melancholy and melody. His wife says that all his songs can be divided into two major categories—*Grim Reapers* and *Grand Weepers*. The latter will knock you to the very floor with sadness. (A devastating little number called "Christmas Card from a Hooker in Minneapolis" comes to mind.) He has never had a hit, though Rod Stewart did take Waits's "Downtown Train" to the top of the charts. But other Tom Waits songs aren't so radio-friendly. (How 'bout this for a catchy pop lyric: "Uncle Bill will never leave a will / And the tumor's as big as an egg / He has a mistress, she's Puerto Rican / And I heard she has a wooden leg.")

It's this darkness and eccentricity that have kept him from being a megastar. Still, he has never vanished into obscurity. For thirty years, as bigger and more conventional rock stars have shimmered and melted away in hot spotlights all around him, Tom Waits has stayed on his dimly lit side stage, sitting at his piano (or guitar or sousaphone or cowbell or fifty-gallon oil drum) creating extraordinary sounds for a loyal audience.

As for the devotion he inspires and how he claimed his unique position in American music, the artist has only this to say:

"There's an aspect of going into show business that's like joining the circus. You come to learn that there's certain people in show business who do the equivalent of biting the heads off chickens. But, then, of course, there's the aerialists . . . and sideshow curiosities. You work with what you came with. Well, maybe I came in with no legs. But I can walk on my hands and play the guitar. So that's just me using my imagination to work within the system."

His is not the voice of the common workingman. It's more like the voice of the common working circus freak. But his voice is heartfelt, epic, and honest, and he represents his peculiar constituency with true honor. Which means this: If only there were as many circus freaks in this country as there are workingmen, Tom Waits would be Bruce Springsteen.

Tom Waits is full of facts. He leans in close to me and says, "The male spider. After he strings four strands of his web, he steps off to the side, lifts one leg and strums them. The chord that this makes? This attracts the female spider. I'm curious about that chord . . ."

Waits keeps these facts jotted down in a small notebook, which is also filled with driving directions and unfinished songs and hangman games he has been playing with his young son. His handwriting is a crazy wobbling of huge, scrawly capital letters. You'd swear it was the penmanship of a crippled man who has been forced to hold his pencil in his mouth.

He thumbs through his notebook like he's thumbing through his own scattered memory. This provided me excellent opportunity to stare at his face. He looks good for a man of fifty-however-many-years-old-he-is. He's been clean and sober for almost a decade, and it shows. Doesn't even smoke anymore. No puffiness along the jaw. Clear eyes. Four deep parallel lines are grooved into his forehead, as evenly spaced as if they'd been dug there with a kitchen fork. He's far better looking (handsome, even) in real life than he is on stage and screen, where—lost in the struggle of performance—he often employs such puzzled facial contortions and shambling postures and spastically waving arms that he looks (and I'm sorry to say this about my hero) something like an oversize organ-grinder's monkey. But here, in this dark old restaurant, he's nothing but dignified. He even looks like he's in shape. Which leads me to try to picture Tom Waits jogging on a treadmill. At a gym. Wearing *what?*

"Ah, here's another interesting fact," he says. "Heinz 57."

He picks up the bottle of Heinz 57 from the table to illustrate his story.

"Between 1938 and 1945," he says, "Heinz released a soup only in Germany. It was an alphabet soup. But in addition to every letter of the alphabet, they included swastikas in every can."

"You're kidding me."

He puts the bottle down. "I imagine it would be called *pastika.*"

It's a great story. Too bad further investigation proves it to be an urban myth. Not that it matters. What matters is that it gets Tom Waits to thinking. Gets him to thinking about a lot of things. Pigs, for instance. He's concerned because scientists are splicing human genes into pigs these days. Apparently, this is to ensure that the animal's internal organs are more accessible for transplant into human bodies. Ethically, Waits thinks this is a horrific notion. It's also having an unsettling effect on the appearance of the pigs. "I saw pictures of these pigs," he muses. "You look at 'em and you say, 'Geez! That's Uncle *Frank!* Looks just like him!' "

Which brings us to his wife. Chances are, it was Tom Waits's wife who showed him the photograph of the experimental pig–humans, because she reads four local newspapers a day and cuts out all the weird stories. You can also bet she's the person who dug up the story about the swastika-noodle soup. And if there's anyone who has ever heard the mating chord of the male spider, it's probably Kathleen Brennan.

But who *is* Kathleen Brennan? Hard to know, exactly. She's the most mysterious figure in the whole Tom Waits mythology. Newspaper articles and press releases always describe her the same way, as "the wife and longtime collaborator of the gravelly voiced singer." You will see her name on all of his albums after 1985. ("All songs written by Tom Waits and Kathleen

Brennan.") She's everywhere, but invisible. She's private as a banker, rare as a unicorn, never talks to reporters. But she is the very center of Tom Waits—his muse, his partner, and mother of his three children. And sometimes, when he is playing live, you will hear him mumble, almost to himself, "This one's for Kathleen," before he eases into a slow and tender rendition of "Jersey Girl."

I've never met the woman, and I know nothing for certain about her, except what her husband has told me. Which means that she is a person thoroughly composed, in my mind, of Tom Waits's words. Which means she's the closest thing out there to a living Tom Waits song.

He has called her "an incandescent presence" in his life and music. She's "a rhododendron, an orchid, and an oak." He has described her as "a cross between Eudora Welty and Joan Jett." She has "the four Bs. Beauty, brightness, bravery, and brains." He insists that she's the truly creative force in the relationship, the feral influence who challenges his "pragmatic" limitations and stirs intrigue into all their music. ("She has dreams like Hieronymus Bosch . . . She'll start talking in tongues and I'll take it all down.") He says, "she speaks to my subtext, not my context." He claims she has expanded his vision so enormously as an artist that he can hardly bear to listen to any of the music he wrote before they met. "She rescued me," he says. "I'd be playing in a steak house right now if it wasn't for her. I wouldn't even be playing in a steak house. I'd be cooking in a steak house.

"She's the egret in the family," he says. "I'm the mule."

"We met on New Year's Eve," Tom Waits tells me.

He loves talking about his wife. You can see it, the pleasure it gives him. He tries not to go too nuts with it, of course, because he does want to protect her privacy. (Which is why he sometimes dodges interviewers' questions about his wife with typical Waitsian nonsense stories. Yeah, he'll say, she's a bush pilot. Or a soda jerk. Runs a big motel down in Miami. Or this: He once claimed he fell for Kathleen because she was the first woman he'd ever met who could "stick a knitting needle through her lip and still drink coffee.") And yet he wants to talk about her because—you can just see it—he loves the way her name feels in his mouth.

They met in Hollywood, back in the early 1980s. Waits was writing the music for the Coppola movie *One from the Heart,* and Kathleen Brennan was a script supervisor on the film. Their courtship had all the drunken, spinning, time-warping delirium of a good New Year's Eve party in someone else's house. When they were first falling in love, they used to drive wildly around L.A. at all hours and she'd purposely try to get him lost, just for the entertainment value. She'd tell him to take a left, then hop on the freeway, then cross over Adams Boulevard, then straight through the ghetto, then into a worse ghetto, then another left . . .

"We'd end up in Indian country," Waits remembers. "Out where nobody could even believe we were there. Places where you could get shot just for wearing corduroy. We were going into these bars—I don't know what was protecting us—but we were loaded. God protects drunks and fools and little children. And dogs. Jesus, we had so much fun." They got married at the Always Forever Yours Wedding Chapel on Manchester Boulevard in Watts. ("It was planned at midnight for a one A.M. wedding," says Waits. "We made things *happen* around here!") They'd known each other, what? Two months? Maybe three? They had to page the guy who married them. A pastor carried a beeper. The Right Reverend Donald W. Washington.

"She thought it was a bad omen that it was a seventy-dollar

wedding and she had fifty bucks and I only had twenty. She said, 'This is a hell of a way to start a relationship.' I was like, 'C'mon baby, I'll make it up to you, I'll get you later . . .' "

There wasn't much of a honeymoon: Soon after the wedding, the couple realized they were dead broke. Waits was already a celebrated musician, but he'd made some serious young-artist mistakes with contracts and money, and now it was looking like maybe he was dried-up. Plus, he was on the splits with his manager. And legal headaches? Everywhere. And studio producers trying to put corny string sections behind his darkest songs? And who owned him, exactly? And how had this happened?

It was at this point that his new bride stepped in and encouraged her husband to blow off the whole industry. Screw it, Kathleen suggested. You don't need these outside people, anyhow. You can produce your own work. Manage your own career. Arrange your own songs. Forget about security. Who needs security when you have freedom? The two of them would get by somehow, no matter what. It's like she was always saying: "Whatever you bring home, baby, I'll cook it up. You bring home a possum and a coon? We will live off it."

The result of her dare was *Swordfishtrombones*—a big, brassy, bluesy, gospel-grooved, dark-textured, critically adored declaration of artistic independence. An album like none before it. A boldly drawn line, running right through the center of Tom Waits's work, dividing his life into two neat categories: Before Kathleen Brennan and After Kathleen Brennan.

"Yeah," Waits says, and he's still all dazzled about her. "She's really radical."

They live in the countryside. In an old house. They have neighbors, like the guy who collects roadkill to shellac and make into art. And then there are the Seventh-Day Adventists and the Jehovah's Witnesses who knock on the door wanting to talk about Jesus. Waits always lets them in and offers them coffee and listens politely to their preaching because he thinks they are such sweet, lonely people. He only recently realized that they must think the same of him.

Waits drives a 1960 four-door Cadillac Coupe DeVille. It's a bigger car than he probably needs, and he admits that. It devours gas, smells terrible, radio doesn't work. But it's good for little day trips, like visits to the dump. Dumps, salvage yards, rummage sales, junk shops—these are his special retreats. Waits loves to find strange and resonant objects hidden deep in piles of garbage, objects he can rescue and turn into new kinds of musical instruments.

"I like to imagine how it feels for the object to become music," he says. "Imagine you're the lid to a fifty-gallon drum. That's your job. You work at that. That's your whole life. Then one day I find you and I say, 'We're gonna drill a hole in you, run a wire through you, hang you from the ceiling of the studio, bang on you with a mallet, and now you're in show business, baby!'"

Sometimes, though, he just goes searching for doors. He loves doors. They're his biggest indulgence. He's always coming home with more doors—Victorian, barn, French . . . His wife will protest, "But we already have a door!" and Waits will say, "But this one comes with such nice windows, baby!"

The Waits household has a family dog, too. Waits feels a special affinity for the animal and believes the two of them have a lot in common: Like "nerves," he says. "Barking at things that are inaudible. A need to mark a territory. I'm kinda like that. If I've been gone for three days, come home, first thing I have to do is take a walk around the house and establish myself again. I walk all over, touch everything, kick things, sit on things. Remind the room and everyone else that I'm back."

He's home almost all the time, because—unlike other dads—he doesn't have a day job. Which is why he's known by the local schools as the guy they can count on whenever they need an adult to do the driving for a field trip.

"I'm down with the field trips," Waits says. "I got the big car. I'm always looking for a nine-passenger opportunity." Recently, he took a group of kids to a guitar factory. It was a small operation, run by music types. "So I'm waiting for somebody to recognize me. OK, I think, someone's gonna come up and say, 'You're that guy, right?' Now, I've been there for, like, two hours. Nothing. *Nothing.* Now I'm getting pissed. In fact, I'm starting to pose over by the display case. Still waiting, but nothing all day. I get back in the car. I'm a little despondent. I mean, it's my field. I expect a nod or a wink, but nothing."

Waits takes a pause to stir his coffee.

"So a week later, we go on another field trip. It's a recycling thing. OK, I'm in. We pull up to the dump and six guys surround my car—'Hey! It's Tom Waits!' "

He shrugs wearily, like he's telling the timeworn story of his life. "Everybody knows me at the dump."

Perhaps the most singular feature about Tom Waits as an artist— the thing that makes him the anti-Picasso—is the way he has braided his creative life into his home life with such wit and grace. This whole idea runs contrary to our every stereotype about how geniuses need to work—about their explosive inter-personal relationships, about the lives (particularly the women's lives) they must consume in order to feed their inspiration, about all the painful destruction they leave in the wake of invention. But this is not Tom Waits. A collaborator at heart, he has never had to make the difficult choice between *creativity* and *procreativity*. At the Waits house, it's all thrown in there together—spilling out of the kitchen, which is also the office, which is also where the dog is disciplined, where the kids are raised, where the songs are written and where the coffee is poured for the wandering preachers. All of it somehow influences the rest.

The kids were certainly never a deterrent to the creativity—just further inspiration for it. He remembers the time his daughter helped him write a song. "We were on a bus coming to L.A. and it was really cold outside. There was this transgender person, to be politically correct, standing on a corner wearing a short little top with a lot of midriff showing, a lot of heavy eye makeup and dyed hair and a really short skirt. And this guy, or girl, was dancing all by himself. And my little girl saw it and said, 'It must be really hard to dance like that when you're so cold and there's no music.' "

Waits took his daughter's exquisite observation and worked it into a ballad called "Hold On"—a song of unspeakably aching hopefulness that was nominated for a Grammy and became the cornerstone of his album *Mule Variations*. "Children make up the best songs, anyway," he says. "Better than grown-ups. Kids are always working on songs and throwing them away, like little origami things or paper airplanes. They don't care if they lose it; they'll just make another one."

This openness is what every artist needs. Be ready to receive the inspiration when it comes; be ready to let it go when it vanishes. He believes that if a song "really wants to be written down, it'll stick in my head. If it wasn't interesting enough for me to remember it, well, it can just move along and go get in someone else's song."

"Some songs," he has learned, "don't want to be recorded." You can't wrestle with them or you'll only scare them off more. Trying to capture them sometimes "is trying to trap birds."

Fortunately, he says, other songs come easy, like "digging potatoes out of the ground." Others are sticky and weird, like "gum found under an old table." Clumsy and uncooperative songs may only be useful "to cut up as bait and use 'em to catch other songs." Of course, the best songs of all are those that enter you "like dreams taken through a straw." In those moments, all you can be, Waits says, is grateful.

Like a clever kid with a new toy, Waits is always willing to play with a new song, to see what else it can become. He'll play with it forever in and out of the studio, in ways a real grown-up would never imagine. He'll pick it apart, turn it inside out, drag it backward through the mud, ride a bicycle over it—anything he can imagine to make it sound thicker, rougher, deeper, different.

"I like my music," he says, "with the pulp and skin and seeds."

He's always fighting for new ways to hear or perform things. ("Play it like your hair's on fire," he has instructed musicians in the studio, when he can't explain his vision any other way. "Play it like a midget's bar mitzvah.") He wants to see the very guts of sound. Just as the architect Frank Gehry believes buildings are more beautiful when they're under construction than when they are completed, Tom Waits likes to see the naked skeleton of song. This is why he finds one of the most exciting sounds in all of music to be that of a symphony orchestra warming up.

"There's something about that moment, when they have no idea what they sound like," he rhapsodizes. "Someone's tightening up the threads of the timpani, someone else is playing snatches of an old song he hasn't played in a long time, someone else is going over that phrasing she keeps tripping on. It's like a documentary photograph—everyone is doing something without knowing they're being watched. And the audience is talking and paying no attention because it isn't music yet, right? But for me, there's lots of times when the lights go down and the show starts and I'm disappointed. Because nothing can live up to what I've just heard."

He abhors patterns, familiarity, and ruts. He stopped playing the piano for a while because, as he says, his hands had become like old dogs, always returning to the same place. Instead, he had fantasies of pushing his piano down the stairs and recording *that* noise. He is known to sing through a police megaphone. He once recorded a song in which the primary instrument was a creaking door. And on *Blood Money,* one of his new albums, he actually recorded a solo on a calliope—a huge, howling, ungodly pneumatic organ, best known for providing music for merry-go-rounds.

"I tell you," Waits says, "playing a calliope is an *experience.* There's an old expression, 'Never let your daughter marry a calliope player.' Because they're all out of their minds. Because the calliope is so flaming loud. Louder than a bagpipe. In the old days, they used them to announce the arrival of the circus because you could literally hear it three miles away. Imagine something you could hear three miles away, and now you're right in front of it, in a studio . . . playing it like a piano, and your face is red, your hair is sticking up, you're sweating. You could scream and nobody could hear you. It's probably the most visceral music experience I've ever had. And when you're done, you feel like you should probably go to the doctor. *Just check me over, Doc, I did a couple of numbers on the calliope and I want you to take me through the paces.*"

He likes a day in the studio to end, he says, "when my knees are all skinned up and my pants are wet and my hair's off to one side and I feel like I've been in the foxhole all day. I don't think comfort is good for music. It's good to come out with skinned knuckles after wrestling with something you can't see.

I like it when you come home at the end of the day from recording and someone says, 'What happened to your hand?' And you don't even know. When you're in that place, you can dance on a broken ankle."

That's a good day of work. A bad day is when the right sound won't reveal itself. Then Waits will pace in tight circles, rock back and forth, rub his hand over his neck, tug out his hair. He and Kathleen have a code for this troublesome moment. They say to each other, "Doctor, our flamingo is sick." Because how do you heal a sick *flamingo?* Why are its feathers falling out? Why are its eyes runny? Why is it so depressed? Who the hell knows? It's a fucking flamingo—a weird pink foreign bird. And music is just that weird, just that foreign. It is at difficult moments like these that Kathleen will show up with novel ideas. (*What if we played it like we were in China? But with banjos?*) She'll bring him a Balinese folk dance to listen to, or old recordings from the Smithsonian of Negro field hollers. Or she'll just take the flamingo off his hands for a while, take it for a walk, try to put some food into it.

I ask Tom Waits who does the bulk of the songwriting around the house—he or his wife? He says there's no way to judge it. It's like anything else in a good marriage. Sometimes it's fifty–fifty; sometimes it's ninety-ten; sometimes one person does all the work; sometimes the other. Gamely, he reaches for metaphors:

"I wash, she dries."

"I hold the nail, she swings the hammer."

"I'm the prospector, she's the cook."

"I bring home the flamingo, she beheads it . . ."

In the end, he concludes this way: "It's like two people borrowing the same ten bucks back and forth for years. After a while, you don't even write it down anymore. Just put it on the tab. Forget it."

* * *

Now, about those two new albums. They are called *Alice* and *Blood Money.* They are recordings of songs Waits has written in recent years for the stage, in collaboration with the visionary theater director Robert Wilson. *Alice* is a dreamy, haunting cycle of love songs based on the real-life story of a middle-aged Victorian minister who fell obsessively (and perhaps pruriently) in love with an enchanting nine-year-old girl. The little girl's name was Alice. The minister's name was Reverend Charles Dodgson, but he is more widely known by his pen name (Lewis Carroll) and for the surreal, not-totally-made-for-children children's story (*Alice's Adventures in Wonderland*) he wrote as a valentine to the girl he adored. On *Alice,* Waits uses his voice as if he were singing tormented lullabies. But singing those lullabies to somebody who's dying, or leaving forever, or growing up too fast.

The second album, *Blood Money,* is completely different. It's based on the German playwright Georg Buchner's unfinished masterwork, *Woyzeck,* about a jealous soldier who murders his lover in a park. (Waits considered calling the album *Woyzeck,* but then he figured, Jesus Christ, who would buy an album with a name like *Woyzeck?*) This album is all rich, complex, mysterious, dark tomes about the concussion of hatred against love. The sound is not quite industrial or grating, but there is a discord to these songs, almost a physical discomfort. These are dirty little dirges, with gritty titles like "Misery Is the River of the World" and "Everything Goes to Hell."

The good people at Waits's label, Anti, struck a bit of genius when they decided to release these two albums simultaneously. Because the contrasts of *Alice* and *Blood Money* perfectly highlight the two aspects of Waits's musical character that have been colliding in his work for decades. On one hand, the man has an unmatched instinct for melody. Nobody can write a more heartbreaking ballad than Waits. On the other hand, he has shown a lifelong desire to unbuckle those pretty melodies, cleave them into parts like a butcher, rearrange the parts like into some grotesque new beast and then leave it in the sun to rot. It's almost as if he's afraid that if he stuck to writing lovely ballads, he might become Billy Joel. Yet he loves music too much to write purely brainy experimental music like John Cage, either. So he does both, going back and forth, sometimes on the same album, sometimes in the same song, sometimes in the same phrase. (In the past, he's explained this schizophrenia as some musical version of the alcoholic cycle—first you're nice; then you punch a hole through the wall; then you sober up and apologize by giving flowers to everyone; then you crash your car into the swimming pool . . .)

This tempestuous struggle with music is the story of his life. Because while Tom Waits and sound have always been infatuated with each other, their relationship has never been a simple one. On the contrary, it's the kind of relationship that leaves broken china in its wake. There was a time, back when Waits was a child, when he had not yet made any kind of peace with sound and he was veritably tormented by the drunken disorderliness of it all. He remembers that the noises of this world felt like insects to him—insects that burrowed through every wall, crawled under every crack, penetrated every room, making absolute silence an absolute impossibility. With hypersensitivity like that (added to his inherently dark nature), Tom Waits could so easily have gone mad. Instead, he embarked on a mission to arrange a truce between himself and sound. A truce that, over the years, has become something like a collaboration and—with these two new albums—finally feels like a real marriage. Because here, on *Alice* and *Blood Money*, you can see it all together, side-by-side. All that Tom Waits is capable of. All the beauty and all the perversity. All the talent and all the discord. All that he wants to honor and all that he wants to dismantle. All of it gorgeous, all of it transporting.

So gorgeously transporting, in fact, that when you listen to these songs, you will feel as if somebody has blindfolded you, hypnotized you, given you opium, taken away your bearings and now is leading you backward on a carousel of your own past lives, asking you to touch all the dusty wooden animals of your old fears and lost loves, asking you to recognize them with only your hands.

Or maybe that's just how it felt for me.

At the end of it all, the dining room in this old inn has emptied and filled and emptied again several times around us. We've been sitting here talking for hours. The light has changed and changed again. But now Waits stretches and says, gosh, he feels like he knows me so well that he's almost tempted to take me on a visit to the local dump.

"It's not far from here," he says.

The dump! With Tom Waits! My mind thrills at the thought—the two of us banging on sheet metal or blowing songs into old blue milk-of-magnesia bottles. Sweet Jesus, I suddenly feel like there is nothing I have ever wanted more than to go to the dump with Tom Waits. But then he notices the time and shakes his head. A trip to the dump is impossible today, it turns out. He was due home hours ago. His wife is probably wondering where he is. And, anyhow, if I'm going to catch that flight out of San Francisco, shouldn't I get moving?

"I still have fifteen minutes before I have to leave!" I say, not yet letting go of the dream. "Maybe we could run over to the dump real quick!"

He gives me a grave look. My heart sinks. I already know the answer.

"Fifteen minutes would not be fair to the dump," Tom Waits pronounces, proving that he is above all things a fair and respectful man. "Fifteen minutes would be an insult to the dump."

FRESH AIR INTERVIEW

National Public Radio, WHYY, May 2002

Terry Gross

This is *Fresh Air*. I'm Terry Gross.

My guest, Tom Waits, is one of the true eccentrics of pop music. In the *New York Times* this month, he was described as "the poet of outcasts." There's always been an element of mystery surrounding his life. The people he sings about are usually loners, losers, hoboes, outlaws, and drunks. The darkness of his lyrics is accentuated by the rumble and rasp of his voice; a voice that sounded old even when he was young. Waits has been recording since 1973. VH1 named him as one of the most influential artists of all time. His songs have been used on the soundtrack of several films, and he's acted in the films *Down by Law, Short Cuts,* and Francis Ford Coppola's *Dracula.*

Waits has two new CDs: *Alice* and *Blood Money.* Each was written for a music theater piece by Robert Wilson. Each has songs cowritten with Waits and his wife, Kathleen Brennan. Let's start with a song from *Blood Money.* This is "Misery Is the River of the World."

(Soundbite of "Misery Is the River of the World".)

GROSS: Music from Tom Waits's new CD, *Blood Money*. Tom Waits, welcome to *Fresh Air*.

WAITS: Oh, thanks. Thanks for having me.

GROSS: What was the music that you grew up listening to because your parents were listening to it? I mean, before you were old enough to choose music yourself, what was the music in your house?

WAITS: Mm-hmm. Really young, mariachi music, I guess. My dad only played a Mexican radio station. And then, you know, Frank Sinatra, and later, Harry Belafonte. And then, you know, I would go over to my friends' houses and I would go into the den with their dads and find out what they were listening to, because I was—I couldn't wait to be an old man. I was about thirteen, you know. I didn't really identify with the music of my own generation, but I was very curious about the music of others. And I think I responded to the song forms themselves, you know; cakewalks and waltzes and barcaroles and parlor songs and all that stuff, I think—which is just really nothing more than Jell-O molds for music, you know. But I seemed to like the old stuff; Cole Porter and, you know, Rodgers and Hammerstein and Gershwin and all that stuff. I like melody.

GROSS: What was the music of your generation that didn't interest you?

WAITS: You know, like the Strawberry Alarm Clock.

GROSS: Right.

WAITS: But later, I liked that stuff. You know, like the Animals and Blue Cheer and—I don't know—you know, Led Zeppelin and all that stuff and the Yardbirds and, you know, of course, the Rolling Stones and the Beatles and Bob Dylan and James Brown. I was really, really hot on James Brown.

GROSS: You said your father listened mostly to the Mexican station and to mariachi music—was your father Mexican?

WAITS: No. My dad's from Texas. He grew up in a place called Sulphur Springs, Texas. And my mom's from Oregon. She listened to church music, you know, all that Brother Springer, all the—she used to send money in to all the preachers, you know. But the earliest song I remember was "Abilene." When I heard "Abilene" on the radio, it really moved me. And then I heard, you know, "Abilene, Abilene, prettiest town I've ever seen. Women there don't treat you mean in Abilene," I just thought that was the greatest lyric, you know. "Women there don't treat you mean." And then, you know "Detroit City"—"Last night I went to sleep in Detroit City, and I dreamed about the cotton fields back home." I like songs with the names of towns in them, and I think I liked songs with weather in them, and something to eat. So I feel like there's a certain anatomical aspect to a song that I respond to. I think, "Oh, yeah. I can go into that world. There's something to eat, there's a name of a street, there's a—OK. Yeah, there's a saloon, OK." So I think probably that's why I put things like that in my songs.

GROSS: When you started listening to older music and relating to that, did other things accompany that, like a certain way of dressing or speaking or behaving?

WAITS: Hmm. Oh, yeah, sure. You know, I wore an old hat and I drove an old car. I bought a car for fifty bucks from Fred Moody next door who's from Tennessee, a '55 Buick Special, and, you know, AM radio in it. I guess. Yeah, sure. I walked with a cane. You know, I was going overboard, perhaps, but . . .

GROSS: What kind of cane was it? Did it have like a silver tip? I mean, how . . .

WAITS: No, no, an old man's cane from a Salvation Army.

GROSS: Uh-huh.

WAITS: Yeah. And I carved my name in it and everything, you know.

GROSS: And what did you think? That that added to your image?

WAITS: It gave me a walk, I guess. It gave me something distinctive. "Oh, who was that guy in here earlier with a cane? Did you see that guy?" It just gave me something that I liked identity wise, I guess.

GROSS: Now I want to ask you about your voice. You have a very raspy singing voice. Was that a sound that you strove for, you know, that you worked on having, or is it what naturally developed?

WAITS: It's that old man thing. I couldn't wait to be an old man; old man with a deep voice. No. I screamed into a pillow . . .

GROSS: Have you ever worried about hurting your voice by . . .

WAITS: Oh, I've hurt it. Yeah, I have hurt it. But I have a voice doctor in New York who used to treat Frank Sinatra and various people. He said, "Oh, you're doing fine. Don't worry about it."

GROSS: Oh, that's good. Now you once said that you wish you could have been a part of the Brill Building era, in which people like Carole King and Leiber and Stoller and Ellie Greenwich and Jeff Barry were writing songs for singers and for vocal groups. What do you think you would have liked about that?

WAITS: Well, I guess writing at gunpoint. It sounds really exciting to me, those kinds of deadlines. I went into the rehearsal building on Times Square in New York one afternoon and a really tiny little room. In fact, it was probably smaller than the room I'm in right now, which is a little larger than a phone booth. There's just enough room for a little spinet piano and then you could just barely close the door and there you were. And you could hear every kind of music coming to you through the walls and through the windows, underneath the door. And you heard African bands and you heard, like, you know, comedians and you'd hear applause every now and then and you'd hear tap dancers. And I think I'd just like the whole mélange of it, you know. I mean, it all kind of mixes together.

GROSS: Mm-hmm.

WAITS: I like turning on two radios at the same time and listening to them. I like hearing things incorrectly. I think that's how I get a lot of ideas, by mishearing something.

GROSS: What are some of the things that scared you as a kid, either that scared you in real life or movies or music, that you found frightening—interesting, but frightening?

WAITS: Oh, I don't know. I guess, like, the plastic covers on sofas scare me—the sound that makes when you sit down on a sofa that's covered with plastic. It crinkles and—I don't know. I used to watch Alfred Hitchcock and *The Twilight Zone.* Those captivate me, those little tales.

GROSS: Mm-hmm. Monster movies?

WAITS: And monster movies, sure. But, you know, things that really scared me—I don't know. I guess, you know, I could conjure up just about anything and scare myself, you know. If I heard a sound at night, you know, and then it would get larger and larger and stranger and stranger, and, you know, it would get—you know, afraid to get out of bed. I think I had some kind of a disorder, the way I heard things. If I moved my hand across in the air, I heard, like . . . [Makes whooshing sound.]

GROSS: Wow, really?

WAITS: And cars going by sounded like planes, and, you

know, very small sounds in the house got enormous. But I think it was just a temporary condition.

GROSS: Did you ever see a doctor about it?

WAITS: [Laughs.] They said they couldn't help me.

GROSS: Now, you dropped out of high school. Why did you drop out? Is there something that you wanted to do instead, or did you just hate going?

WAITS: Oh, I wanted to go into the world, you know? Enough of this. Didn't like the ceiling in the rooms. I didn't like the holes in the ceiling, those little tiny holes and the cork board and the long stick used for opening the windows.

GROSS: Oh, God, yeah, we had one of those in my elementary school. Yeah.

WAITS: Oh, I just hated all that stuff. I was real sensitive to my visual surroundings, and I just—you know, I just wanted to get out of there.

GROSS: Did any adults try to stop you, either your parents or teachers?

WAITS: I had good teachers. I had some—my folks broke up when I was about eleven, and so I had teachers that I liked a lot, that I kind of looked up to. But then they seemed like they couldn't wait to get out into the world themselves and do some, you know, banging around and learning and growing. And so I thought maybe they were encouraging me to leave.

GROSS: So did you succeed in kind of getting out into the world, so to speak?

WAITS: Pretty much, yeah.

GROSS: What'd you do?

WAITS: Oh, I hitchhiked all over the place . . . and I don't know . . .

GROSS: What's the craziest ride that you got when you were hitchhiking that you would shudder to think about now?

WAITS: Well, actually, I had some good things that happened to me hitchhiking, because I did wind up on New Year's Eve in front of a Pentecostal church, and an old woman named Mrs. Anderson came out of the—I was stuck in a town with, like, seven people in this town, and trying to get out, you know? And my buddy and I were out there for hours and hours and hours getting colder and colder, and it was getting darker and darker. And finally she came over and she says, "Come on into the church here, where it's warm and there's music, and you can sit in the back row." And we did. And they were singing and, you know, they had a tambourine, an electric guitar and a drummer.

And they were, you know, talking in tongues, and then they kept gesturing to me and my friend Sam; said, "These are our wayfaring strangers here," and so we felt kind of important. And they took up a collection, they gave us the money, bought us a hotel room and a meal. And we got out the next morning and we hit the first ride, seven in the morning, and we were gone. It was really nice. I still remember all of that. And it gave me a good feeling about traveling.

GROSS: Tom Waits, thank you so much. It's really been great to talk with you. Thank you.

WAITS: Oh, oh, we're all done.

GROSS: Yeah.

WAITS: Oh, OK. Nice to talk to you, Terry.

THE ONION INTERVIEW

The Onion, May 29, 2002

Keith Phipps

Tom Waits was born on December 7, 1949, in the back of a truck (or a taxi, depending on which account, if any, is to be believed) in the Los Angeles suburb of Pomona. True or not, it's an appropriate origin for a man whose music contains so much transience and questionable sanitary conditions. Waits began performing Beat-inspired songs in clubs around the time he reached legal drinking age, though his gravelly voice seemed incongruous with his youth. Experience and albums followed, as he became a sort of hipster outsider cousin to the seventies California music scene. After meeting frequent collaborator Kathleen Brennan, who eventually became his wife, Waits adopted a more experimental approach only suggested by his previous work. His cluttered, clamoring new style, first fully developed on 1983's *Swordfishtrombones,* led him to a new audience and a new label. Around the same time, Waits began curbing the lifestyle detailed in his gutter-trolling songs, tried his hand at acting, and found new collaborators, most notably director Jim Jarmusch and Robert Wilson, a longtime fixture of avant-garde theater. After a six-year silence following 1993's *The Black Rider*, Waits returned with *Mule Variations*, then disappeared again. From a carefully guarded location somewhere in rural California, Waits spoke to the *Onion A. V. Club* shortly after the simultaneous May release of *Alice* and *Blood Money*, both soundtracks to Wilson works.

The Onion: When you do theatrical projects, do you worry at all about them translating to albums?

Tom Waits: Gee, I don't know. What do you think? How did it go? I don't think it really matters much. I mean, by the time it's a record, it's just a record. It either works in that way or it doesn't. I don't think the backstory really dignifies anything, or solves any problems that you tried to solve during the recording. "Oh, this is all based on the John Wilkes Booth story, and that third song is when he was trapped in the barn." I mean, I could tell you anything. "Helen Keller made an appearance in the last tune, and it's sung by her mother." "Oh, okay." Your mind will make sense of anything. The fact that *Blood Money* is about Woyzeck . . . I didn't know anything about Woyzeck. Kathleen knew more than I, but I didn't really know the story or anything. I was just told the story in a coffee shop in Boston over eggs a few years ago. You try to create some sort of counterpoint for this story, but you're still dealing with song logic. When people listen to songs, they're not . . . It's like a form of hypnotism that goes on during the listening process, so you're taking it up through a straw. It's like a separate little world in the world. You go in there and then you pop back out. Those musicals always sound so corny when somebody stops and thinks of something and goes back to life.

O: You've said before that the stories behind songs are less interesting than the songs themselves. Have you ever written a song where the opposite was true?

TW: Oh, gee. I don't know. Most songs have meager beginnings. You wake up in the morning, you throw on your suspenders, and you subvocalize and just think. They seem to form like calcium. I can't think of a story right off the bat that was that interesting. I write things on the back of my hand, usually, and sing into a tape recorder. I don't know.

O: Many of your albums are filled with references to sailors and the sea. Do you think there's a reason for that, beyond growing up in San Diego?

TW: I think all songs should have weather in them. Names of towns and streets, and they should have a couple of sailors. I think those are just song prerequisites. [Laughs.]

O: For yours, or for all songs?

TW: Oh, all songs. Most of them fail miserably. I go looking in other people's songs for their sailors and their towns. I don't know, everybody has things that they gravitate towards. Some people put toy cars or clouds or cat crap. Everybody puts something different, and it's entirely up to you what belongs and what doesn't. They're interesting little vessels of emotional information, and you carry them in your pocket like a bagel.

O: When *Mule Variations* came out, it seemed like the first question most people had for you was, "What took you so long?" Does that annoy you?

TW: Well, I submitted myself to the questions, so it's hard to be annoyed. But, yeah, when people want to know what you've been up to, how can you possibly explain to a stranger what you've been doing for seven years? Would they truly be interested? [Laughs.]

O: It seems artists with a devoted following are under pressure to turn out albums regularly. Does that pressure ever get to you?

TW: Not really. It's not like I'm one of those expensive, high-powered pop groups on the road eight months out of the year, talking to *Teen Beat*. I finally discovered that my life is more important than show business. But, yeah, people are curious about all kinds of things, which takes your mind off that which is really important. They usually ask questions about things that don't matter to them, or to me, or to anybody else. Just to take up time, I guess, and distract them from the important questions, like "Who won the World Series in 1957?" or "Who said, 'Today you will play jazz, tomorrow you will betray your country'?"

O: Is there an answer to that one?

TW: It was on a Soviet propaganda poster in the thirties. Did you know that honey is the only food that won't spoil? They found it in King Tut's tomb. Jars of honey. They said it was just as fresh as it was on the first day.

O: Did they actually try it?

TW: They tried it, yeah. Wouldn't you? If you found a jar of
honey in a thousands-of-years-old tomb, would you put
your finger into it and taste it?

O: So, why did it take you so long to record the songs on
Alice?

TW: The songs were written around '92 or '93, 'round in
there. It was done with Robert Wilson in Germany.
We stuck 'em in a box and just left 'em there for a
while. They were aging like the honey. And we locked
in the freshness. They were hermetically sealed. You
move on to other things, you know? And then you go
back and say, "Well, this was okay."

O: It was kind of developing a reputation as the great lost
Tom Waits album.

TW: I bought a copy of the bootleg on eBay. 'Cause I didn't
know where those tapes were.

O: How does the bootleg hold up?

TW: Okay. There was stuff that didn't make it on to the
record.

O: How many songs are usually left over on any given record?

TW: Oh, there's always a bunch of them that don't make the
boat. That's normal. You just stick 'em all together later
and put 'em out by themselves. Those *Alice* songs were

all in a briefcase that got stolen out of the back of my car, and they were ransomed by these radicals who thought they really had something. We had to pay a couple of grand to get the briefcase back, but I think they copied the tapes.

O: What was the exchange like? Did you get to meet them somewhere?

TW: Yeah, some dark café, you know, everybody was wearing sunglasses, it was really cold. They said, "We're gonna leave the briefcase by the trash can. Put the money in a bag . . ." It added a little intrigue to the whole project.

O: What's your collaborative process like with Kathleen Brennan?

TW: [Chuckles.] Oh! Well, you know, "You wash, I'll dry." It all comes down to making choices and a lot of decisions. You know, are we gonna do a song about our cruise ship, or a meadow, or a brothel, or . . . just a rhapsody, or is it a parlor song or a work song or a field holler? What is it? The form itself is like a Jell-O mold. It's like doing anything that you would do with someone. "You hold it right there while I hit it," or the other way around. You find a rhythm in the way of working. I trust her opinion above all else. You've gotta have somebody to trust, that knows a lot. She's done a lot of things. I'm Ingrid Bergman and she's Bogart. She's got a pilot's license, and she was gonna be a nun before we got married. I put an end to that. She knows about everything from motor-cycle repair to high finance, and she's an excellent pianist. One of the leading authorities on the African violet. She's a lot of strong material. She's like Super-woman, standing there with her cape flapping. It works. We've been at this for some time now. Sometimes you quarrel, and it's the result of irritation, and sometimes it comes out of the ground like a potato and we marvel at it. She doesn't like the spotlight. She's a very private person, as opposed to myself. [Laughs.]

O: You have kind of developed a reputation as a recluse. Does that bother you?

TW: Hell, no. I think that's a good one. It wards off strangers. It's like being a beekeeper. No, if people are a little nervous about approaching you at the market, it's good. I'm not Chuckles the Clown. Or Bozo. I don't cut the ribbon at the opening of markets. I don't stand next to the mayor. Hit your baseball into my yard, and you'll never see it again. I just have a close circle of friends and loved ones—the circle of trust, as they say.

O: There's actually a section on your Web site about fans who have spotted or encountered you in public. Do you have a problem going out?

TW: I go where I feel like. Funny little story . . . I drove on a field trip once, to a guitar factory, to show all these little kids how to make guitars. So we're standing there, and I'm looking around, and folks are looking over at me, and I'm just waiting for someone to recognize me—you know, "Hey, aren't you that music guy? That singer guy?" Nobody. Nothing. We're there for, like, two hours, watching them put the frets on and all that, and I'm waiting and waiting . . . A week later, I took the same group of kids on a field trip to the dump, and as I pulled up, don't ask me how, but my truck was surrounded by people that wanted an autograph. It was a dump, for Christ's sake. I guess everybody knows me at the dump.

O: It kind of proves that you never know who your audience is.

TW: You don't really know. I guess one should not even assume that one has an audience, and allow it to go to your head.

O: Your early stuff is influenced by the Beats, and your later stuff seems equally influenced by older, harder-to-define influences. Do you think you're slipping further back into the past as you get older?

TW: I don't know. I hope I'm not slipping at all.

O: I don't mean that in a negative sense. I mean, do you think you're drawing on older influences as you get older?

TW: I really don't know. What you rely on . . . I think you kind of take the world apart and put it back together. The further you get from something, the better your memory is of it, sometimes. Who knows how that works? Those are big questions about the nature of memory and its influence on your present life. I don't know. Consider this: The number of cars on the planet is increasing three times faster than the population growth. Three times faster. I mean, there's eleven and a half million cars in Los Angeles alone.

O: What are you driving these days?

TW: Oh, I got a beautiful 1959 Cadillac Coupe DeVille four-door. No one will ride in it with me.

O: Why's that?

TW: It's unsafe. But it looks good. I take it to the dump. We spend a lot of time in our cars. You know what I really love? The CD players in a car. How when you put the CD right up by the slot, it actually takes it out of your hand, like it's hungry. It pulls it in, and you feel like it wants more silver discs. "More silver discs. Please." I enjoy that.

O: Do you have one in the Cadillac?

TW: No, I have a little band in there. It's an old car, so I have a little old string band in the glove compartment. It's grumpy.

O: You used a lot of unusual instruments on these albums. Can you tell me about any of them? I was intrigued by the stroh violin [a violin with a trumpetlike bell attached to it].

TW: Well, you know, there were stroh basses, and there were stroh violas, stroh cellos. Have you ever seen one?

O: No, I don't think so.

TW: It's a horn attached to the bridge, and it has a hinge on it. It's like a brass flower designed in the same configuration

371

or shape as the old 78 players. You could aim it at the balcony. The string players were disgruntled. They felt they were constantly competing with the brass. It gave 'em a little edge. I don't know, you don't hear it anymore. I guess because before the advent of amplification, you were dealing purely with physics all the time. It's an interesting solution to that problem.

O: Are there any instruments that you've wanted to use that you haven't had a chance to yet?

TW: Well, we tried to find a theremin for *Alice,* but we were unable to find anyone locally that was really accomplished. The woman that played in the original *Alice* orchestra we found was the granddaughter of Leon Theremin. She was really amazing. You would imagine someone like that would have some really sophisticated instrument, but she brought this thing that looked like a hot plate with a car aerial coming out of it. She opened it up, and inside, all the connections between the circuits were established with cut-up little pieces of beer can wrapped around the wires. All the paint was worn off, but when she played it, it was like Jascha Heifetz. They're doing experiments with the theremin now. The sound waves you experience when you play it have therapeutic value.

O: How so?

TW: I don't know, just the fact that you don't touch it—that you play the air and you're in contact with the waves—somehow does something to you on a more genetic level, and can heal the sick. Raise the dead. Apparently.

You know the average person spends two weeks over their lifetime waiting for the traffic light to change?

O: Really? I would actually guess a little more.

TW: I would guess more, too. I'm thinking, two weeks, you know . . .

O: That sounds like a bargain.

TW: During your whole lifetime, though. You know mosquito repellents don't actually repel anything? They actually hide you because they block the mosquito's sensors. They don't know that you're there. It's like blinding them.

O: It used to be that, like you, a lot of musicians took a hard-line stance against having their music used in advertising. That seems to have shifted. Why do you think that is?

TW: I don't know. They're all high on crack. Let's just say it's a sore subject with me. I went to court over it, you know . . . You know, you see a bathroom-tissue commercial, and you start hearing "Let the Good Times Roll," and the paper thing's rolling down the stairs. Why would anybody want to mortify and humiliate themselves? Well, it's just business, you know? The memory that you have and the association you have with that song can be co-opted. And a lot of people are really in it for the money. Period. A lot of people don't have any control over it. I don't own the copyrights to my early tunes. So it is unfortunate, but there are a lot of people that consciously want their songs exploited in that way, which I think is demeaning. I hate it when I hear songs that I already have a connection with used in a way that's humiliating. I mean, in the old days, if somebody was doing a commercial, you used to say, "Oh, gee, too bad, he probably needs the money." But now, it's like hocking cigarettes and underwear with rock 'n' roll. I guess that's our big export. It's like how a good butcher uses every part of the cow. I don't like hearing those Beatles songs in the commercials. It almost renders them useless. Maybe not for everyone else, but when I hear it I just think, "Oh, God, another one bites the dust."

O: I still can't hear "Good Vibrations" without thinking of Sunkist.

TW: Oh, wow, yeah. That's exactly what they want. They want to plug your head into that and change the circuitry. While you're dreaming about your connection with that song, why don't you think about soda or candy or something? It's too bad, but it's the way of the world. They love to get their meat-hooks in you.

O: Your kids are old enough to have their own musical tastes now. Do you approve of what they listen to?

TW: Oh, sure, yeah. As long as they're listening. You know, what happens is that as you start getting older, you get out of touch. I'm like a turtleneck sweater. And then your kids kind of enlighten you: "Dad, have you heard Blackalicious?" I take 'em to the show, but I drop them off. I'm not allowed to go in. It'd be too embarrassing.

O: Do you have a favorite cover version of one of your songs?

TW: Johnny Cash did a song called "Down There by the Train," Solomon Burke did one. But, you know, cover versions are good. I used to bark about it, and then I said, "Oh, it's good." If you write songs, you really do kind of want someone to hear it and say, "Hey, man, I could do that." So if they're not doing your songs, you wonder, "Why aren't they doing my songs?" If it's too individual, too personal, then it can't be reimagined.

O: What's the most outrageous lie you've ever told a reporter?

TW: That I'm a medical doctor.

O: Did the reporter buy it?

TW: I started talking anatomy with the guy, and I think I strung him along pretty good for a while. But then I realized . . . He told me his dad was a doctor, and he tripped me up on something. I mispronounced "femur" or something. I do like books on anatomy. I have to say I'm an amateur physician, I guess.

O: You've never practiced?

TW: I practice at home, on the kids. Interestingly enough, there are a lot of musicians who are also doctors, or a lot of doctors who are also musicians. There is a connection. Surgeons work in a theater, and they call it a theater. All medical procedures require two hands, so in a sense it's like when you play an instrument. That's what they call things that they use in their work: They call them instruments. I've played with a lot of musicians who are also doctors. I worked with a bass player who was a doctor. You know, I suppose there is a connection. A lot of people start out majoring in medicine and drop it and change their major to music. I don't know, it's just one of those things.

O: Any last words for our readers?

TW: Famous last words? Lemme think here. All right, here we go. Umm . . . I'm looking down my list. Never have I waltzed to "My Country 'Tis of Thee," nor met anyone who did. Still, it's a waltz, for it's written in waltz time.

PROUST QUESTIONNAIRE

Vanity Fair, November 2004

For more than thirty years, singer-songwriter (not to mention actor and playwright) Tom Waits has been the godfather of the gravelly-voiced barroom ballad. With a new album—*Real Gone,* his twentieth—in stores this month, the gruff Renaissance man pauses to reflect on his affection for lies, the bliss of washing dishes, and his favorite Journey.

VF: What is your idea of perfect happiness?
TW: Happiness is never perfect.

VF: What is your greatest fear?
TW: Being buried alive.

VF: Which historical figure do you most identify with?
TW: Cantinflas.

VF: What is your favorite journey?
TW: Actually, I don't own any of their records.

VF: What do you consider the most overrated virtue?
TW: Honesty.

VF: On what occasions do you lie?
TW: Who needs an occasion?

VF: Which words or phrases do you most overuse?
TW: "Do as I say and no one will get hurt."

VF: What or who is the greatest love of your life?
TW: My wife, Kathleen.

VF: When and where were you happiest?
TW: Nineteen sixty-three, 1:00 A.M., washing dishes on a Saturday night in the kitchen of Napoleone Pizza House, 619 National Avenue, National City, California.

VF: Which talent would you most like to have?
TW: Being able to fix the truck.

VF: If you could choose what to come back as, what would it be?
TW: A bull in Wyoming.

VF: What do you regard as the lowest depth of misery?
TW: The floor just below that.

VF: Where would you like to live?
TW: Hotel Esmarelda, Storyville.

VF: What is your favorite occupation?
TW: Blacksmith, ventriloquist, magician, jockey, train conductor, tree surgeon, and lion tamer.

VF: What is your most marked characteristic?

TW: My ability to discuss, in depth, a book I've never read.

VF: What is the quality you most like in a man?

TW: Generosity, irony, bravery, humor, madness, imagination, and the ability to take a punch.

VF: What is the quality you most like in a woman?

TW: Good bones, sharp teeth, big heart, black humor, full of magic, plenty of forgiveness, and a good sport.

VF: What do you most value in your friends?

TW: Jumper cables and a tow chain.

VF: Who are your favorite writers?

TW: Rod Serling, Breece D'J Pancake, Charles Bukowski, Woody Guthrie, Bill Hicks, Fellini, Frank Stanford, Willie Dixon, Bob Dylan, O. Henry.

VF: Who is your favorite hero of fiction?

TW: Frankenstein. And Dumbo.

VF: How would you like to die?

TW: I don't think I would like that very much at all.

NIRVANA

Black Sparrow Press, 1992

Charles Bukowski

———————————

Note: In a 2002 interview with SOMA *magazine, Waits mentioned that the following by Bukowski was among his favorite poems.*

not much chance,
completely cut loose from
purpose,
he was a young man
riding a bus
through North Carolina
on the way to
somewhere
and it began to snow
and the bus stopped
at a little cafe
in the hills
and the passengers
entered.

he sat at the counter
with the others,
he ordered and the
food arrived.
the meal was
particularly
good
and the
coffee.

the waitress was
unlike the women
he had
known.
she was unaffected,
there was a natural
humor which came
from her.
the fry cook said
crazy things.
the dishwasher,
in back,
laughed, a good
clean
pleasant
laugh.

the young man watched
the snow through the
windows.

he wanted to stay
in that cafe
forever.

the curious feeling
swam through him
that everything
was
beautiful
there,
that it would always
stay beautiful
there.

then the bus driver
told the passengers
that it was time
to board.

the young man
thought, I'll just sit
here, I'll just stay
here.

but then
he rose and followed
the others into the
bus.

he found his seat
and looked at the cafe
through the bus
window.

then the bus moved
off, down a curve,
downward, out of
the hills.

the young man
looked straight
forward.
he heard the other
passengers
speaking
of other things,
or they were
reading
or
attempting to
sleep.

they had not
noticed
the
magic.

the young man
put his head to
one side,
closed his
eyes,
pretended to
sleep.
there was nothing
else to do—
just listen to the

sound of the
engine,
the sound of the
tires
in the
snow.

TIMELINE AND DISCOGRAPHY

DECEMBER 7, 1949

Born to Jesse Frank Waits and Alma Johnson McMurray (both school-teachers), in Pomona, California.

1960

Parents divorce.

1965

Lands first job at Napoleone Pizza House in San Diego. Later sings about it on "I Can't Wait to Get Off Work," from *Small Change*.

1965

Plays in band called the Systems (R&B and Soul).

NOVEMBER 1970

First paid gig at the Heritage Stage. Paid $25.

1971

Herb Cohen becomes his manager. Moves from San Diego to Los Angeles. Does demo recordings for Straight/Bizarre (Cohen's label). Tracks later released on albums *The Early Years I & II*.

1973

Releases album *Closing Time* (Elektra Entertainment).

1974

Releases second LP, *The Heart of Saturday Night* (Elektra/Asylum Records). Later in the year he releases the single "San Diego Serenade."

1975

Moves to the Tropicana Motel on Santa Monica Boulevard. Releases double album *Nighthawks at the Diner* (Elektra/Asylum Records).

1976

Releases *Small Change* (Asylum Records), and later in the year releases single "Step Right Up" / "The Piano Has Been Drinking (Not Me)" (Asylum).

1977

Arrested in Los Angeles with Chuck E. Weiss at Duke's Tropicana Coffee Shop for disturbing the peace. Later found not guilty. Also releases album *Foreign Affairs* (Elektra Entertainment) and begins an affair with Rickie Lee Jones.

1978

Appears in first movie alongside Sylvester Stallone, *Paradise Alley*, as Mumbles, a pianist. Releases album *Blue Valentine* (Elektra Entertainment), and later in the year records single "Somewhere."

1979

Releases single "Somewhere" / "Red Shoes by the Drugstore" (Asylum). Breaks up with Rickie Lee Jones.

1980

Marries Kathleen Brennan. Releases *Heartattack and Vine* (Elektra Entertainment).

1983

Releases soundtrack album *One from the Heart* (Columbia Records/Sony Music Entertainment) for Francis Ford Coppola movie, on which Crystal Gayle shares vocals. Leaves Asylum and Herb Cohen, and signs with Island Records. Moves to New York City. Daughter, Kellesimone, is born. *Swordfishtrombones*, first album produced by Waits, comes out on Island Records.

1984

Meets Jim Jarmusch and John Lurie. Albums *Anthology* (Elektra) and *The Asylum Years* (Asylum) are released, though Waits is now with Island Records.

1985

Rain Dogs comes out on Island Records, as well as the single "Downtown Train" / "Tango Till They're Sore." Son, Casey Xavier, is born. Named "Songwriter of the Year" by *Rolling Stone.*

1986

Releases single "In the Neighborhood" / "Jockey Full of Bourbon" / "Tango Till They're Sore" / "Sixteen Shells from a Thirty Ought Six" (Island). Stars in Jim Jarmusch's film *Down by Law* with John Lurie and Roberto Benigni.

1987

Album *Frank's Wild Years* released (Island). Appears in screen version of *Ironweed* with Jack Nicholson and Meryl Streep.

1988

Release of concert album and video *Big Time* (Island Records).

1990

Wins $2.5 million judgment against Frito-Lay for its unauthorized use of his music in a 1988 Doritos commercial.

1991

Unauthorized release of 1971 recordings for album *The Early Years I* (Bizarre/Straight Records).

1992

Release of album *Night on Earth* (Island Records). Also, a second unauthorized album, *The Early Years II* (Bizarre/Straight Records), is released, as well as *Bone Machine* (Island Records). Plays Renfield in Coppola's *Dracula*. At the end of the year, he wins Best Alternative Music Album Grammy for *Bone Machine*.

1993

Collaborates with William S. Burroughs on the album *The Black Rider* (Island Records), which becomes a stage production directed by Robert Wilson. Appears in Robert Altman's film version of Raymond Carver's stories, *Short Cuts*. Son, Sullivan, is born.

1998

Album *Beautiful Maladies: The Island Years* (Island Records) is released, and Waits leaves Island Records.

1999

Album *Mule Variations* (Epitaph) is released.

2000

Awarded Best Contemporary Folk Album Grammy for *Mule Variations*.

2002

Two albums released on Epitaph, *Alice* and *Blood Money*. Collaborates again with Wilson on stage drama, *Woyzeck*.

2004

Releases album *Real Gone* (Epitaph), to great critical acclaim.

ACKNOWLEDGMENTS

Without the following people and places, this book would never have made it to closing time.

Jofie Ferrari-Adler for having the great idea of this book and telling me about it in the kitchen that day.

John Oakes for recognizing how good Jofie's idea was.

Rachel Mehlsak, who is so fantastically more organized than I could ever be.

Naomi Sablan for being really patient with me and good with the celebs.

Nancy Dillon for schlepping me to work (and having the *Vanity Fair* with the Waits piece in her car library).

Isaac Guzman for his foreword thinking.

Aaron Goldman and April Peveto, for loving music as much as they do.

Jim Jarmusch for showing me my first images of Waits.

Melissa Lo for her help out West.

Pieter Hartmans, keeper of the unofficial Waits Web site, the Tom Waits Supplement, www.keeslau.com/TomWaits-Supplement/, for this exhaustive, invaluable research tool. If you are a fan, go there now.

Billy and Pinn for being radical. Always.

San Francisco and Los Angeles for going so well with Waits.

Aaron Ruby for our Waitsian years together on Cherokee, Spalding, and Detroit.

Heather Chaplin, Plato Hieronimus, Peter Cavagnaro, and Jeremy Kasten for being who they are.

The Clash, the Replacements, Serge Gainsbourg, and any

other music that makes you feel cooler than you are.

Mom and Dad, who played me *Abbey Road,* Pete Seeger, and the *King Kong Compilation* when I was a kid, and taught me to love music.

Catherine and Oona for being absolutely the sweetest, greatest family a guy could ever want.

Black Francis, for his kindness and for lending his considerable talent to this project.

Tom Waits for making some of the most beautiful and sad music the world has ever heard.

CREDITS

Grateful acknowledgment is made for permission to reprint the following copyrighted works. We have made every effort to trace and contact copyright holders. If an error or omission is brought to our notice we will be pleased to correct the situation in future editions of this book. For further information, please contact the publisher.

Bradley Bambarger: "Tom Waits Joins Indie Epitaph for *Mule* Set," *Billboard*, March 20, 1999. Used by permission of *Billboard* magazine.

Johnny Black: "Tom Waits: Waits and Double Measures," *London Trax*, March 18, 1981. Used by permission of music author and critic Johnny Black, who also runs www.backonthetracks.com

Brian Brannon: "Tom Waits," *Thrasher*, February 1993. Used by permission of the author and *Thrasher* magazine.

Rob Brunner: "No Tom Like the Present," *Entertainment Weekly*, June 21, 2002. Used by permission of *Entertainment Weekly* magazine.

Charles Bukowski: "nirvana," from *The Last Night of the Earth Poems* by Charles Bukowski (Black Sparrow Press, 1992). Copyright © 1992 by Charles Bukowski. Reprinted by permission of HarperCollins Publishers Inc.

Charles Bukowski: "one for the shoeshine man," from *Love Is a Dog from Hell: Poems 1974–1977* by Charles Bukowski (Black Sparrow Press, 1977). Copyright © 1977 by Charles Bukowski. Reprinted by permission of HarperCollins Publishers Inc.

Betsy Carter with Peter S. Greenberg: "Sweet and Sour," *Newsweek*, June 14, 1976. Copyright © 1976 Newsweek, Inc. All rights reserved. Reprinted by permission.

David Fricke: "The Resurrection of Tom Waits," *Rolling Stone*, June 24, 1999. Copyright © Rolling Stone LLC 1999. All rights reserved. Reprinted by permission.

Elizabeth Gilbert: "Play It Like Your Hair's on Fire," *GQ*, June 2002. Copyright © 2002 Elizabeth Gilbert. Reprinted with the permission of The Wylie Agency, Inc. The article originally appeared in the June 2002 issue of *GQ*.

Terry Gross: "Fresh Air," National Public Radio, WHYY, May 2002. Reprinted by permission of Fresh Air with Terry Gross, produced in Philadelphia by WHYY.

Geoffrey Himes: "Tom Waits," *Washington Post*, October 29, 1979. Copyright © 1979 Geoffrey Himes. Used by permission of the author.

Jim Jarmusch: "Tom Waits Meets Jim Jarmusch," *Straight No Chaser*, October 1992. Used by permission of the author.

Don Lane: "The Don Lane Show," Channel Nine, April 1979. Used by permission of Channel Nine.

Robert Lloyd: "Gone North: Tom Waits, Upcountry," *L.A. Weekly*, April 23, 1999. Copyright © 1999 Robert Lloyd. Used by permission of the author.

Craig MacInnis: "Waits Never Lets Guard Down," *Toronto Star*, October 7, 1987. Copyright © 1987 *Toronto Star*. Used by permission of Torstar Syndication Services.

David McGee: "Smelling Like a Brewery, Lookin' Like a Tramp," *Rolling Stone*, January 27, 1977. Copyright © Rolling Stone LLC 1977. All rights reserved. Reprinted by Permission.

Glenn O'Brien: "Tom Waits for No Man," *SPIN*, November 1985. Copyright © 1985 Glenn O'Brien. Used by permission of the author.

Steve Oney: "Tom Waits, 20 Questions," *Playboy*, March 1988. Copyright © 1988 by *Playboy*. Reprinted with permission. All rights reserved.

Steve Packer: "In the Words of Waits," *Weekend Australian* March 27, 2004. Copyright © 2004 Steve Packer. Used by permission of the author.

Jon Pareles: "Pop Review: Romance in Tall Tales of Drifters and Drunks," *New York Times*, September 27, 1999. Copyright © 1999 by The New York Times Co. Reprinted with permission.

Clark Peterson: "Tom Waits: The Slime Who Came in from the Cold," *CREEM*, March 1978. Copyright © CREEM Media Inc. 1978/2004. Used by permission of Creemmagazine.com.

Keith Phipps: "Tom Waits," *The Onion*, May 29, 2002. Reprinted with